Podcast Academy™:
The Business Podcasting Book

Podcast Academy™: The Business Podcasting Book

Launching, Marketing, and Measuring Your Podcast

Editor-in-Chief
Michael W. Geoghegan

By:
Greg Cangialosi

with:
Ryan Irelan
Tim Bourquin
Colette Vogele

Focal Press
Taylor & Francis Group

NEW YORK AND LONDON

First published 2008

This edition published 2013
by Focal Press
70 Blanchard Road, Suite 402, Burlington, MA 01803

Simultaneously published in the UK
by Focal Press
2 Park Square, Milton Park, Abingdon, Oxon OX14 4RN

Focal Press is an imprint of the Taylor & Francis Group, an informa business

Library of Congress Cataloging-in-Publication Data

Podcast academy : the business podcasting book / Michael Geoghegan ... [et al.].
   p. cm.
Includes index.
ISBN 978-0-240-80967-0 (pbk. :   )
1. Webcasting. 2. Marketing. I. Geoghegan, Michael W. (Michael Woodland), 1968–
TK5105.887.P63 2008
659.20285'67879—dc22

2007031291

British Library Cataloguing-in-Publication Data
A catalogue record for this book is available from the British Library.

ISBN: 978-0-240-80967-0 (pbk)

Typeset by Charon Tec Ltd (A Macmillan Company), Chennai, India

Contents

Section 1: Podcasting Overview: Understanding the Medium and Its Impact on Business

Section 3: Producing the Podcast: Production, Delivery and Legal Issues

Foreword

Welcome to the first series of Podcast Academy™ books. While many books have been written about podcasting, you hold in your hands the first book written specifically with the *business* user in mind. For those of us who have been involved in podcasting from its very first days—in some cases since before the term had even been coined—podcasting has been a wild ride. While fueled early on by a true sense of community born of its grass-roots creation, it became clear that the medium offered new opportunities for companies, educational institutions, churches, and organizations of all sizes to better connect with customers, constituents, and the people they serve. What was missing, however, was a guide to help them embark on their podcasting endeavors. It is out of this need that we assembled the contributing authors for this book.

The Podcast Academy™ is the longest-running professional podcast training event in existence. While each Academy has a slightly different focus, our primary purpose is always to train those in need of professional-level podcast education and expertise. Held at locations such as Duke University, Boston University, the Yahoo! campus, and the Podcast & New Media Expo, the Academies offer a 1- or 2-day long course that our attendees have appreciated and found effective because of its methodical and practical approach.

For this book series we have asked some of our top instructors to commit to paper the course materials they have presented during our Academies. Unlike other trade shows and events, the Podcast Academy features instructors that are not merely "presenters" on a topic, but who practice what they preach. Our instructors are chosen from among the podcasting vanguard, the ones who are forging the way for this new medium's continued growth and innovation.

In addition to this book series, we offer a number of ways to further your knowledge of podcasting. Whether through our Web site at www. podcastacademy.com, our forums at http://www.podcastacademy.com/ forum, or through free podcasts of previous events at http://pa.gigavox. com, The Podcast Academy™ is here to help.

Additionally, we can target and create Podcast Academy events for private groups, with instructors selected to address the topics most relevant to the audience assembled. Whether you're working on a corporate initiative, higher education deployment, or an organizational undertaking, please feel free to contact us regarding a Podcast Academy™ for your group or organization.

Sincerely
Michael W. Geoghegan
Editor-in-Chief, The Podcasting Business Book

About Michael W. Geoghegan

Michael W. Geoghegan is co-founder and CEO of GigaVox Media, a technology company that provides a production, publishing, and advertising platform for audio/video media companies and podcasters.

Michael also founded Willnick Productions, creator of some of the first corporate podcasts, including the official podcast of the Disneyland Resort. Michael's other podcasting endeavors include Reel Reviews: Films Worth Watching, Grape Radio, and PrivaCast, an enterprise-level solution for secure RSS currently used by Duke University. He is also co-author of "Podcast Solutions: The Complete Guide to Podcasting."

Michael speaks frequently on podcasting's impact on new media and its corporate applications and is often quoted by the media including The New York Times, USA Today, CNN, and Wired Magazine.

About the Authors

Greg Cangialosi

Greg Cangialosi is President and CEO of
Blue Sky Factory, Inc. As an ambassa-
dor of email marketing and new media,
Greg Cangialosi has built a reputation
as a pioneer in today's online marketing
landscape. Cangialosi is a seasoned email
marketing veteran, developing and exe-
cuting successful strategies for a wide
and diverse client base. His organization,
behind some of today's most successful
email marketing initiatives, works with
brands of national and international scope, from leading Fortune 500 com-
panies to performing artists such as Justin Timberlake. In addition to email
marketing strategy, he has pioneered corporate podcasting initiatives for
companies including Verizon Wireless, GM/Pontiac, Disney, Dow Chemical,
and Ortho-McNeil.

Cangialosi is a seasoned lecturer on the topic of email and podcasting,
and producer of ROI Radio (www.roiradio.com), a popular podcast focused

on what's next in online media and marketing. He is also an active blogger, authoring his personal blog, The Trend Junkie (www.thetrendjunkie.com) since 2003. Cangialosi has been involved in online communication projects for today's most recognized brands including The PGA Tour, Under Armour, Improv Comedy Clubs, The McGraw-Hill Companies, and TIG Global.

Cangialosi received his BA in English from UMBC (University of Maryland Baltimore County) where he currently serves on the university's alumni board of directors.

Ryan Irelan

Ryan Irelan, Web developer, podcaster, and writer, is located in the quiet confines of Raleigh, NC. He launched his first podcast, an indie music show, in December 2004.

Ryan created, maintains, and writes for Podcast Free America (www.podcastfreeamerica.com), a Web site dedicated to providing authoritative information on podcasting for people of all technical levels. Ryan also publishes a short podcast of the same name that offers actionable podcast advice for the beginner. He has helped individuals and businesses with their podcasting concerns through consulting and speaking.

Ryan is a Web developer with the nationally recognized Web shop, Airbag Industries, based out of Aliso Viejo, CA.

Tim Bourquin

Tim Bourquin is Founder and CEO of TNC New Media, Inc., an online media company that has developed, launched, and grown several advertising-supported podcasting sites. Among the portfolio is EndurancePlanet.com, for triathletes, marathon runners, and adventure racers, SmallBusinessPodcast.com with content for entrepreneurs and TraderInterviews.com, a podcast site for online investors. Under Tim's leadership, TNC New Media has also used podcasting and other forms of New Media as a promotional tool for everything from corporate events and tradeshows to product launches.

Tim is also the Founder of the Podcast and New Media Expo (NewMedia Expo.com), an annual conference and tradeshow for digital content creators.

Tim started his tradeshow and media company while he was a police officer with the Los Angeles Police Department. It quickly grew to the point where he needed to make a choice—promote to Detective with the LAPD or become an entrepreneur. He chose the latter and has never looked back.

Tim's expertise in building communities and creating audio content for community Web sites has allowed TNC New Media to develop niche content that is attractive to both the listener and advertisers wanting to reach a highly targeted audience.

Colette Vogele

Colette Vogele practices intellectual property law specializing in technology, new media, and the arts. She heads Vogele & Associates (www. vogelelaw.com) where she represents numerous bloggers, podcasters, and businesses building Web 2.0 social networks and interactive communities as they navigate the seas of contract and licensing issues, copyright, fair use, trademark and brand management, litigation, and government regulations.

Vogele speaks and writes regularly on issues related to intellectual property and the Internet. Vogele also holds a non-residential fellowship at Stanford's Center for Internet & Society (cyberlaw.stanford.edu) where she co-authored the *Podcasting Legal Guide* (2006) with Creative Commons and Harvard's Berkman Center for Internet & Society. In January 2007, Vogele launched *Rules for the Revolution*, an audio podcast offering commentary on the legal questions faced by podcasters, video bloggers, and others engaged in new media innovations. Her writings also include *Podcasting for Corporations and Universities: Look Before You Leap* (with Professor E. Townsend Gard, Tulane Law School; October 2006 in *Journal of Internet Law*/Aspen Publishers), and contributing authorship for this book by Greg Cangialosi and GigaVox Media Inc., entitled *Podcast Academy: The Business Book—Launching, Marketing, and Measuring Your Podcast* (Focal Press/Elsevier, Inc.).

Prior to establishing her own law firm, Vogele litigated IP cases with two national law firms, Weil Gotshal & Manges and Preston Gates & Ellis (now, K & L Gates). She has extensive experience in management, enforcement, and defense of intellectual property rights. She is admitted to practice in California and maintains active memberships in the American Bar Association, the Ethics Committee of the Bar Association of San Francisco, and California Lawyers for the Arts. Vogele is also a board member of San Francisco-based non-profit INFORUM, a division of the Commonwealth Club of California, and a member of the Board of Editors for the *Journal of Internet Law* (Aspen Publishers). She is an Honors Program graduate in Political Science from the University of Washington (Seattle), and earned her law degree with honors at George Washington University Law School (Washington, DC).

Introduction

I was honored when Michael Geoghegan asked me if I would write the first Podcast Academy book that was focused on the business applications of podcasting. From my experience as a presenter and instructor in several Podcast Academies, my on-going dialog with many of the corporate attendees both before and after these great events, and my daily role as the owner of an online marketing company, I could see that there was not only an interest, but also a need for more resources on podcasting for the business world.

I first met Michael back in early 2005, just 1 day before we had the unique pleasure of working together on the first three Disneyland 50th Celebration podcasts. Looking back now, just 2 short years later, it is truly amazing just how far podcasting has come. Today, podcasting is not only used for entertainment, education, and outreach, but has evolved into a viable communications platform for businesses and organizations of all sizes and sizes to embrace for marketing, public relations, internal communications, and countless other functions.

What was interesting to both Michael and I as we initially discussed the book was the clear void that existed in the marketplace for a resource that addressed the *business* world in particular. There was no other book or resource on the market that explained podcasting in its most simple and basic elements, and more importantly made the case for why businesses and organizations should not only understand the power of podcasting, but also why they should incorporate it into their own communication efforts.

On the other hand, both Michael and I agreed that podcasters were the best served market in regards to the books and resources available today. So right up front, I would like to be clear that this is not a "how-to" book, nor is it a step-by-step guide to podcasting. Although it offers plenty of practical information and instruction that readers can put to use, it is intended to be an educational overview of the medium, designed to help them understand the entire podcasting ecosystem—not just the what and how but the why.

The book is separated into three main sections. The first, "The Case for Podcasting," begins with a high-level and historical look at both podcasting's history and its place in the rapidly changing landscape of Web 2.0 and social media, then focuses on how successful companies and organizations are currently using podcasting to their advantage.

The second section, "The Podcast Production Process," gets down to nuts and bolts of a podcasting initiative, from planning and pre-production to distribution and legal issues. Here, we explain the various steps you'll have to take before you even record your first podcast, the myriad production decisions you'll have to make along the way, and the workings of RSS, the technology that delivers your podcasts to your audience.

Finally, the last section, "Launching and Measuring Your Podcast," is focused on the question I most often get asked: "How do you market podcasts?" In short, there is no one simple answer, no single fail-safe strategy, but rather a combination of tactics you should use in order to get the word out. The last few chapters of the book are focused exclusively on getting the word out about your podcast and, once the word is out, how to measure your efforts.

Knowing that we wanted to produce the best possible product for our readers, I reached out and recruited some of the brightest minds in the podcasting field to help as co-authors and contribute to this book. First, Ryan Irelan, from Podcast Free America (www.podcastfreeamerica.com) and Airbag Industries (www.airbagindustries.com) took on almost the entire second section of the book. Ryan does an incredible job explaining each of the various steps involved in producing a professional podcast. Everything you need to consider for your own planning and production process is covered in this section.

Ryan was also joined by Colette Vogele, of the law firm Vogele & Associates, (www.vogelelaw.com). Colette contributed an excellent and detailed chapter that will help you navigate your way through the potential legal minefield that awaits the business podcaster. Colette is also the producer of Rules of the Revolution (www.rulesfortherevolution.com) and co-author of Creative Commons' Podcasting Legal Guide, both of which are invaluable tools for understanding the legal implications of social media.

In Section 3 of the book, I am joined by Tim Bourquin, of TNC New Media (www.tncnewmedia.com). Tim is the producer of the Podcast & New Media Expo (www.podcastexpo.com) as well as the Podcast Brothers (www.podcastbrothers.com) podcast to name just a few. Tim contributed an incredibly detailed chapter on the various ways to monetize your podcast. Tim speaks from a solid base of experience, having launched the EndurancePlanet podcast in 2005 and, after growing its audience and building its reputation, later selling it to USA Triathlon in 2007.

The book has several common elements in it to make it easy to maximize your takeaways and lessons. The first element of the book that you will see in every chapter is the use of author tips and author warnings. These boldfaced tips are represented to alert you to key points within each chapter. The author tips are key takeaways for consideration, and the warnings are just that: things you want to either avoid or be very aware of as you think about your own podcast initiative.

You will also notice several sidebars, which are used to highlight particular case studies and company profiles. And, where appropriate, we've used graphics and imagery appropriately to help illustrate the subject matter or to highlight a screen shot from a particularly successful podcast initiative.

One important element that you will find at the end of every chapter in the book is a section called "Lessons Learned." Here you will find several bullets of information that summarize all of the key points and lessons within the chapter. These are in place as a point of reference and as a summary for each chapter of the book.

So now, I invite you to sit back and learn as we discuss and explain how your business or organization can embrace this exciting new medium. Podcasting is no passing fad—it's here to stay and will be an integral part of the new media landscape for quite some time to come. It is our goal that this book will show you how to implement this exciting new medium for your own benefit, and help take podcasting to the next level.

Happy reading!

Greg Cangialosi
Cancun, Mexico
June 2007

Acknowledgments

I have many people to give thanks to for this book.

First and foremost, I would like to thank the following individuals:

Michael Geoghegan for believing in me and giving me such an incredible opportunity to write this book. Angelina Ward and the rest of the team at Focal Press for being a visionary publisher and identifying the need in the market for a resource like this. Eric Schumacher-Rasmussen, my development editor, thank you for helping out a first-time author. Your guidance, assistance, and feedback during this entire process was invaluable. Thank you for helping me get to the finish line; it has been a true pleasure working with you. And Lauren Witlin, thank you for your incredible assistance with helping me research, edit, and stay on track during a very fast process. You are a true rock star!

I would also like to thank my contributing authors, Ryan Irelan, Tim Bourquin, and Colette Vogele for taking the time to share their expertise and insight. I couldn't have done it without you.

I would also like to thank the following people for their assistance, feedback, insight, and experience in helping me write this book.

Chris Penn (Financial Aid Podcast, Podcamp.org), Chris MacDonald (Libsyn & Indiefeed), Mike Spataro (Visible Technologies), Andy Mueller (ROI Radio), Dave Kawalec and Matt Snodgrass (Porter Novelli), Jonathan Cobb (Kiptronic), Kris Smith (Room 214, Croncast), Doug Kaye (Gigavox/ Conversations Network), Greg Galant (Radio Tail), Chris Brogan (chrisbrogan.com, Podcamp.org), Giovanni Gallucci (Dexterity Media, MediaSwamp), Gary Vaynerchuk (Wine Library TV), Jeff Beringer (Golin Harris), Keith Nickoles, and my entire staff at Blue Sky Factory, Inc., Todd Storch (Center for Sales Strategy), Jason Van Orden (jasonvandorden.com), Rick Klau (Feedburner), Susan Bratton (Personal Life Media, ADM).

I would also like to thank the incredible PR teams at Weber Shandwick Worldwide and Golin Harris for giving me the unique opportunity to get involved with corporate podcasting early in the game, and trusting me with your clients. Thanks also to the following companies that I have worked with through their PR agencies on various podcasting initiatives: Disney, Ortho-McNeil Neurologics, GM/Ponitac, Verizon Wireless, Waters Corporation, Dow Chemical, and Raytheon.

And finally, I would like to thank my family. First, my mother and father, Carol and Jerry Cangialosi, for always believing in me at every stage of my life. Thank you both dearly for always letting me march to the beat of my own drummer. And my loving wife Theresa, thank you for being the incredible person that you are, and thank you for being my best friend.

SECTION 1: PODCASTING OVERVIEW: UNDERSTANDING THE MEDIUM AND ITS IMPACT ON BUSINESS

The Podcasting Revolution

Greg Cangialosi

Early in the fall of 2004, the word "podcasting" made its entrance into the consciousness of early Web 2.0 adopters and those on the fringes of Internet technology. Although the medium had been around for many months prior, the term first surfaced online and throughout the blogosphere in late 2004.

A few months later the term "podcasting" was one of the most popular buzzwords in both the technology and media sectors. For most of us in the business world, this "new" medium initially seemed to be nothing more than just audio on the Web. What was all of the hype about? Haven't we been doing this for a while? These questions were valid when podcasting first emerged, and even throughout 2005 and 2006 as it began to develop into a viable medium. But now, a deep understanding of the power of podcasting is essential to any individual involved in marketing, public relations, or business communications. It is important for companies and organizations of all sizes to understand why podcasting can and should be a key element of their strategy moving forward.

The medium of podcasting is truly revolutionary. Although we may not have even realized it at that time, the advent of podcasting symbolized the beginning of a new era of communication. The blogosphere was ripe with conversation, outreach, and dialog in all realms, both consumer and business, and with the emergence of podcasting, the next step in the development of citizen media was solidified. The concept and practice of "we the media" is now coming to you in audio and video format, and being syndicated all over the globe.

Podcasting promises to change the way we think about communications. Individuals have been podcasting for some time now, and businesses and other organizations are now beginning to realize the importance of the medium. Corporate communications can no longer be simply dictated to an audience. Rather, the audience can, and is, talking back, commenting on content and products, and voicing their opinions on corporate policies and practices. Podcasting is changing the roles of "us" and "them," instead creating the space for "we" as conversations between businesses and consumers become a common practice.

Initially, podcasting was not crucial to understand from a business standpoint. The first wave of podcasters was also the same group that made up the audience—a very selective, technological crowd that embraced the newest way of sharing information. But then something happened—as iPods infiltrated millions of homes across the globe, Apple's iTunes music store began offering a directory of podcasts that was available to everyone. Today it is one of the largest, if not the largest, podcast directories available online. Suddenly, podcasts had a platform, and people began listening to it.

As podcasting continues to become more pervasive in popular culture, it is more important than ever to understand what exactly this medium is, how it evolved, and why it matters to your organization today. Most importantly, it's essential for you to understand how you can take advantage and reap the benefits of this exciting new communications tool.

A Brief History

Without getting into a long and detailed history of exactly how podcasting came to be (you can find that on Wikipedia), I should note that several

bright individuals are mainly credited with developing and bringing podcasting to the mainstream. Dave Winer, a well-known software developer—
founder of Userland Software and author of ScriptingNews (www.scripting.
com)—and Adam Curry, professional broadcaster and technology entrepreneur, are responsible along with a few others for making the necessary
technological advancements and popularizing the medium through their
early dialog and experimentation. From their initial efforts back in early
2004, a revolution was born.

The term "podcast" was first coined early in 2004 as a means of describing how a media file could be subscribed to via an really simple syndication (RSS) feed, and automatically downloaded to a user's computer, and
then to a portable media device like the iPod. Without much warning, the
term "podcasting" was soon all over the place, by causing controversy with
Apple over the use of the word "pod" to the development of podcast directories, books and Web sites dedicated to helping people get started with
the medium.

Since the fall of 2004, podcasting has grown so rapidly that it can be hard
to follow all of the moving pieces, let alone grasp some of its most basic
benefits. Only now it has become critical to understand why we should be
thinking about the benefits of podcasting as a business tool.

Over the past 2 years an industry has emerged. Look around today and
you will find an abundance of companies who are helping take podcasting to the next level. You will come across podcast directories, production
companies, advertising networks, sponsorship models, content distribution
networks, technology companies, tradeshows and conferences, etc. All of
them are based on the medium of podcasting and new media.

**Podcasting has rapidly developed into its own industry, and the market and tools
for production continue to become more accessible to organizations of all sizes.
The barriers to entry are very low.**   GREG'S TIP

The Evolution of Podcasting

With all of the activity in what has become a rapidly evolving industry, there still is a common misperception on what exactly podcasting is. A large percentage of people still believe podcasting to be nothing more than an audio or video file that one can simply download from the Web. While it is understandable why many people view it this way, it really is so much more than that.

Let's go back to the beginning and look at how podcasting evolved and what it really represents in terms of an emerging communications medium for businesses and organizations.

When I first discovered podcasting, I was simply fascinated by the pure power and possibilities that it presented. Understanding podcasting—what it is and how it works—can be boiled down to one simple concept: podcasting allows any person or organization to get behind a microphone or a video camera, record content on any subject matter and in any format they choose, and then globally syndicate that content using the power of RSS, giving a truly global audience the ability to subscribe to that content and be alerted when new information has been published.

The piece of the puzzle that most individuals have not fully embraced is the RSS component of podcasting. RSS is what makes podcasting so unique. This is the element of the equation that gives podcasting "game changer" status. RSS has revolutionized the way that content is delivered on the Internet, giving users control over how and when they receive the information they are interested in.

Later in this book, there is an entire chapter dedicated to RSS that will delve into detail on all of the important aspects and what you need to know about it, but for now it is important to have a base understanding of the role RSS plays in podcasting.

GREG'S TIP

Podcasting is much more than just a downloadable audio or video file that is online. RSS (Really Simple Syndication) is the differentiator, because it not only notifies subscribers of new information, but also actually delivers it to them, or offers a direct link.

Podcasting is more than just an audio or video file on the Web that can be viewed or listened to. This type of technology has been around for many years. As mentioned earlier, what makes podcasting different and more powerful is that it allows the content creator to syndicate their message, and allows the listener to subscribe to that content and consume it at their own leisure.

Think back to the time when blogs and blogging first became mainstream. Blogs had been around for many, many years, but their real entrance into the mainstream occurred between 2001 and 2003. Individuals had a place online to quickly post thoughts, insights, trends, opinions, etc.; businesses soon followed suit. There were places to converse with each other in the comments of blogs, and conversation was born.

What we know today as "the blogosphere" developed from the dialog created from all of the blogs from around the globe, and continues to evolve every day. Outside of great content and pure interest from blog readers and authors alike, what really helped fuel the blogging phenomenon was the power of RSS. Whether the author knew it or not, most blogging software enabled each blogger with an RSS feed that accompanied it. To keep things basic for now, presence of an RSS feed allowed other individuals to be able to "subscribe" to your blog, so that every time you wrote something new, your subscribers would be notified. From there, they could choose to read your content at their leisure. RSS began to quickly solve a big problem. With the growing amount of content on the Web, it was virtually impossible to visit all of the Web sites and blogs that one wanted to read on a daily or even weekly basis. RSS allowed people to pick and choose the content they wanted to receive, be alerted when there was something new to check out, and then read it when it was convenient for them.

The Emergence of Web 2.0

The presence of RSS changed the game in that, suddenly, we were all being syndicated. Our words were out there, more and more people began to subscribe to feeds, and the conversations continued to evolve from there. The business world quickly followed the citizen journalists and the publishing world, and soon corporate blogging emerged as an effective way for businesses to communicate with their customers, prospects, and the media. These developments were taking place as the terms "Web 2.0" and "social media" began to surface in the mainstream.

In short, the terms "Web 2.0" and "social media" broadly define the next generation of Internet, a generation where online tools encourage active participation, interaction, and community between individuals. Podcasting plays the role of one of the tools of social media and Web 2.0.

Shortly after blogging went mainstream, the RSS protocol evolved further, and the next version was enhanced with the ability to carry along media files known as "enclosures." These files consist of audio MP3s and video files. This was how podcasting was born. Instead of just simply syndicating text content, the next generation of RSS opened up a whole new world of syndicating audio and video. Just think about how audio and video syndication over RSS will change the way we think about *consuming* media. But also think about the possibilities that it presents to us to be able to *publish* our own media.

Since the beginning of podcasting, my interest in the medium has shifted to focus around my core area of expertise, which is marketing communications. Over the past couple of years, I have spent a lot of time exploring how businesses and organizations are using podcasting to further extend their communication and outreach efforts.

Over the past few years, I have had the opportunity to participate in many unique podcasting projects for companies such as Disney, Verizon Wireless, General Motors/Pontiac, Ortho-McNeil Neurologics, among many others. I have also employed podcasting as a branding and marketing medium for my own business, Blue Sky Factory, Inc. Through my collective experience, and from the experiences of others, I have learned several lessons and best practices that I hope to bring to you throughout the course of this book.

It is clear that today a very low barrier to entry exists for businesses and organizations to create audio and video content. When you extend that ability to everything from small businesses to Fortune 100 corporations, podcasting can be used for education, outreach, marketing, advertising, and public relations. Include the power of globally syndicating that content via RSS, and you have a very powerful medium for organizations to embrace. Let's take a look at why you should be considering podcasting for your organization.

Why Podcasting Matters to Your Organization

One of the main goals of this book is to not only give readers a good understanding of what podcasting is, but more importantly why it matters to your organization and the various ways you can use the medium to your advantage. As I have laid out above, and as you will see for yourself throughout this book, this medium is not just a passing fad. It's a communications revolution.

As I mentioned earlier, podcasting is the natural extension of blogging. It is an evolution that puts sound and video at the fingertips of our companies. Communications that were once only words are now infused with energy, excitement, and entertainment in addition to (hopefully) engaging content. These are some of the key things that engage individuals and develop audiences around other traditional media outlets such as terrestrial radio and television. Never before has a company or an organization been able to seriously consider developing and syndicating audio- and video-based content globally, unless they were a Fortune 500 enterprise with seriously deep pockets.

We have entered into a new era where any company or organization with minimal investment can begin to extend their communications outreach online. Just like many other marketing and communications mediums before it, podcasting is beginning to make its mark and prove its effectiveness as a targeted and measurable medium.

GREG'S TIP

Podcasting is a natural extension of blogging. Developments in the new media landscape are now empowering organizations to go beyond the written word, making syndicated audio and video available for the communication mix.

No matter what kind of organization you are part of—corporation, non-profit, association, academic, religious—there is one common thread amongst them all: the need to communicate, and communicate effectively. All organizations need to talk to their current and prospective customers, members, constituents, the media, employees, etc., and podcasting opens the door to take these communications to the next level, beyond the simple written word.

As we progress through the book we will be highlighting several examples of organizations that are currently utilizing podcasting for a variety of reasons. There are a few functional areas into which most podcasts fall: advertising and branding; education and outreach; media and public relations; and internal communications. You will see these come up again and again throughout the book simply because they are the key areas for any organization's outreach. Within each of these there are unlimited amounts of executions where podcasting can be used. There are many facets to creating a successful podcast for each of these areas. Of course, good, relevant content is at the top of the list. The voice and style of the podcast has to be easy to listen to or watch. And ultimately, creativity plays a significant role as well. We will discuss all of these elements and much more as we move forward.

GREG'S TIP   As a part of social media, podcasting is easy to engage in and is versatile enough to be incorporated into the workings of many different types of organizations for a wide array of purposes.

Why Start Now?

There are a several reasons why your organization should consider launching a podcasting initiative, no matter what sector you are in. The versatility of podcasting makes it an excellent medium that can adapt to your business or organizational needs quickly and effectively, and can be utilized in a variety of ways.

There is a quote from a company called OneUpWeb that resonated with me: "Perhaps the single greatest appeal of corporate podcasting is its potential to enhance and amplify all of the other marketing efforts undertaken by a company." I couldn't agree with that statement more, and we will explore the many ways to do just that throughout this book. Now let's take a look at some of the basic advantages of implementing a podcasting strategy for your company or organization.

Build Your Reputation as a Market Leader

One reason to begin podcasting is that doing so establishes you as an innovator and a pioneer in new communications. The media landscape has begun to shift in recent years from traditional mediums to social media like blogs, wikis, and podcasting. Social media represents change in the playing field between businesses and consumers, corporations, and individuals. It creates dialog like never before, and embracing podcasting demonstrates your organization's willingness to participate in this dialog. You clearly establish that you are on the cutting edge of communications and are following the trends of consumer demand.

Build the Future of the Medium

Beginning your podcast initiative now also allows you to have a part in shaping the future of the medium. Podcasting is still a young medium and it has not yet reached its full potential. By engaging in podcasting now, you are joining the ranks of the pioneers, exploring new ways to utilize podcasting in creative and exciting ways that will distinguish your organization from your competitors. Becoming a pioneer creates the opportunity for you to develop the importance of podcasting within your industry, and will help you to start building a relationship with your consumers through this medium.

> **Companies and organizations of all sizes are most commonly using podcasting for; advertising and branding, education and outreach, media and public relations and internal communications.**

GREG'S TIP

Build a Relationship with Your Customers

Part of having a successful podcast is your relationship with your audience, who are also your customers. Starting to publish a podcast sooner than later allows you to begin to develop your audience now, and begin to build a base of subscribers through a variety of marketing and outreach efforts. The sooner you start, the bigger advantage you will have over your competitors. Producing the show is only one step in the process. Once you have this growing arsenal of content, you have to then get the word out and develop your audience. It should be no surprise that this can take time. Several of the chapters in Section 3 are dedicated solely to marketing and getting the word out about your show.

The reality is that it may take you a couple of trials to producing a podcast before you perfect the format and content to make it pertinent and exciting enough for your particular audience. But in starting your podcast initiative now, you have the opportunity to start appealing to your audience now and develop a following long before you have swarms of competitors. Podcast consumers are hungry for good content, and the market for podcasts is only increasing. Building an audience now will give you an advantage over others in your industry.

Build a Library of Content

Because the podcasting market is growing at an incredible rate, starting a podcast now provides you with another benefit. With each show you produce, your company or organization is building a continuously growing library or archive of media content. This content can always be accessed by both your current and future audience, and can be an incredible asset to any organization. Fox example, if you did a weekly podcast on various topics that are relevant to your industry, in just 1 year you would have 52 shows that are filled with your organization's insights and analysis on your industry. This content would be available to anyone, all over the globe. That would certainly be impressive to anyone from the outside looking in and would provide your organization with specific timeless or "evergreen" content that will always be of interest to your constituents.

An archive of podcasts is a valuable tool because it can help attract new subscribers. Should someone conduct a search for a particular topic that you have already covered, they may come across your podcast and subscribe to it as well. An archive of podcast content also allows you to monitor the shows that you have already covered, allowing you to see what was popular and what was not.

Take a look at IT Conversations (www.itconversations.com) for example. It is the longest running podcast on the planet, featuring over 1800+ episodes of quality content, with interviews and discussions with some of the pioneers of technology. IT conversations features content that was recorded over 3 years ago that is still getting major downloads. Their library and archive of content is rich, and growing every single day. This content library serves the current audience of IT Conversations and helps them to continually be attracting new listeners.

Knowing your audience is a crucial factor in developing your podcast. As I mentioned earlier, when starting your podcast you might put out some shows that are homeruns, bringing in subscribers and hitting high download numbers, whereas others may only offer a slight impact. As with any new initiative, there is a certain degree of trial and error. There is no foolproof recipe for success, largely because every audience in every market is different. A successful podcast for one type of audience could be a failure for another.

You will need some time to sort out what works for you and your audience. Your initial format may not "click." You may want to solicit feedback and engage with your listeners or viewers and make them an active part of your content production process. All of the various elements of podcasting take time to develop if you are going to do it right. And as you will see as we go through this book, podcasting is here to stay, so the sooner you can figure out how to make it work for your organization, the sooner you will begin to reap the benefits.

> **GREG'S TIP**
>
> Much of what you will need to know in order to produce the best podcast stems from knowing your audience. What do they want? What are they looking for?

The Growth and Validation of Podcasting

We wouldn't be writing a book on the importance of podcasting if it were something that only a small percentage of the population thought was a cool new Internet technology. One of the more intriguing things about podcasts is the sheer number of individuals who are actively downloading and listening or viewing them. The numbers are there to support the growth and validation of the medium, and it is clear this is no fly-by-night passing fad.

eMarketer recently published research that stated over 10 million people downloaded podcasts in 2006 alone, and that number continues to grow rapidly. In addition to that data, the Pew Internet & American Life Project found that the number of people who download podcasts increased by 71 percent in just 6 months. That is an incredible adoption.

We also can't forget about the advertising and sponsorship side of podcasting. There are many advertisers who are looking to get in front of the many unique and niche audiences that podcasts offer. eMarketer projects that ad spending on podcasting hit $80 million in 2006 and is projected to reach $300 million annually by 2010 (see Figure 1.1).

What is truly validating podcasting as a viable communication medium is that it has proven itself to encompass three key elements of any highly successful media. That is that it has to be targeted, relevant and most

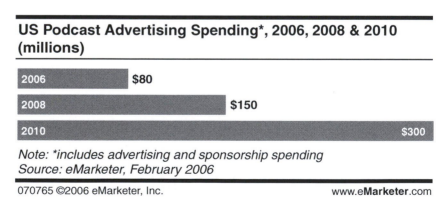

US Podcast Advertising Spending*, 2006, 2008 & 2010 (millions)

2006	$80
2008	$150
2010	$300

Note: *includes advertising and sponsorship spending
Source: eMarketer, February 2006

070765 ©2006 eMarketer, Inc.   www.**eMarketer**.com

FIGURE 1.1
eMarketer's US Podcast Advertising Spending. *Source*: eMarketer, February 2006.

importantly measurable. Think about the evolution that email marketing, search engine marketing, and online display advertising had to go through in order to receive widespread buy-in from marketers. Today, all three are highly successful online channels that deliver positive return on investment (ROI) to those marketers who use them. And in most cases, they are now part of the standard annual marketing budget. But this wasn't always the case; each one had to first prove its effectiveness to the marketing world. Podcasting, like all other online mediums before it, is now maturing into a viable medium for marketers to take advantage of.

Embracing the Shift

The number of podcasts, podcasters, and listeners continues to grow at an accelerated rate. With each contribution to the medium, new lessons are being learned and the nature of communications is evolving. The rules of the communications game are changing. Consumers no longer wish to be inundated with superfluous information, but instead want just the information they desire or need—when they want it, wherever they choose to enjoy it.

Being tied to a computer or television to enjoy your favorite programs or get information is rapidly becoming a thing of the past. While podcasting will neither eliminate the need nor obviate the use for these other mediums, it is creating a new way of communicating that will certainly change the way in which businesses and consumers relate to each other. Consumers are being endowed with power like never before, having the opportunity to express what content they want and control how they get it. Just as TiVo has changed the way in which people watch TV, podcasting is changing the way audiences get their audio and video fix.

> **GREG'S TIP**
>
> Changes in popular culture (on-demand information, portable media devices) have made the media environment prime for the onset of podcasting.

Including podcasting in your business or marketing strategy now will give your business or organization the benefit of being at the forefront of this new medium. At this particular moment in time, we are witnessing the emergence of a new medium that is having a profound impact on the way people communicate with each other, and the way organizations reach out to their markets.

From Theory to Practice

The rules of the communications game are changing and evolving. With the explosion of social media in recent years, individuals who had never before expressed themselves online are now doing it *en masse*. Opinions, thoughts on life, product reviews, jokes ... everything can be and is being syndicated or shared through blogs, social networks, and podcasts. This communications revolution is not only affecting the way individuals communicate with each other, but also signifies that businesses and organizations need to reevaluate how to reach their audiences.

Traditional forms of media and communication, while not rendered useless or ineffective, are experiencing a change in roles. Social media has caused a shift in the way we receive our information, taking it from something that was prepared and presented to the audience on the publisher's terms to an on-demand format that consumers control. Audiences can tune out or ignore the information they don't want and access mountains of information and entertainment of their choosing.

In the subsequent chapters, we will take a closer look at understanding social media and the role that podcasting plays in it. We will discuss the rise of corporate podcasting and discuss the various ways you can use podcasting within your business or organization. And, in Sections 2 and 3 of this book, we will show you how you can launch, market, and measure your own podcast.

Lessons Learned

- Podcasts are part of a communications revolution that is a result of shifts in new media consumer demand.

- Podcasts are a means of reaching the audience through more than just words, bringing the ability to produce audio and video content to businesses and organizations of all sizes.

- RSS is what makes podcasting unique. It allows your audience to subscribe to content and consume at their own leisure.

- Publishing a podcast is one way to use social media as a viable marketing tool.

- Companies are using podcasting as a form of marketing, advertising, public relations, education and outreach, and internal communications.

- Starting a podcast now sets your organization apart as a pioneer, and gives you a head start on building an audience and an archive of valuable content.

Leveraging the Shift to Social Media

Greg Cangialosi

As mentioned in the last chapter, the term "social media" is quickly becoming a common phrase in today's world. According to Wikipedia (www.wikipedia. org)—itself an example of social media—social media encompasses the online technologies that people use to share insights, experiences, and opinions with one another. You may be a participant in social media and may not even realize it. Accessing Wikipedia, adding or editing an entry, posting a comment on a blog, sharing a video on YouTube—all of these activities fall into the social media context. Popular culture thrives off of social media, as the need and ability to share information globally becomes increasingly more available to everyone, not just the technologically competent.

The advent of social media has influenced the development of a new highly interactive culture in which everyone can have their own "soapbox" to stand on and share their ideas and opinions. This puts a great deal of power in the hands of the consumer. More and more companies are becoming aware of the business implications of the new consumer paradigm. Consumers now have access to the same market that companies do, enabling them to share rave reviews of a product or service, or to launch a slanderous campaign against a company should they feel slighted or taken advantage of. The emergence of social media has created a double-edged sword that can work either for or against a company.

Social Media and the Changing Consumer–Business Relationship

Social media forces a dialog between businesses and consumers in a way never seen before. Traditionally, businesses would extend information to the consumer through standard mediums like newspapers, television, and magazine advertisements. Through these mediums, businesses rarely received immediate feedback from their consumers, if they received any at all. This perpetuated a one-way, very passive relationship between businesses and their customers. Should a consumer wish to provide feedback, their options for communication were limited to calling customer service, writing a letter, or sending an email. Businesses, likewise, were left without information pertaining to the success of their ad campaigns, their products, or their services. Social media changes the playing field by giving more communication power to the consumers. A very basic example of how businesses have embraced this changing landscape is the corporate or product blog, where customers can respond to corporate initiatives almost instantly and the business can dialog back with the customer through the comments. Conversation between businesses and customers is now possible, allowing businesses to create a product to the desired specifications of their markets.

Most businesses view the onset of blogs, podcasts, and other mediums as a new opportunity to communicate with consumers. Advertisers are seeking new ways to engage social media and use it to reach new markets. Marketers and public relations professionals are seeing the vast opportunity of utilizing popular blogs and social networks to promote their company or different events. Social media is being incorporated within the office, using blogs and wiki's to encourage collaboration between departments and podcasts for internal communications or announcements. Those businesses that are resisting the changing consumer culture will soon find themselves scrambling to catch up as the importance of social media continues to grow and begins to overshadow traditional media.

> To become familiar with the various tools people are using to engage in social media, check out company blogs, download and listen to podcasts, and visit various social networking and news sites like www.digg.com
>
> **GREG'S TIP**

Embracing Social Media

This is not the first time in history that technology has forced cultural shifts, or vice versa. The new social media is also most certainly not the last change we'll see as technology and consumer demands continue to evolve. However, social media is here to stay, and so businesses have to evolve and learn to adapt to this new medium, much as they have in the past. Think of how businesses have evolved thus far, from print, radio, and television spots to online marketing and all of its channels. Now, businesses have to take the next step and embrace social media marketing and advertising.

A recent study conducted by the University of Massachusetts Dartmouth Center for Marketing Research reveals that Fortune 500 companies are on the forefront embracing social media. Forty percent of respondents said that social media is an important part of their business/marketing strategy (see Figure 2.1).

In the realm of internal communications, there is an increasing awareness and usage of other mediums that fall into the social media toolset, such as podcasting. As social media continues to evolve, corporations are increasingly using the available mediums to foster growth, training, and collaboration within themselves.

The role of social media within corporate communications can be very diverse. Most corporations, for example, like to keep tabs on when they make headlines or have important information to share, both internally and externally. Traditional means of obtaining and disseminating this information involve extensive reports, internal office memos, email blasts, and newsletters. Social media allows for an evolution of the processes

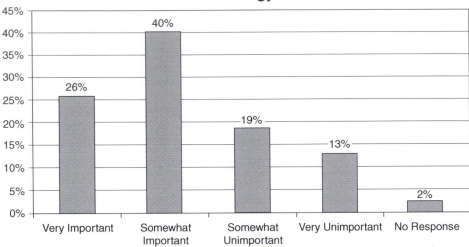

FIGURE 2.1

How important is social media to your business/marketing strategy? *Source*:
University of Massachussets, Dartmouth Center for Marketing Research.

currently involved in corporate communications. The presence of internal
or corporate blogs allows for open dialog. Podcasting creates the space for
the arrival of new media in the form of audio and video, moving beyond
just words. Each component of the social media spectrum can, or already
does, serve some sort of role within corporate communications.

Social media within a company is also a valuable means of gaining feedback from employees. An internal corporate blog is a place where issues
can be discussed and evaluated before taking action, and such a blog is
certainly less cumbersome and time consuming than a company-wide
meeting. Additionally, social media can lend itself to collaborative efforts,
particularly across departments. Anyone who is involved in the corporate
structure knows how challenging it can be to set a meeting that fits everyone's schedule and how difficult it can be to get anything accomplished
during that time frame. Social media affords the opportunity for different departments to collaborate at their own pace, as ideas come to them.
Issues can be worked out over the Internet from individual desks instead
of in a conference room.

Understanding the Role of Social Media in Corporate Communications

There are chances that you already have started to see opportunities to use social media within your own organization. There are many ways to include some of these tools in your day-to-day business operations, and people are constantly developing new ways to expand the use of podcasts, blogs, wikis, and social networking. Major advances are being made both internally and externally in terms of corporate communications. It is very likely that many of your employees are already a part of the social media landscape that is expanding rapidly. They may follow particular blogs (or even have one of their own), subscribe to podcasts, or watch and share videos on YouTube. If they are involved in this new world of on-demand free speech, outreach, and entertainment, then your company should also be aware of how to take advantage of this evolving landscape.

Social media has shifted the audience with whom businesses interact. Companies are no longer communicating solely through printed mediums in hopes of reaching customers. Fewer third parties—think traditional media— are involved in the deployment of social media; instead, companies now have the opportunity to interact directly with their consumers. Potential customers and clients have increasingly more control over the content they receive, particularly by way of advertising and online media. Consider anyone who has ever used TiVo to record a program. Most of these viewers fast-forward through all the commercials—which then translates into a loss of hundreds of thousands of dollars for the company paying for the advertising spot. This shift in the consumer–business relationship necessitates that companies embrace the on-demand nature that social media offers in terms of communication.

Shifting corporate communications to include the tools of social media is one of the most critical challenges facing businesses over the next few years. Technological developments within the field are coming rapidly, and consumers are adjusting to them just as fast. This forces a company to reconsider current marketing and business strategies and evaluate how a podcast or blog might add to their press coverage and brand image. Many major corporations are already making this shift. Some companies have experienced great success with huge amounts of positive feedback regarding their use of social media, either for branding, marketing, or general public relations.

Sun Microsystems, for example, has been praised for its use of blogging to communicate not only internally, but externally to consumers as well. Blogs are available to all associates at Sun Microsystems, which aids in internal communication and collaboration. CEO Jonathan Schwartz posts on his blog regularly, using it to share personal experiences with technology as well as introduce new innovations that are on the horizon (see Figure 2.2). Access to these blogs is not restricted solely to Sun employees—they are open for any individual to read and subscribe to. Sun has embraced various elements of social media for both internal and external benefits. In the next chapter, we will see in detail some specific and successful uses of podcasting within this landscape.

FIGURE 2.2
Sun Microsystems CEO Jonathan Schwartz posts regularly on his blog, which is available for viewing both inside and outside of the company.

Other corporations have not had the same success. Wal-Mart, the leading discount superstore, received some severe backlash from an attempted public relations campaign via social media in 2006. "Wal-Marting Across America" was a blog kept by two people traversing the US in a recreational vehicle who parked overnight in Wal-Mart parking lots and conducted employee interviews. Posts on the blog were often very upbeat, describing how content Wal-Mart employees are with their jobs. (Great controversy has existed over this very issue, with one side arguing that employees are underpaid and poorly treated, and the other arguing the opposite.) *BusinessWeek* soon revealed that the two bloggers were actually being sponsored by Edelman Public Relations, which was responsible for Wal-Mart's public relations campaign at the time. The explosion of outrage regarding the blog that followed was spawned by the same "social media" that initially supported the campaign. The moral of the story: be open, honest, and upfront when engaging with the social landscape.

As with any emerging medium, it is important to learn from failures as much as successes. The experience of Wal-Mart demonstrates an unsuccessful attempt to use social media for public relations. Why did Wal-Mart fail? Because it did not hold true to the core definitions and values of social media. Social media relies on the experiences of real people with their own thoughts and opinions. The blog put out by Jonathan Schwartz of Sun Microsystems is a real blog, by him, about his experiences and opinions. Sure, he may highlight new technology or point out the benefits of Sun Microsystems products, but at the heart of the blog is his opinion. Successful social media demands nothing less.

Extending the Blogosphere: More Than Words

One of the main drivers of social media is the blog. In the past, blogs have been at the forefront of the new culture that shares ideas and opinions freely. The written word bore all the weight in conveying emotions, passions, and information. Anyone who has ever written a persuasive piece of material knows how challenging it can be to convey the intensity of emotion or the true tone of voice solely through writing. There is much to be said for the inflections of the human voice (as well as facial expressions and body language) in making a point or expressing concern. Fortunately, as social media has continued to evolve, other means of communicating have become available.

Audio and video are becoming a more popular means of sharing information on the Internet. Their surge in popularity is largely linked to the emergence of podcasting and really simple syndication (RSS) feeds. Why only read your favorite blog, which ties you to your computer, when you can listen to your favorite blogger's podcast while you are working out or commuting to work? Podcasts and video podcasts certainly will not replace blogs as a means of sharing ideas (after all, everything has its place). They do, however,offer something that blogs lack—an actual human voice, and now video.

Offering information in a portable way is essential to reaching consumers as social media continues to evolve. People are no longer content to receive media and information in a manner that requires them to remain in one spot. BlackBerry's, iPhones, Treo's, iPods, and even portable gaming systems provide the tools for the public to be both completely connected and completely mobile. Information and media now needs to be as "on-the-go" and "on-demand" as the people accessing it, otherwise you risk the message not reaching the intended audience. Similarly, because consumers are constantly in motion, they often do not have the time or the will to search their favorite sites to see if new information is available.

Syndicating blogs and podcasts has been a key part of the evolution of social media. RSS technology has played a key role in the skyrocketing popularity of blogs in the early years of the new millennium. As RSS became more sophisticated and capable of carrying media files, syndicating an audio or video message has a very low barrier to entry. Consumers are able to subscribe to the information they want, rather than being distracted by superfluous media. The effects of syndication on social media have been both broad and deep.

Social media has become even more of an on-demand phenomenon because of the ability to syndicate content. People no longer have to search deep for information; in most cases it is simply delivered to them. What's more, it is only the information that they *want*. No more searching through pages of irrelevant articles or bad search results. Instead, the consumer has exactly the information they want as soon as it becomes available. The only waiting involved is the time it takes to download the file or for the text or HTML to load. Syndicating a message is not only powerful for the people downloading podcasts or following a blog, but it is also an incredible door to the consumer market for businesses.

What syndication does for businesses is narrowly target a niche subscriber base. Consumers subscribe to a particular medium for specific reasons, most commonly because they have an interest in the content being offered. This makes them selectively join consumer markets that allow businesses to target them directly. What's more, businesses can tailor their message in such a way that is more appealing to this audience because it is so specific, rather than a broad and general message that is cast into the media in hopes of getting the attention of the consumer. The power of syndication, RSS in particular, will be discussed in depth in a later chapter. For now, it is merely important to understand that syndication has been another catalyst for the birth and expansion of social media. It is this ability to syndicate audio and video that makes podcasting so alluring.

Podcasting in the Social Media Landscape

Podcasting is a crucial new force in social media. Presently, most corporations that are using podcasts favor using them for things such as branding, marketing, and public relations. Podcasts are not necessarily as useful as blogging in terms of being collaborative tools, but they are very effective at disseminating important information. As we will discuss more in depth in the next chapter, podcasting has yet to reach its full potential in regards to corporate communications. It is still in its infancy, but it is rapidly maturing as a means of communicating not only within a corporation, but with the consumer market as well.

Podcasts are an attractive form of communication not only because of their portability, but also because they are relatively easy to produce. Essentially, anyone can create and syndicate a podcast so long as they have some basic audio equipment and a basic knowledge of RSS (neither of which is expensive nor hard to obtain). Because podcasts are part of the social media landscape, they do not need to be like formal broadcasts, and more often than not the best ones out there are not scripted at all, but are rather variations on a theme; each episode of the same podcast will have a similar format, but beyond that, it's not planned out to the letter. A real human voice with a personality combined with solid, unique content is what creates a successful podcast. Because of these features, podcasting has changed the impact consumers can have on businesses.

The Impact of the Consumer Podcast

As mentioned before, just about anyone can create a podcast. This shifts a great deal of power into the hands of individuals. People can literally voice their opinions on any topic they choose, including businesses, products, and services. The effects of individual podcasting on different organizations can vary greatly. As with blogs and other forms of social media, there is no filter in place to control the content of podcasts. This means that a consumer can review a product put out by your company and say whatever he or she chooses, be it positive or negative. The impact of a review such as this is largely dependent on the audience to which the reviewer has access. Right now, the podcasting audience is a rather niche market, so the impact of a message is limited only to those who have subscribed to, or may come across, the podcast.

The audience that subscribes to a specific podcast is most likely to be very selective. It is narrowed down by a combination of technological know-how and tools, in addition to an interest in the topic. The first part of the equation, technology, is rapidly dispersing through the population, across all kinds of demographics. Podcasts are not just a form of media used by teens and twenty-somethings. The required interest in the topic is a more qualifying feature, narrowing the audience not necessarily by age but by personal interest and relevancy. Within the vast social media landscape are where podcasters find their audience, and where businesses will find their niche market.

Obviously there is some concern regarding the complete lack of control your business can exert over an individual's podcast. However, this is not a reason to shun podcasting. Rather it is an opportunity to become involved in podcasting on a business level. A positive podcast by a popular producer within your company's consumer market is a form of good publicity that reaches consumers that are already interested in your company's product, service, or brand.

Consumers that are podcasting can actually be strong assets to a corporation. These individuals are informing your market about new advances in the field, providing insider tips, creating calls to action, defending a position, and so on. A successful podcast will increase its subscriber base, perhaps even create new interest in the area of the market that your company was originally unable to access. It is this ability of podcasts to reach into the consumer base and extend a message beyond traditional market boundaries that makes them so valuable as a new means of corporate communications.

Like other forms of social media, podcasting is creating a dialog between business and consumers like never before. Podcasts produced by consumers can offer a cross section of consumer interests and perceptions of your organization. Using this information, you can complement or even compete with existing podcasts to get your message out. So, as you consider podcasting for your business, it is important to learn how you can participate, how to respond to consumer demands, and what kind of information you should be podcasting.

Responding to Consumer Demands

A major component of social media is the forum for conversation and dialog. This extends beyond conversations among individuals, and has evolved to include business to consumer dialoguing. Businesses need to be aware of the podcasts that are out there, particularly the ones that may be covering their activities or their industry. The information that comes out of these podcasts is useful to a company in many ways. One reason is that it provides a snapshot of how the company or industry your are in is perceived within a particular market. You can gauge from this type of content how well respected your organization or your industry is to specific groups of individuals.

Another useful effect of podcasting is that podcasts offer a unique cross section of the consumer market. As mentioned earlier, a podcast audience is specific and targeted. A cat lover will not subscribe to a podcast about dogs. They might, however, be a subscriber to podcast on pet health care tips like those found on Purina's Web site. Purina offers "Petcasts"—video podcasts of funny dogs and cats, different competitions, and advice. While not every podcast might appeal to every subscriber, there is enough relevant content to keep them interested. Furthermore, by tracking which podcasts have more downloads, Purina can produce more Petcasts of a similar content to keep the audience coming back for more.

Many companies that are currently podcasting offer a link on their website requesting feedback from their audience. They directly ask their audience to tell the company exactly what they wish to hear via podcasts. As more consumers report back to the company about their demands, the business not only can produce higher quality podcasts, but also learns valuable consumer information. Keep in mind that the audience is a highly selective group, usually very knowledgeable in their particular area. Feedback from this group provides the business with insights as to what new products might interest the consumer, what sort of products they require now, or what kind of information are they thirsting for that the business can provide them.

Conversing with the consumer has traditionally been localized to surveys and focus groups, which often provide an inaccurate portrayal of true customer sentiments. Podcasting and other social media provide the tools to actively seek out and learn more about your particular consumer market, and perhaps even reach out to a market that you had not initially considered. After a business has gathered all of this information from what is being said online, and through direct audience feedback, it should go into production creating viable content to be distributed as a syndicated audio or video file.

> **Always include some way for your audience to communicate and engage with you in your podcast. Offer them a feedback form, a place to post comments, a quick poll, or a simple email link to start a dialog and find out what your audience is thinking.**

GREG'S TIP

Selecting the format for your content to be shared is an important factor to consider. This can be an evolving process that stems from consumer dialoging. Podcasting audiences have preferences toward format, and certain content is better suited for an audio file than video file, or the other way around. For example, a podcast covering a sporting event is perhaps best delivered as a video podcast rather than an audio file, whereas interviews "behind-the-scenes" can be just as easily shared as an audio podcast instead of video. It is also vital to consider when and where your audienceis going to listen to or view your podcast when determining whether audio or video will be more successful. Many people multitask while enjoying their downloaded podcasts. They may work out, do laundry, drive a car, etc. While video podcasts can be fun and entertaining because of the visual and audio stimulus, they may not always be practical since they require visual attention, limiting a person's ability to multitask. Likewise, a recording of a press conference may be interesting audio, but it is probably not well suited to video podcast production.

Consumers are not interested in wasting time checking to see if new information is available. Many have several Web sites or blogs or podcasts that they are interested in, so taking the time to check all of them is something that rarely happens. RSS feeds that are available with many forms of media offer a solution, providing updates on all the relevant content that an individual is interested in. This streamlines the information process not only by sending notification of updates, but also providing links to the files and downloads so that the subscribers can access this new information at their leisure. It's on-demand information, brought directly to the consumer.

The timeliness of getting your podcasts and video podcasts out to the public can also be a huge factor in your success. Bear in mind the allure of podcasts to the consumer—instant access to information and entertainment. Thus, depending on the nature of your content and subject matter the timing of your publishing can be critical. Podcasts that cover an event need to be posted almost immediately after the event, or at least well within 24 hours. Any time later than that for event coverage makes the podcast "old news" as the consumer may have already redirected their attention elsewhere. Other podcasts, such as tips and advice on issues that are not time sensitive, can be posted at a slightly more leisurely rate. Even then, consistent posting of podcasts keeps the consumer engaged and interested to see what information the next podcast will hold.

There are many components of podcasting that make it such a heavy favorite as the new means of participating in social media. The ease of creation and distribution of podcasts, make them an affordable means of communicating whether you are an individual expressing your opinion or a business seeking deeper market penetration. From the business stand point, podcasts offer a unique view into the consumer market. The demographic data that can come from monitoring a podcast subscriber base offers details pertaining to who is interested in the topic, what age group, what their interests are. From this information a corporation can develop content that specifically targets their market and engages in direct dialog with consumers to better understand their needs. Clearly, the stronger the content, the more subscribers you will attract, and the greater the audience, the more powerful the impact of your message will be.

Lessons Learned

- Social media is defined as the technologies and practices that people use to share information, insights, experiences, and opinions with one another.

- Consumer culture has shifted to one of empowerment, with the ability to spread information globally in a variety of ways.

- Changes in the business–consumer relationship are forcing companies to consider using social media for corporate communications both internally and externally.

- Consumer demands influence the content of the podcasts being produced, and will generally determine their success.

- Dialoging with consumer markets is now possible because of mediums like podcasting and the feedback that is mandated by it.

The Emergence of Corporate Podcasting

Greg Cangialosi

What is it about podcasting that distinguishes this technology from so many trends that have come and gone before it? Why will podcasting become a new medium for information dissemination where others have failed? In order to understand why podcasting is here to stay, we must first define the difference between a trend and a fad. Many technologies that burst forth into the consumer markets can be quickly discarded as a fad—the proverbial "flavor of the month." A prime example of a fad is the CueCat. You may find yourself asking, "What is a CueCat?" As well you should, since this passing fad never caught on. The CueCat is a scanner (one that is still sometimes deployed in library applications) that was designed to scan bar codes that were printed in magazine advertisements. Once scanned, the CueCat would redirect users to the advertiser's Webpage. Despite being distributed to hundreds of thousands of magazine subscribers, very few actually took the time to use it. The CueCat has now been relegated to the ranks of passing technological fads, same as the iSmell and Nintendo Power Glove.

In contrast, a trend is something that merges new and evolving consumer demands into one product or service and will last for a very, very long time. "Consider the iPod," wrote Chris Pentilla in the June 2004 issue of Entrepreneur, "which draws on multiple trends, ranging from our desire for more mobility, instant gratification, and customization to our craving for all things fashionable." Through the iPod and iTunes, Apple has cornered the market on digital music, offering an easy-to-access online music store and a variety of means of carrying around your favorite music and now, audio and video podcasts. Many competitors have failed to break through Apple's overwhelming presence in the portable music industry simply because their products are too technical or too many obstacles exist to obtaining quality music downloads. Apple has successfully read the consumer market and developed a product that is certainly not a fad, but a trend that will last until the next big evolution in portable media.

Podcasting: More Than a Fad

Past experience has demonstrated that when something is overly hyped, it often fails to live up to expectations. When podcasting first emerged in early 2003, it was relatively localized, mainly within the technical and early adopter community, and unknown to the mainstream. Podcasting has had the luxury of being developed by the technological community under the radar and away from the masses, slowly emerging as a new information medium. Even though podcast production has been available to everyone from the very beginning, only a particular community engaged in producing podcasts. Now, with major players like Apple and Yahoo! supplying podcast directories, what is to prohibit podcasting from becoming over commercialized and going the way of the CueCat?

Perhaps one of the best things going for podcasting is that the industry is still so young, which means there is a lot of ground yet to be explored. There is still a lot of room to develop and deploy the medium in new ways. Simply put, there are no rules. As the technology continues to develop, consumers are actively seeking out podcasts based upon their content. The better the content, the more likely listeners will subscribe to and download future podcasts by the same producer.

Because of its gradual emergence into the world of new media, podcasting has been able to mature and grow without being abused in the process. Often times when a technology becomes available to the masses, it is overused and misused before it is completely understood. This can lead to an erosion of trust in the medium, which can then have an adverse affect on its success. Consider email marketing, for example, a medium I know very well in my role as the President of Blue Sky Factory, Inc. We have been in the email marketing business for almost 7 years, and today we know that email has one of the highest return on investment (ROI) of any direct-response medium, in both the traditional or interactive media worlds. While email marketing is one of the most effective channels for marketers, there is no denying that it has gone through, and continues to go through, trials with the abuse of spam and, subsequently, spam filters that can have an impact on the deliverability of legitimate marketing email. The abuse of the medium with unsolicited commercial mail has even spawned separate industries to deal with security, filtering, and delivery management and monitoring. Because of the way podcasts function, and how the widespread adoption of really simple syndication (RSS) is developing, they are not subject to the same challenges as email in regards to permission or subscription based messaging. That said, as mentioned earlier, things are still developing, and every medium has its own unique issues to work through. In today's world, the average user wants functionality and control. If a new medium fails to deliver on these points, it will be cast aside and left in the technological wake of a more stable, reliable and useful one.

Podcasting, like the iPod and blogs, converges the desires of the consumer with the delivery of media and information. It feeds off of the needs of the public, and provides them with means to download and enjoy programming and information wherever and whenever they desire. As information continues to become more accessible and portable, the need to publish your organization's message in an effective manner will become increasingly paramount. Podcasting fills this need, and because of its young age has incredible potential to not only meet current demands, but also to evolve and expand as new uses for it continue to emerge.

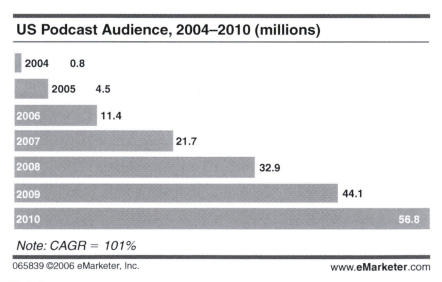

GREG'S TIP

Podcasts offer access to very targeted, niche audiences, and embrace the changing face of consumer media demands.

Branching Out by Reaching Out

Podcasting is becoming the new means of sharing information over the Web. More and more people are downloading podcasts each year. According to a report conducted by The Diffusion Group (May 2005), less than one million people downloaded podcasts in 2004 (see Figure 3.1). One year later, in 2005 a recorded 4.5 million people comprised the podcast audience.

US Podcast Audience, 2004–2010 (millions)

Year	Value
2004	0.8
2005	4.5
2006	11.4
2007	21.7
2008	32.9
2009	44.1
2010	56.8

Note: CAGR = 101%

065839 ©2006 eMarketer, Inc.   www.**eMarketer**.com

FIGURE 3.1

According to eMarketer, nearly 60 million people will be downloading podcasts by 2010. *Source*: The Diffusion Group, May 2005.

By 2006, the number of people downloading podcasts had more than doubled to over 11 million. Projections for the years to come suggest that by 2010, the number of consumers downloading podcasts will approach 60 million. The growth of podcasting is huge and the opportunities to become involved are vast.

In earlier days, independent content producers were primarily the ones creating podcasts. People make their mark with their own show as a form of news, outreach, and entertainment. Today, that group of content producers continues to grow at a rapid pace. Podcasting is opening up many new opportunities for emerging talent. As a business tool, however, podcasting is still a relatively new phenomenon and can be used as an effective means to share internal communications with employees, increase brand awareness, promote products, and disseminate relevant press information, to name just a few examples. Podcasting is also finding its way into the educational arena, as more colleges are embracing the technology as a means to share lectures of their classes with their students, and as supplemental material to the curriculum. Let's take a look at how podcasting can be utilized in these areas, as well as others, in following sections.

Internal Communications

Every business, whether large or small, has a certain degree of internal communications. Human Resources needs to keep employees up to date on the latest health care information, the latest facts and figures in the industry, news from the CEO, and the list goes on and on. Traditionally, this sort of information goes out in the form of a newsletter, email, or interoffice memo. The information usually is read because it is required somehow—for instance, an employee is not likely to disregard an email regarding changes to the payroll system. However, there's no guarantee the information will be accessed in a timely fashion, and it is extremely difficult to track. Employees are generally forced to stop and take time to read these materials, reducing their efficiency at the work place.

Most people prefer to multitask and like to have options on how they consume information. By providing certain company information in the format of a podcast you are expanding the ways in which an employee can receive information. First of all, by creating a podcast, employees will be able to access the information when it is convenient for them. They can listen to the information at their desk, or download the podcast and listen to it when it is convenient to them.

Using podcasts in the workplace is a very efficient means of sharing information, from the reduced amount of paper, to the ease of creating the podcast. A podcast can be utilized by specific departments to broadcast information in a manner suitable to each. Many businesses are discovering that podcasts are a very effective training tool. A training department can quickly setup and share a podcast that relates to a new selling tactic or a slight change in an operating procedure. For a large retail corporation with locations across the country, a podcast could be deployed to update the staff in the field of upcoming campaigns or changes to the merchandising.

In 2006 a study conducted by Edelman's Change and Employee Engagement practice involving 111 Fortune 500 companies found that 35 percent were actively using podcasts for internal communications (see Figure 3.2). Podcasts were cited as being an effective means of communication since they can be scripted and edited, offering a structured content (see Figure 3.3). Additionally, podcasting is favored over other mediums like blogging, because user comments regarding the material are private and inaccessible to other users. This affords a greater degree of control over the information being shared.

During this study, the companies were asked to rate different mediums regarding their effectiveness for different tasks. Podcasts were most highly regarded with respect to training, rated just under traditional print materials. In fact, the Edelman report (see Figure 3.4) notes that several large companies such as Capital One, Xerox, and National Semiconductor have

Does your organization use podcasts?

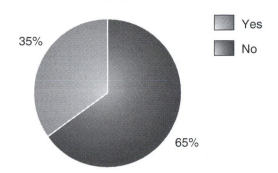

FIGURE 3.2

A study by Edelman in 2006 indicated that 35 percent of the 111 Fortune 500 companies surveyed were using podcasts for internal communications. *Source*: New Frontiers in Employee Communications, Edelman 2006.

Provide your opinion of the usefulness of each channel as a tool to communicate with employees*

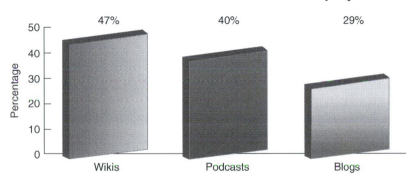

Percent listing useful or very useful

FIGURE 3.3

The same Edelman study found that nearly 30 percent of the companies surveyed cited podcasts as effective means of communications. *Source*: New Frontiers in Employee Communications, Edelman 2006.

begun issuing MP3 players to employees to encourage the usage of podcasts for training purposes.

The popularity and effectiveness of podcasting for internal communications is not strictly limited to training. Brad Bellaver, an internal communications

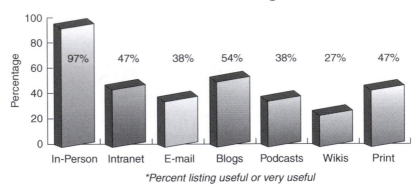

Rate each communications channel with regards to culture change*

Percent listing useful or very useful

FIGURE 3.4

The Edelman study found that employees rank podcasts ahead of wikis and equal to email as impetus for culture change. *Source*: New Frontiers in Employee Communications, Edelman 2006.

specialist at Wells Fargo, has stressed the importance of internal communications to the functions of any organization. He states that developing cross-departmental communication that drives home the goals of higher management is paramount. Furthermore, this information dissemination needs to be streamlined and incorporate new media as much as possible. Information management is an important and challenging part of internal communications. A common challenge for many businesses is getting employees to access information that is posted on the corporate Web site or Intranet. Pushing information through email helps in this area, but overusing this medium can cause employees to ignore it. Podcasting offers an additional way to engage employees with new information. By subscribing to the company's RSS feeds, new feed items alert them when new content is posted.

Bellaver points out that with the current inundation of internal communication through memos and emails, the effectiveness of these mediums is rapidly disintegrating. In such instances, the content has become so cumbersome as to cause the reader to stop reading after only a few sentences. Podcasting avoids this problem by delivering information via audio, in which a human voice can engage employees in a way that emails cannot.

The incorporation of podcasts in internal corporate communications is still relatively new. One of the leaders in introducing podcasts as a means of internal communication as well as for the public is Southwest Airlines. Southwest has posted on its Web site several podcasts from company officers, including different vice presidents, the president, and even the CEO from their Media Day on November 1, 2006. In these podcasts, you are able to garner the five performance measurements Southwest uses to gauge their success and quality of service. Additionally, you can find out what qualities Southwest looks for in employees and what it takes to succeed in that company.

CASE STUDY
SOUTHWEST AIRLINES

Who They Are?

Southwest Airlines is one of the largest airlines in the United States, based in Dallas, TX. The goal of Southwest is to provide high quality yet affordable service to its passengers.

Purpose of Podcasting

Public relations and internal communications. Convey information to customers and employees about the company's mission, employee traits for success, etc.

Approach

Southwest Airlines held a "Media Day" back in November of 2006. There, the speakers were recorded and the information was posted as podcasts for their employees and the public. Ongoing podcasts are posted in the media gallery and highlighted on the corporate blog, www.blogsouthwest.com

Benefits

The podcasts offered a unique way of reaching out to Southwest's customers and 32,000 employees. Due to the large dispersal of staff, podcasts were a natural fit to share the information internally. Employees received direct messages from the President, CEO, and other executives that offered motivation, support, and tips to get ahead.

Podcasts such as the ones put out by Southwest are an effective means of driving home the mission and core values of a corporation. In having upper management speak out to the employees, it reinforces goals and can even help motivate by generating a sense of camaraderie. Using podcasts has a humanizing effect on the dissemination of corporate information, offering a voice instead of the written word. Perhaps even more importantly, creating a podcast is a much easier way for a CEO or upper level manager to get a message out than blogging or emailing. Both blogging and emails require time at the keyboard, carefully constructing the message so as to not lose any impact. Communicating in this way can be quite time consuming, particularly if it is to be something that is updated weekly. The ease of generating a podcast means that the CEO must simply get himself/herself in front of a microphone and a computer with recording software. Podcasts can be scripted ahead of time, although a more natural flow and tone is often the preferred method of producing a podcast.

Internal communications, when used effectively, not only inform but also make the employee base a more cohesive, functioning team. Over usage of existing mediums such as email and print newsletters have lost some of their edge in bringing information to employees. More often than not, the information can go unread. Podcasts offer a means to circumvent the norm and create a new opportunity to communicate with employees and move them toward a common objective.

Branding, Marketing, and Advertising

Perhaps one of the most exciting new venues available for podcast experimentation is marketing. The specific content-driven nature of podcast audiences singles out particular markets simply based on the type of media that a listener is subscribing to. For example, a company that sells vintage car parts can immediately connect with their specific group of consumers by sponsoring podcasts about vintage cars, or even better, begin to produce their own podcast on the subject. Once the market is specified, an effective podcasting strategy can be developed.

In creating a branding strategy with podcasts, it is essential to first define the objective. What is the intention behind the podcast? Is it meant to inform and increase awareness? Do you want it to sell? Motivate? Are you trying to increase your company's credibility in your industry? Defining the objective will help you develop the podcast in an appealing manner that corresponds with the target audience.

How are podcasts able to support branding efforts? First of all, podcasts have already weeded out a specific, targeted marketing group. Offering an informative podcast helps establish within the consumer market a reputation as an expert in the field or as the leader in the industry. Take Wine Library, for example, a popular wine store located in Springfield, NJ. Director of Operations Gary Vaynerchuk has fully embraced podcasting by producing Wine Library TV, (tv.winelibrary.com), a video podcast that Gary produces 5 days a week. His goal with the podcast is centered around "breaking the stereotypes and providing his viewers with a new outlook on wine." Or as Gary says on every one of his shows "we are changing the wine world together."

On each episode, Gary features and tastes a variety of wines from a particular region or varietal, discusses and rates them. Having already produced over 300 episodes Gary has featured over 60 percent of the wines that his 40,000 square feet retail wine shop sells. Wine Library also does about 50 percent of its business through its online store (www.winelibrary.com). Instead of being a sales platform for his store, his video podcast is entertaining, engaging, and educational. He focuses his content not only on the quality, but also on the quantity. Gary is serious about the podcast, running it like a completely separate business and ensuring he publishes the show 5 days a week. In fact, when Gary was interviewed for this book he was about to leave for a 10-day cruise and had just finished a marathon filming session to make sure there was one show a day being published while he was gone, just like his viewers would expect. The end result is that Gary has built an incredibly strong brand recognition for his store Wine Library, an engaged community around his podcast, and an audience that results in over 25,000 unique downloads each day and growing.

CASE STUDY
WINE LIBRARY

Who They Are?

New Jersey-based wine store that started in 1983 and changed its name to Wine Library in 1998. In 1997 the business launched an ecommerce Web site www.winelibrary.com. Currently, online sales represent 50 percent of their overall business.

Purpose of Podcasting

To build loyalty and awareness around the Wine Library brand, to break the stereotypes around wine, and provide viewers with a new outlook on wine.

Approach

Started in February 2006, Wine Library TV is produced with a one camera shot. Host Gary Vaynerchuk sits behind a table and tastes a variety of wines, commenting on them and rating them. The show is informative, educational, and engaging.

The podcast is treated like its own business, with new episodes being put out 5 days a week. The focus is not only on quality content but also on quantity. After a year and a half, Gary has published over 300 episodes of Wine Library TV. Check out episodes No. 18, No. 125, and No. 148 to get a good feel for the show.

Benefits

Wine Library has built an incredible community around its video podcast and its brand. The audience has grown to the point where Gary had to have someone dedicated to moderating the comments and forums on his sites. At the time of publishing, the video podcast had an audience that resulted in over 25,000 unique downloads per day, and over 17,000 subscribers.

When they published their first *Thanksgiving* episode it featured a redeemable code for free shipping for the wines they highlighted on the podcast. The show was picked up and placed on the Yahoo! home page for 4 hours, and resulted in over 4200 redemptions of the free shipping code.

Wine Library TV shows us that content truly is king.

Podcasts can have many other applications in the world of marketing and advertising as well. Many corporations, non-profit organizations, community groups, and other associations are implementing podcasts not only to inform and increase awareness, but to sell goods or services as well. Marketing via podcasts is increasing in popularity in the corporate world. Again, podcasting offers access to targeted consumer markets that is otherwise hard to specify. There are several ways to become involved in podcast marketing.

Another way to use podcasting as an advertising and marketing medium is to sponsor a show that has access to your target market. This can be an extremely effective means of advertising if your company chooses not to actively create its own podcast. There are several ways to sponsor and get your message on a specific podcast, or a network of podcasts. Companies such as Kiptronic (www.kiptronic.com), and Podtrac (www.podtrac.com), offer advertisers access to a wide variety of podcasts, covering various targeted topics and reaching unique niche audiences. Companies can utilize such a service to find the right podcast, target the audience, and sponsor the show with an audio ad. While participating in this way is not actually podcasting, it is a means of involving your company in the new medium without producing a show yourself.

The increase in podcast marketing raises the question of podcast advertising, which is still a relatively unexplored venture. Because podcasting is such a new medium, measuring the effectiveness and ROI of podcasts in terms of advertising is still a great challenge. We will be discussing this topic in detail later in the book. However, advertisers are already focusing on developing different means of advertising through podcasts. As mentioned earlier, sponsorship is one way for a company to engage in podcast advertising. A 10-second ad at the beginning of a podcast leaves you with a captive audience since the file has already been downloaded due to the appeal of the audio content. A small advertisement for a related product will not cause the listener to disengage. Even though this format is similar to terrestrial radio, remember the consumers chose the content and downloaded it based on their interest. A short ad or sponsorship at the beginning and end can be very effective for advertisers.

According to Gregory Galant, CEO of RadioTail, there are several things that an advertiser needs to bear in mind when creating an ad for podcasts—one that will not be passed over. First and foremost, he recommends that podcast ads be kept brief and relevant. Studies have shown that podcast listeners do not mind listening to an advertisement so long as it is kept short. After all, they downloaded the program for the content, not the ads. A short ad is less likely to be fast-forwarded through, particularly if the content of the ad is relevant to the podcast itself. It is simply not worth the effort to bypass the ad.

Another key point in advertising via podcasts is to understand the audience. Because individual podcasts have a very specific and narrow audience, the ads included in these mediums need to be equally as targeted. Take for example Grape Radio (www.graperadio.com). Grape Radio is another podcast that specifically targets wine aficionados. In their media kit to advertisers, Grape Radio specifically notes that over three-quarters of their audience consumes wine on a daily basis—a fantastic marketing opportunity for producers of wine and wine-related products.

Research firm eMarketer predicts that more than $400 million per year will be spent on advertising through podcasts by 2011. Because of the huge projected increase in podcasts being downloaded, advertising through podcasting creates a whole new medium to reach consumers. Although the measurement and effectiveness of podcast advertising is still developing, it is sure to become a large part of the booming industry. We will cover podcasting advertising and sponsorship in depth later in this book.

Clearly, the most effective way for a company to engage in using podcasting as a marketing medium is to simply publish their own podcast. This is ideal because the company controls the content and builds the audience. Offering a podcast with interesting content that relates to your product or service will create more interest among consumers. Much in the same way as podcasting supports brand awareness, podcasting also generates the traffic to a Web site that hopefully results in higher conversion rates. Additionally, creating a podcast for a specific product helps generate interest and buzz, and with any luck, if your content is compelling enough, the podcast will spread and reach a larger audience than anticipated.

General Motors, for example, has been using podcasts to market new cars since 2005. I was asked to cover the launch of the Pontiac Summer Solstice Party in Times Square, New York City, in the summer of 2005. This was at a time when using podcasts for marketing and branding purposes was still new and relatively unexplored. The intention behind the podcast was to convey the excitement of the event—being in Times Square, meeting the bands, and capturing the buzz around the new Pontiac Solstice roadster. It was an experimental podcast for General Motors, and an extension of what the company was already doing. General Motors was one of the first corporations to explore both blogging and podcasting as extensions of their

> **Podcasts offer companies unique advertising and sponsorship opportunities. This fast-growing market is expected to surpass $400 million by 2011.**
>
> GREG'S TIP

communications outreach (fastlane.gmblogs.com). Since then, many other car companies have begun using podcasts and video podcasts as well.

Education and Outreach

One market that has embraced podcasting with open arms is education and academia. Podcasts have been employed in a variety of ways by many universities and didactic institutions. The opportunities with podcasts are seemingly endless in an environment where lectures and lessons are key to disseminating information. Incorporating podcasting into lesson plans is not only possible but already occurring at some institutions.

The content offered up by university lectures is prime podcast material. It is relevant, informative, and what student wouldn't welcome the opportunity to listen to a lecture of a class they missed or a review of lecture material at their leisure. Some universities are already employing podcasts in their lessons. Duke University launched the Duke Digital Initiative, outfitting over 160 incoming first-year students with 20-GB iPods. The initiative was followed closely over the course of an academic year. The results broke iPod usage into five different means of usage: course content dissemination, classroom recording, field recording, study support, and file storage. According to the university's report evaluating the first year of use, the initiative was highly successful, supporting the effectiveness of podcasting as an educational medium.

Not surprisingly, the use of podcasts was highly useful in language learning and other audio-dependent courses. The applications of the podcasts in language learning are vast, since students can obtain multiple audio feeds in a foreign language that they can then take with them instead of being locked to a computer. The Duke report found that in certain courses, in particular language courses, students reported benefits in being able to multitask and replay lectures to increase comprehension. Certainly, the portability of the information appeals to the student lifestyle, and the ability to repeatedly access a lecture allows for greater absorption of information after listening multiple times.

Podcasting has proven useful for educational institutions in other ways as well. College admissions offices are beginning to see the value of using podcasts to reach out to high school juniors and seniors. Because high school students are busier than ever, particularly trying to build up their résumé to get into college, putting admissions info into a podcast is a logical move. Not only does the information reach the target audience, but it also demonstrates awareness of changes in technology on the part of the institution. Universities are also using podcasts to reach out to graduate students. The University of California, Berkeley not only offers a blog for MBA candidates, but also offers a podcast with tips and insights regarding the admissions process. Which graduate school candidate wouldn't want tips on how to get accepted? Berkeley uses the podcasts to offer curriculum information as described by the actual professors, admission tips, financial aid, and even career search information. Offering these pearls of wisdom not only reaches a wide audience of people seeking their MBA, but also keeps Berkeley in their mind as an option.

The way educational institutions disseminate information is changing. Professors have been posting lecture notes, media links, and PowerPoint presentations for years. Now, the trend is shifting to include podcasts of the entire lecture. As podcasts continue to emerge as a viable means of sharing information, we will see more students plugged in that ever before.

The success of podcasts in university learning is comparable to training in the business world. For instance, with the amount of commerce being conducted internationally, many companies are stressing the importance of language training for their employees. Just as universities are finding podcasts useful in language courses for their students, businesses are able to incorporate the same technology to train their employees. The dissemination of information through podcasting allows for a variety of resources to be sought out and shared throughout a corporation. As noted before, many Fortune 500 companies are favoring podcasting as a training tool in the corporate world. These businesses are finding that podcasts are an excellent way to pass on new training information, much as professors have found them useful in sharing lectures.

Like their educational counterparts, companies are utilizing podcasts as a means of outreach as well. Ortho-McNeil Neurologics, Inc. embraced podcasting during National Headache Awareness Week, by producing three separate podcasts that covered topics related to migraine headaches. These podcasts featured calls with experts in the field detailing the nature, symptoms, and treatments available for migraines. The intention behind these podcasts was to raise awareness regarding migraine headaches. As a result Ortho-McNeil, which is the maker of the popular migraine drug Topamax, gained more public awareness. Reaching out to the community with a public awareness message is a means of free publicity, and doing it through podcasting allows your business to specifically target your market. Ortho-McNeil's podcasts not only offered valuable information to people currently suffering from migraines, but also informed others who may be new to the symptoms, and are just starting to learn about migraine treatment. Regardless, the podcasts set Ortho-McNeil apart as an authority on headaches and have been able to build off their outreach campaign.

CASE STUDY
ORTHO-McNEIL

Who They Are?

Ortho-McNeil is a healthcare company that offers pharmaceutical treatments to health providers and patients, as well as products specializing in women's health, urology, migraine treatments, epilepsy, and Alzheimer's.

Purpose of Podcasting

Reach out to consumers to raise awareness of migraine symptoms during National Headache Awareness Week. Increase public knowledge of available treatments.

Approach

Ortho-McNeil put together three individual podcasts that were available during NHA Week. These podcasts offered tips and information from headache experts detailing the symptoms and causes of migraine headaches. Treatments were also discussed.

Results

The three-podcast series has been downloaded direct from their Web site and through iTunes more than 15,000 times.

Benefits

As a result of these podcasts, Ortho-McNeil set themselves apart in the pharmaceutical industry as an authority on migraine headaches and management of this ailment. Not only were consumers better informed about migraines, but they became more aware of the medications available, particularly those provided by Ortho-McNeil. Podcasts allowed Ortho-McNeil to reach their target audience directly.

Public Relations

Another area in which podcasts have extreme potential is the field of public relations. As any public relations representative knows, you are constantly dealing with the media and the dissemination of information. Often times, it is vital to get information out as quickly as possible, with the clearest message, to the widest possible audience. On the other hand, you have no way of knowing which publications will have the greatest interest in your information or products and therefore are the most important to reach out to.

Podcasting offers a means of getting the information out there quickly, and to a very broad audience. Imagine being able to get information typically found in a press release to the media without having to draft a press release. In the very near future, almost any publication that is interested in your company's activities will have subscribed to your RSS feed and will be notified when new information arrives. Better yet, using podcasts for public relations allows a company to completely bypass mainstream media and communicate directly with its market. Podcasting has become a time-saving, efficient way to conduct public relations.

The ability to reach the market directly is perhaps the most alluring reason to consider podcasting in your public relations strategy. In delivering your message directly to consumers and skipping over the media, you gain complete control over the message being delivered to your audience. Creating a consistent podcast with interesting, relevant content will encourage consumers to download your podcast, thereby increasing public awareness of new products and services, events, or business developments.

Many companies offering public relations podcasts rely on audience feedback since they are now communicating directly with the public. This increases the transparency of the information shared. A company will put out a podcast or video podcast and ask for reviews and input from those who are downloading the files. As we discussed in the last chapter, engaging the audience and creating the dialog with the consumer is how an organization can actively participate in the shifting social media landscape. Those providing feedback and engaging with your company offer a specific segment of the market that you are ideally trying to reach. Hopefully, this communication will aid the business in producing better, more relevant, and more desirable content, which should then increase the number of subscribers that are both gained and reached.

Hewlett Packard has produced a wide array of podcasts available on their Web site. The links are found on their news page, a prime location for public relations traffic. Information available there ranges from digital photography and image printing to Hewlett Packard's history and tips for small and medium-sized businesses. The variety of information appeals to many different markets, some of which overlap, but at the core of the podcasts is the attempt to connect with individuals who own or work within small and medium-sized businesses. Hewlett Packard also extends information out to their non-business clients—think the soccer mom with her digital camera—through their product-related podcasts. Overall, Hewlett Packard is reaching out to as much of their market as possible by offering up varied but pertinent podcasts and video podcasts.

Many of Hewlett Packard's podcasts are related to new products and the benefits that will be delivered to the consumer as a result of using them. For instance, one podcast is specifically targeted toward realtors and how the broadband network capabilities of a Hewlett Packard notebook will directly help their business. Another podcast relates the personal story of a customer who has experienced amazing success with the Tablet PC. This is a prime example of public relations via podcasting. Public relations is a vital means of increasing new product awareness. Hewlett Packard is using consumer experiences and personal stories to draw attention to existing products, but is also reaching out and creating allure for the technology that is to come by offering insights as to how these new products will create a better lifestyle or business for consumers.

Hewlett Packard has also included on their podcast Webpage a link asking listeners to "tell us what you want." On this page, aside from obtaining certain consumer details, Hewlett Packard asks a pointed question—what sort of podcasts does the listener want them to offer? Hewlett Packard offers several categories, such as tips on product use, ideas for business or the home, or new products. There is room for comments and dialog between the consumer and the business, helping Hewlett Packard produce more podcasts that will attract more listeners. If consumers are requesting more tips and tricks for the products they have purchased, Hewlett Packard will be able to produce more "how-to" type media, and in the process can introduce new initiatives and products that are on the horizon, ready to revolutionize the way in which we work from home and manage our businesses.

As podcasting continues to come into its own, we are sure to see a surge in the amount of public relations conducted through this medium. The ability of podcasts to communicate not only to the media but also directly to the desired market as well makes it an easy choice. Podcasting affords a greater degree of control over the message going out to the public since it does not need to go through the filter of mass media. Additionally, it opens the channels of communication between businesses and consumers, allowing them to dialog over podcast content and possibly even the direction of product and service development. A business can learn a lot about their consumers through engaging them with podcasts.

Business to Business and Business to Consumer

Podcasting is also finding its niche in business to business (B2B) and business to consumer (B2C) commerce. For both, podcasting offers the opportunity to break into new markets. Consider B2C marketing, which is ripe with the chance to win over new customers. Virgin Atlantic, for example, has developed podcasts as travel guides for the 20 destinations available on Virgin Atlantic Flights. Similarly, Purina has published a variety of audio and video podcasts, attracting more pet owners to their RSS feeds and gaining entry into larger markets. In B2C podcasting, the content is directed at reaching not only deeper into the existing market, but searching for those customers on the fringe who may not yet see that your business can offer something they want.

B2C podcasts will often highlight the consumer's interests rather than directly promote a product or service. Speedo, for example, has launched a biweekly podcast that offers insight into the world of swimming. The programs often include interviews with the professionals of the industry, news regarding international swimming events, and professional insights on competitions. Speedo entices listeners to subscribe with the promise of in-depth information and insights from the top performers in the sport, as well as exclusive video podcasts that "bring you up close and personal with some of today's swimming superstars." Podcasts like these speak directly to the consumer. The type of person who subscribes to this podcast is likely a serious swimmer, more than likely a competitor. As a result, they most likely are inclined to know about Speedo, a leader in the industry, and by offering these podcasts and video podcasts, Speedo increases its image as an authority in the swimming community.

For B2B marketing, podcasts are proving useful in reaching new markets as well. A typical B2B podcast show usually involves interviews with the proverbial "rock stars" of an industry. The average B2B podcast subscriber is looking for insights and tips—perhaps they want to learn why your company's product line is better suited for their business, or what the latest industry trends and thinking are in a particular sector. Regardless, the content you include in your podcast will determine the type of markets you reach. Hobson and Holtz, a biweekly public relations podcast, points out that podcasts can be used to stimulate communication with new markets, creating a sense of community and increasing the chances of successful business.

As with the other areas we have already examined, podcasts are useful in the world of B2B marketing to establish a presence and credibility in your field. Podcasting to a B2B audience does not mean that you have to divulge major industry or trade secrets, but sharing a small tidbit of information will draw attention. Furthermore, podcasts allow you to use this information to allude to the fact that your business not only has this information and is a thought leader, but that it can also expand the listener's business. A successful B2B podcast baits the market and opens the door to dialoging between businesses.

The cost value of B2B podcasting is great. According to Dana Gardner, author of the blog BriefingsDirect, "the cost savings come in both the ability to capture a lot of knowledge (via phone calls) and then package and distribute it globally via a network as diverse-yet-targeted as iTunes." The costs of producing a podcast are minimal, especially when compared to a traditional B2B campaign complete with brochures, ad campaigns and trade shows. Because they are so cost effective, podcasts are rapidly becoming a staple marketing tool for B2B industries.

IBM has developed several different RSS feeds containing podcasts on various topics. One that reaches out specifically to other businesses is

"IBM Business Consulting Services." This feed boasts podcasts that divulge business insights regarding customers, CFOs, and the changing global business dynamics. These podcasts are directed at corporate executives across a wide array of fields and industries. IBM has taken note that many of the concerns of top executives are the same, regardless of their specific industry. They face similar issues regarding changing workforce demographics, or understanding the consumer, or new discoveries regarding outsourcing. These topics, along with interviews with the CEOs of major businesses and other experts are all available on the IBM Web site. The allure of this information attracts more businesses to subscribe to the feed and learn more about what IBM may be able do in assisting their growth and development.

Lessons Learned

· Podcasting is a trend with staying power, not a fad.

· The audience downloading podcasts is increasing quickly, with a projected 60 million listeners by 2010 vs. 10 million in 2006.

· Internal communications is being revolutionized by podcasts by creating an easier means of notifying employees of new information, sending it directly to their inbox instead of through memos and newsletters.

· Branding is possible through podcasts by sharing information that demonstrates expertise in the field.

· Podcasts offer valuable support as a marketing tool, providing access to specific, targeted markets.

· Advertisers are examining more ways to utilize podcasts due to their targeted, content-driven nature.

· Universities and corporations are using podcasts to promote themselves and reach out to broader audiences.

· Using podcasts for public relations offers complete control over the delivery of the message, getting it direct to the consumer.

SECTION 2: PODCASTING FUNDAMENTALS: PLANNING AND DEVELOPMENT

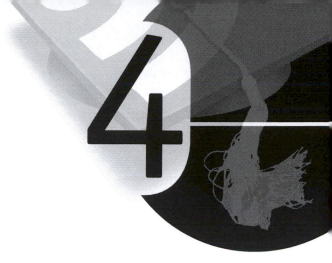

Internal Considerations for Podcasting

Greg Cangialosi

By now you should understand the shift in media, the changes in the business–consumer relationship, and the essence of podcasting and its potential uses. We saw several examples of businesses that have been successfully podcasting for a few years now, and others that are just beginning to embrace this new medium. You are probably wondering by now if podcasting is the right fit for your business, and if so, how you will incorporate it.

Integrating any new technology into your business can be a challenge. There are many factors to be considered, such as the receptiveness of your staff, the costs of the infrastructure, the practicality of the new processes, etc. There is no doubt that it can be incredibly daunting. We have already revealed some of the challenges in creating podcasts from sources outside of your business. We have also discussed several key points to keep in mind when adding podcasting to your marketing and communications mix that will help your company transition into a fully functioning, podcast-capable corporation. But before you can launch your own podcast, you will need to look at the potential challenges within your organization that can hinder adding podcasting to your communications mix.

One of the principle challenges facing any change in corporate communication is the challenge posed by old habits and mindsets. Typically, many people fear change and only embrace it after the change has been forced upon them and they begin to reap the benefits. Hopefully, introducing podcasting in your corporation will not be such a traumatic experience. With new technologies constantly being developed and arriving on the consumer market, people are now more willing to adapt to using different technologies, especially if they build on tools they are already familiar with. Podcasting builds on audio and video technologies and portable MP3 players—things that most people in the work place today are aware of.

Still, in spite of the familiarity of the tools, you may find resistance to podcasting into your corporate environment. One reason is that some people may inherently prefer or be more comfortable with traditional forms of media. As more and more new technology infiltrates our daily lives, some people are left wishing for the "good old days" when memos arrived on paper instead of via email, or when the president of the company held a corporate-wide meeting instead of posting updates on his blog. This can be a great challenge to overcome since it breeds contempt and dissatisfaction among this group of employees.

The Role of the Internal Champion

Not everyone is enamored with social media, and so it is important to understand your audience before you launch headlong into podcasting. Your staff needs to fully understand the value of including podcasting into the corporate strategy in order to successfully execute it as an extension of your communications. Crucial to overcoming this resistance can be the presence of an internal champion within your organization.

By "internal champion" I am referring to a person who is willing to make the case for podcasting, and make the cause their own. Preferably, you will have more than one internal champion, so that you have a team that you are able to rally for support. Regardless, the function is the same—create enthusiasm and cohesive efforts to garner support for the podcasting initiative. Without cohesive actions and support from all sides, the message behind the podcast will be lost and ineffectively communicated.

Consider some of the lessons learned from Verizon Wireless's first foray into the world of podcasting. Verizon embarked upon its podcasting path with the intention of producing brief shows that promoted the new phones that are available through their network. I was the host of the podcasts, and my team produced them from start to finish. Although the idea was sound, in hindsight it becomes clear that there wasn't enough cohesive action on the part of the end client, so the message lost its power and wound up sounding more like a commercial than a podcast. If you were to go and look for the podcasts on Verizon Wireless's Web site today, you would find the links buried somewhere on their "News" page rather than placed prominently on the home page or on some of their other public-facing Web properties. In addition, both podcasts we produced were around major product launches, but due to internal approvals and input on editing, not to mention the slow moving nature of a large organization, one of the podcasts didn't go live until weeks after the product was launched. If Verizon had an internal champion driving the development of the podcasts, they likely would have been able to promote the products more successfully, made cohesive parallel moves, and streamlined communication in between the departments.

CASE STUDY
VERIZON WIRELESS

Who They Are?

Verizon Wireless is a leading wireless cell phone network provider.

Purpose of the Podcast

Inform consumers of new phones and services available through Verizon Wireless, focusing on the network's reliability and the company's service features.

Approach

Verizon produced two podcasts, one covering the launch of the V Cast music service and the other the launch of the LG 9800 phone. Interviews and discussions with college students, random individuals on the street, and Verizon Wireless employees were conducted to impart information on the technology and consumer perspectives.

Benefits

Verizon Wireless was one of the first corporations to explore podcasting, pioneering new territory for corporate communications. Because the podcast was not given a prominent spot on the company's consumer Web properties, and because of the more commercialized feel to the episodes, however, these podcasts did not offer the impact that was hoped for. The number of downloads was not significant enough to suggest that Verizon Wireless should forge ahead and embrace the medium. This was due more to poor execution than the medium itself.

GREG'S TIP — Having an internal champion will keep your efforts focused and efficient. When selecting your internal champion, look for someone who is a self-starter and will bring enthusiasm and dedication to the task at hand.

Overcome Resistance to New Media

Internal champions for new media are essential for overcoming the difficulties posed by traditional media and institutionalized biases toward it. Right now, new media is comparable to certain forms of traditional media back in their early days, such as radio, televisions, CDs, and DVDs. Each of these mediums, now considered part of "traditional" media, faced developmental challenges in the face of the most popular medium of the time. At its onset, television challenged radio. There were many who refused to embrace the new "picture box" in place of their classic radio programs.

Gradually, as the technology spread and more and more information of same or greater quality became available via television than radio, people made the shift and a new mainstream media was born.

Currently we are witnessing a similar shift from traditional forms of media into the new social media that are blogs, podcasts, wikis, photo sites, news sites, and social networks. Podcasts, at present, do not have the "mega audiences" boasted by some of the more popular social networking Web sites, but the audience is growing rapidly as the content and availability of the information continues to expand and increase in quality. Again, I will make the analogy to earlier forms of media, such as the transition from cassette tapes to compact discs. In the 1980s, you were most likely to head out and buy your favorite band's latest album on tape. Slowly, listeners switched to CDs as the technology became more affordable and the higher sound quality more broadly appreciated. Now, trying to locate a place to purchase cassette tapes is near impossible.

To bring this back to your business, you must be aware of the media shift, recognize that it is irreversible, and begin encouraging your team, and overall staff to consider the value of embracing social media. Because consumers in social media are also producers, this creates a greater opportunity for participation among staff members in utilizing these new tools. Social media tools open new lines of communication not just for businesses to their customers, but also for management to their staff.

New media forms allow for a degree of interaction between staff and management across departments, which until now, was very challenging to achieve. In fostering the use of these tools within your office, you are creating a space for the sharing of ideas on an equal playing field. Businesses often find that employees are more inclined to work hard when they feel an emotional connection to the project or company. By allowing for this level of participation to occur, you are not only gaining the maximum amount of collaboration but also creating the opportunity for employees to feel that they have an integral role in the objectives of the company.

Advocate for Gradual Change

In instituting these new tools in corporate communications it is important to introduce the mediums gradually. Shock therapy in terms of technological introductions rarely works. In other words, do not change the company newsletter from standard print format to a podcast overnight. Gradually make the new technology available and, if possible, keep both as options for accessing the information for a period of time. This allows your company to become accustomed to the presence and use of new mediums without taking away the comfort of the familiar. Rapidly and unilaterally making the change is likely to create anxiety and frustration among the staff, and ultimately will work against your objective of creating a successful corporate podcast initiative.

Encourage Collaboration, Not Specialization

For larger organizations, another potential challenge that your company faces is the way in which podcasting challenges the traditional corporate setup of independent (or loosely linked) departments. Traditional forms of media were often developed separately by different departments: press releases are handled by public relations or an outside agency; email campaigns are launched by the marketing or in some cases the IT department; advertising strategies are developed by marketing and/or advertising departments. Developing a successful podcast initiative forces a level of intimacy between departments that was never a major requirement when using older forms of media. Starting a podcast production can require that the Web and marketing departments work extremely closer together. Overcoming the traditional mindset of separately functioning departments may prove quite challenging for your staff to master. Collaboration between departments is never easy to orchestrate, particularly with busy schedules and different departmental agendas.

Coordination across departments can be difficult to achieve, but is absolutely essential for producing an effective podcast. This is because of the importance of timing and knowledge gathering when you are producing a corporate podcast. Podcasts are on-demand in nature, and sometimes the most successful ones can be incredibly timely, so having solid communication across company departments is key in a quick, timely production. This requires reducing the time that usually goes into combing through and refining traditional media communications. A poorly coordinated team will be unable to deliver a clean, powerful podcast in a quick turn around time situation. Thus, coordination among your Web, marketing, and public relations staffs—and every other member of the team—needs to be streamlined. Without coordination, even the most well-produced podcast can be rendered irrelevant when not posted in a timely manner.

GREG'S TIP

If you're in a larger organization, you can streamline coordination between departments by having clear deadlines on production elements. The use of other social media tools like internal blogs and wikis can increase collaboration among different departments.

Determine Whether to Produce Internally or Externally

An additional issue to consider when looking at incorporating podcasting to your business strategy is the natural desire to keep production internal and whether or not that's a realistic goal. It is possible to produce podcasts internally at your company, or you can use an external production company and an outside personality for your host. There are certain components essential to any podcast, and as a business owner you must objectively look at the capabilities of your company in meeting these needs. We will briefly examine this challenge later in this chapter, and more in depth in the next section of the book. For now, you must simply bear in mind the real capacity of your company to produce a podcast. Do you, right now, have the hosting talent? Do you have someone knowledgeable in communications? Can you offer the resources to edit and publish your podcast files to the Web and create and manage your really simple syndication (RSS) feed?

If the answer to these questions is not a resounding "yes" do not despair. Podcasting is still entirely within your reach, either as an internal production or as an external one. By introducing podcasting to your business, you will begin to uncover hidden talents of your staff members (perhaps you never knew that your lead sales person was the most popular DJ at her college radio station), and reveal the strengths of your teams. Or you may find that adding podcasting requires more time than your current staff is able to devote, and so outsourcing the production is the more appealing option. Regardless, there are certain factors you must consider before deciding if you should podcast, and how you should approach the task.

Developing Your Team

Think of your current staff. If you were to choose your podcasting champion(s), who would they be? This is a more difficult question to answer than you may think. It is not always the most ambitious person who should be on your team, nor the one most infatuated with podcasting, nor solely one department. The ideal team will represent a cross section of your company, and in the case of a bigger company, should involve more than one department. You will face some challenging decisions in selecting your developmental team, regardless of whether you have four employees or four thousand.

The Core Team

Regardless of the size of your business, there are certain components of your core team that you must have if you are to successfully add podcasting to your business strategy. The team you put together will determine whether your efforts will flourish or fail, whether podcasting will be an invaluable asset to your business or a detriment to your strategy. Let's take a look at the reasoning and importance behind building your team with certain core ingredients.

The team leader

The first component you need to consider for your team is the team leader, who often turns out to be the "internal champion." Depending on the overall objective of your podcast, you will want to select your team leader based on which sector will be best able to support that objective. For instance, if your goal is to increase brand awareness, your team leader should come from your marketing department rather than human resources. You may also be considering starting more than one podcast, each one around a different topic or approach. In selecting someone who is familiar with the topic and content, you are ensuring that the message being conveyed by the podcast is on point with your objective. Regardless, a strong team leader who understands the goals and objectives in implementing podcasting as part of the business strategy is crucial.

Your team leader should ideally have a base understanding of communications, even if his or her background and area of expertise have nothing to do with this field. Bear in mind that at its core, a podcast is a communication, and thus as it relates to business, involves conveying some sort of message to the consumer or business to business market. However, podcasts are a new breed of corporate communications, which means that they do not always fall under the ownership of traditional communication specialists like public relations. Your internal champion may very well come from a communication background, but it is not essential so long as they have a functioning knowledge of how to reach out to your specific audience. If your choice for team leader is not the most experienced communicator with the public, you can select the other team members to offset that weakness. Still, the ideal person should understand the basics of communication and have a grasp on the new media shift to accurately produce and deliver the message to the end audience.

Where do you find this leader? Identifying the right person to spearhead your podcasting initiative can be a challenging task. There are certain qualities you will want to look for in this individual. Your team leader needs to have a clear understanding of your organization's overall goals, and support and believe in them completely—there can be no room for doubt. As mentioned earlier, ideally this person is the "internal champion" within your company who can motivate others to produce the best possible product. Additionally, your team leader needs to be someone who can coordinate cross-departmentally. Your optimum team will likely not be confined to one department, but rather will incorporate opinions and expertise from various executives and experts. Thus, whomever you entrust with the task of developing and maintaining your podcast needs to be able to work well with others and understand how to maximize cross-departmental knowledge and influence.

In some cases, especially with small organizations, your team leader may be the only member of the team, filling the job description for the additional components that make up a successful podcast team. Such a situation is neither rare nor problematic. In some cases, having one person comprise the entire team can make things more cohesive and streamlined. But in order for this to be effective, the person selected must be absolutely able to handle all aspects of podcast production, from the content and format development to the hosting talent, all the way through to the publishing components. In short, so long as the team you select has the required knowledge and know how, and is working toward the ultimate objective— a high quality, successful podcast that is in line with the organization's objectives—you need not be concerned with the size of the team.

Other team members

Assuming your team leader is not the only person required to produce a podcast, you have to select the additional members of the team. You should also carefully consider the size of the team. Would you prefer a larger team, which may not be able to move as fast but will be able to combine various points of view into a singular, unified message; or would you prefer to have a smaller, more efficient team that will offer a slightly narrower vision? There are benefits and drawbacks to each, but so long as you select the appropriate team members, you will be able to produce a quality product regardless of your company's size.

GREG'S TIP

Podcasts are a form of corporate communications in which you are talking to your market directly. Adding someone who is familiar with communications concepts to your team will help keep your podcast's message on track.

The talent

Whether it's someone from inside the organization or outside, one key member of your team will be of your talent or host(s). Keeping in mind that podcasts should not sound like commercials, you will need to locate someone who can offer a quality voice, and who can deliver the message in an easy to listen to manner. Often times the person who has the talent is also another member of the team—perhaps someone from your public relations group or someone from the Web team. Whoever fills this role should have some basic knowledge of podcasting as a medium. You will not want to choose someone who is locked into the traditional media mindset, or someone who believes that your company's podcast is nothing more than a commercial. While the objective of your podcast can be parallel to the goals of a commercial, the format must be entirely different. The podcast should offer stellar content, and not just shameless self-promotion. That said, you will want to make sure the host of your podcast has an easy to listen to, professionally sounding voice. And in the case of video podcasts, you should have someone who presents well in front of the camera. Before sounding "professional" like a radio DJ, the person's voice should simply be easy to listen to. The content has to be good, but it must also be easy to consume for a listener or viewer.

Locating this talent may be a challenge, or it may be one of the easier factors to uncover. If you feel that you do not have the appropriate talent within your organization, it is possible to outsource the talent, perhaps by linking up with an established podcaster. For instance, I have been recruited by several companies as the talent/host for their podcasts. As mentioned earlier, through their public relations firm, GM hired me to produce their podcast for the Pontiac Summer Solstice party, when podcasting was just emerging as a part of new media. They were looking for someone from the outside to bring in the voice talent and familiarity with podcasting instead of seeking the voice internally since the medium was so new.

The technical guru

In addition to talent, since you will be producing an audio or video file to be shared over the Web, you will want at least one technical team member who is familiar with audio and visual recording equipment. This person could come from your IT department, or from your Web team, or any other department—so long as they have an understanding of how to record and publish content via audio or video equipment. Entrusting the A/V requirements to someone who is not well versed in the technology can jeopardize the quality of the production. Someone who is knowledgeable in recording technologies will be able to make recommendations as per the format, file size, etc., and will know which tools to use in correspondence with these decisions.

With any luck, the person who brings their knowledge of A/V production to the team will also be the person who will know how to handle the Web publishing and RSS feed component as well. Having someone who is comfortable with the Web side of podcasting will be essential to your success. Without proper placement and publication on your Web site, the point in producing your podcast becomes useless. Typically, your Web team will have best person to recruit for both A/V production and management of podcast inclusion on the Web.

Having someone from your Web team involved in your podcasting team is critical, since they control all the content that is published on your Web site. They will be the ones to create the "home" for your podcast, the section of your Web site dedicated to your podcast initiative. Having your Web team work with the marketing and/or public relations team, will make it much easier to discover the best place for your podcast to live, and other strategic locations to link to it, for example from the news or press section, etc. You will want to develop several inbound links to your podcasts to help your audience access the information quickly and easily. Having a cohesive team that's all on the same page makes this process flow.

After going through these necessary components, you may feel that you need a rather sizable team to launch a podcasting initiative. But before you panic or begin thinking you need to reallocate resources to make this happen, keeping in mind that the beauty of podcasts is that they are relatively easy to produce—meaning that many if not all of these roles can be handled by one person. It is not uncommon to have one person be able to produce an entire podcast on his or her own. After all, podcasts were largely produced and supported by individuals before corporations began incorporating them into their communications strategy. Just look at the slew of podcasts out there that are put out by the independent content producers, some of which are very popular. Because podcasts do not necessitate the super-polished look of traditional corporate communications, they can be produced by a small team of savvy individuals, or by one person.

The key to a successful team is not the size of it, but rather its efficiency. The timing and regularity of podcasts is paramount. Information and content needs to be gathered, edited, and published quickly and accurately. This can only be achieved by a cohesive, well-defined team, be it an individual or 20 who work well together. If your team is larger than one or two individuals, you must ensure that communication across multiple departments is streamlined and clear. Your team must be able to dedicate the necessary time and resources to producing your podcasts. If you find that one staff member is qualified to produce the entire podcast on their own, you must be sure they have the time to devote to it without sacrificing their current workload. These are all the important considerations when selecting your team.

> **Your podcasting team does not need to be a large team. So long as the required skill sets are present, your team can range in size from one person to five.**

GREG'S TIP

Internal Team vs. External Team

Naturally, selecting your core team is only relevant if you decided to keep podcast production in-house. You may decide that you do not have the right resources to produce in-house, or that your resources are limited enough or too valuable to assign staff members to such an initiative. In such a situation, outsourcing your podcast can be a very effective solution. In the coming chapters we will talk in detail about making this decision, and the pros and cons of each. There are many ways in which you can engage in external podcasting, alleviating some of the production concerns by way of putting together a team. Often times it is possible to seek out a well-established podcaster in your field, someone who already has an audience and credibility as an authority on the content that is being put forth. Going to an external producer can streamline the production and gain immediate access to a market. There are plenty of great podcast consultants and production companies available to help you craft your podcast message, format, and production.

Keeping production internal offers other benefits and challenges. Having members of your own staff working on the podcasting initiative affords you a greater degree of adherence to the corporate image. In keeping the production internal, the personnel working on production will understand the goals and objectives of the podcast, and also your current brand image and overall corporate goals. However, while you are developing your podcast, you will also need to consider how you will develop your audience. It may take some trial and error before the right format for the podcast has been developed and for an audience to form. When you take on podcasting internally you have greater control over the content and quality of the message, but your staff may lack the experience and knowledge of getting the word out and measuring your success. This is why it is important when starting your podcast to set realistic goals to gauge your success.

Making the decision to go out of house to produce a podcast vs. keeping it in-house is a purely subjective decision that varies from business to business. One is not inherently better than the other, and each offers a different set of pros and cons. When evaluating your choices, consider the resources you have available and the costs of production. We will examine these options more thoroughly later in this book.

Developing Your Goals and Objectives

Now that your team is in place and you have decided if you are going to pursue in-house production or use an external service, you must develop some goals and objectives for your podcast initiative. During this initial stage, there are several things to consider. First, you have to define who your audience is and how you will appeal to them through your podcast. You must also consider your market perception, how you wish to be perceived by your audience, and how it relates to your marketing and communications strategy. Finally, and perhaps most importantly, you need to define the main purpose of the podcast. Are you selling? Branding? Educating? All of these considerations must be carefully examined and well thought out before embarking upon podcast production.

Defining Your Market Perception

In creating your podcast, you must consider how you desire your message and your company to be represented in the market. Podcasts are a new form of corporate communications, and although they are less formal than traditional mediums, they are still very much a reflection of your corporation and what you represent. How you define your market perception will determine how podcasting will be merged with your existing communication outreach efforts. For instance, if you are looking to reach deeper into your existing market, you will probably produce a podcast that is very much in line with your current market perception. However, if you are looking to reach a new demographic, you can use podcasts to develop and craft a different market perception, one that may appeal to new consumers.

Developing a position for your podcast initiative from the onset will eliminate wasted hours trying to refine your message and goals. In determining your market perception, you must consider your target audience and what it is you are going to offer them through your podcast. What is the problem facing your audience, or what information are they missing or anxious to receive? How is your podcast going to resolve these issues for your audience? Answering these questions is crucial to developing the communications platform from which you will launch your podcasting initiative, and will serve to define corresponding communications to your audience.

To determine your market perception, you must clearly understand what it is that your audience desires. Podcasts create the space for dialoguing with the consumer, but it may prove very useful to conduct some research into similar podcasts that already exist to see what sort of information your target audience is currently downloading. Podcasting appeals to very niche markets, so understanding the consumers in this area is even more crucial than with traditional mediums. Their desires and needs are even more targeted than that of the average consumer. Not only must your podcast offer excellent content, but it must also be timely, accurate, and well produced.

Who's Listening? Determining Your Audience

As described in Chapter 3, there are many different uses of podcasts. Each use dictates a different audience. Now that you have considered who your market is, you need to define your audience and their needs. Are you reaching out to consumers to build customer loyalty, or maybe to inform them of new products? Are you trying to create a younger image for your brand, and therefore are trying to reach out to the younger crowd to market your goods or services? The recipients of your message will largely dictate the tone and content of your podcast. After all, an information podcast on financial services that is geared toward an older generation will not impact the rising stars in the field in the same way, since those people in their 20s and 30s have different desires, needs, and considerations than their counterparts who are in their 40s and 50s (see Figure 4.1).

So who is it that you are reaching out to? Are you sending a message to consumers? Are you trying to build stronger business-to-business communications? Perhaps you are considering redefining your public relations strategy and reaching beyond traditional media to get your message out. Regardless, you must know who your target audience is in order to create your message. It is important to remember that *podcasting appeals to niche markets*, so you must completely understand your audience since it is most likely composed of a very specific group of individuals.

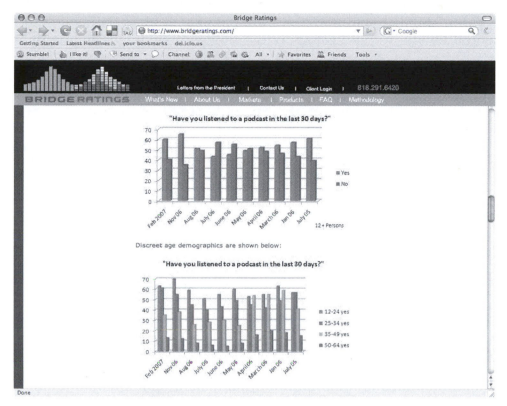

FIGURE 4.1

Breakdown of podcast usage within 30 days by age. *Source*: Bridge Ratings (www. bridgeratings.com) "Podcast User Survey" conducted in February 2007.

There are certain basic statistics you will want to know about your audience when producing your message. First and foremost, you will want to determine your audience's interests. Why should your audience listen to your podcast? You must uncover what they desire and build your podcast around that. Whole Foods Market offers various podcasts to their consumers. The typical market that Whole Foods reaches out to is very interested in natural and organic foods and nutritional supplements. Knowing this, Whole Foods has produced two separate podcasts, one that informs people of seasonal foods and organic products, as well as recipes for these foods. The other podcast appeals to the more nutritionally conscious crowd, offering tips and information from experts on the value of different natural supplements. The organic, naturally driven food market is very specific, and the consumers in it are much vested in receiving quality information about the food and supplements they put into their bodies.

CASE STUDY
WHOLE FOODS MARKET

Who They Are?

Whole Foods Market is an Austin, TX-based company that offers organic foods and natural products to consumers. They offer specialty foods, wines, cheeses, fish, and natural body products and supplements. Whole Foods Market has almost 200 locations in the USA, Canada, and the UK.

Purpose of Podcasting

Increase awareness and knowledge of organic foods and new products. Inform listeners the benefits of natural supplements.

Approach

Whole Foods Market offers two different podcast categories, one focusing on the foods offered by the store and ways to prepare those foods, and the other focusing on offering natural supplements for total body health. For the first category, Whole Foods offers podcasts relating to seasonal foods and different recipes. A new podcast is offered every few weeks. The second group of podcasts reaches out to consumers who focus not just on organic foods, but also natural supplements and herbs for total body health. Whole Foods Market enlists the help of experts in the field to inform listeners about the different supplements available and their benefits.

Benefits

In offering podcasts that cover the wide variety of food available at Whole Foods Market, the company is able to generate interest in products that the consumer may not have initially been aware of or willing to try. Regarding the podcasts that cover natural body care, Whole Foods is able to establish itself as an authority on natural health and body products, and as a provider of those goods.

A common marketing strategy employed by traditional media is to make a message very general so as to rope in as much of the consumer market as possible in one attempt. Unfortunately, this does not work with podcasting. Instead, the opposite is true. The more specific and targeted the content, the more successful the podcast will be. This is because in narrowing your focus you are appealing to a niche market, which is the essence of podcasting. Several programs put out by National Public Radio (NPR) are currently some of the most downloaded podcasts available on iTunes. Shows like "Fresh Air," "Car Talk's Call of the Week," and "Wait, Wait, Don't Tell Me" are among the top 10 downloaded podcasts. These particular podcasts appeal to a very narrow, specific audience—well-educated, upper middle-class, socially conscious listeners. With podcasts, narrow focus works very well.

You can learn more about your audience by doing a little competitor research as well. Tracking the different podcasts that your competitors produce or support can give you insights into what is already out there and what kind of information your consumers are looking for. Aside from learning about consumer interests, studying competitor podcasts will allow you to see what is out there, what others are doing, and what you can do better or differently to distinguish yourself. Being able to differentiate yourself from your competitors is incredibly important and will give you an edge in reaching out to your new podcasting market.

GREG'S TIP

The success of a podcast is directly linked to the quality of its content. The more specific and engaging your content is, the more appealing it will be to your niche audience. Don't be afraid to be specific and have a narrow focus.

To study your audience further, it is wise to search blog and podcast directories to see what people are discussing and downloading. Conducting searches covering your topic will offer insights as to the potential size of the audience as well as reveal what has already been done before. Although it is important to have a specific, niche-focused podcast, you want to ensure that there is a market for it, which is what research such as this will help you achieve. A search that returns a number of relevant hits linking to solid sources of information would suggest that there is an active audience for that particular topic. As with traditional marketing strategies, you want to ensure that your venture will succeed, and so the more information you can obtain on your market, the better. You will want to determine the demographics of your market from age group to income to location. Much of this can be achieved by conducting online research, or better yet, conducting a listener/viewer survey to refine your message once you have an audience. You don't need to know everything about them, but the more you know, the better you can tailor your content.

In producing your podcast, you must also bear in mind a more general idea of your audience. Are they consumers? Business partners? Your own employees? Obviously the type of podcast you produce to attract new consumers will differ from the kind that you develop to inform your employees of the new health insurance policy. Knowing your audience in this sense will again help you define your strategy. Podcasting as a form of internal communications is much different than podcasting as part of an advertising campaign. Your audience is quite distinct and requires a different pitch and delivery of the information. For example, a podcast to a new consumer market may highlight the benefits of purchasing a product from your company, whereas a podcast geared toward B2B may offer tips and insights that allude to the knowledge and expertise of your company, thereby encouraging more business. This type of broad understanding of your audience is what will allow you to clearly and accurately define the goals of your podcast.

What's the Point? The Objective of Your Podcasting Initiative

You have developed a market perception. You know you have a viable audience for your particular podcast subject matter. Now what are you going to do with it? As you may have begun to notice as we delved into the topic of your audience, the group of people you are podcasting for largely dictates the purpose of your podcast. You are not going to try and push the hard sell on your own employees, nor are you going to offer training tips to the consumers you are trying to win over.

The final step before launching into production of your podcast is to determine what your ultimate goal is. Are you trying to increase the sales of a particular product? Would you like to improve customer service by offering training advice? Or is the purpose of the podcast simply to create brand awareness in a saturated market? It is essential to evaluate the main objective of your podcast before you begin recording; otherwise you risk having a podcast that, no matter how well it is put together, fails to deliver the desired results.

> **Having a clear goal for your podcast will direct the tone and voice of your content, as well as set up the means for measuring success.**

GREG'S TIP

Each component we have discussed up to this point segues into this final piece. You must be completely clear on what it is you wish to accomplish with your podcast. While one podcast can produce multiple positive results (for instance, a podcast meant for branding could also generate additional sales), it is important to develop the message for one key purpose. This is so important largely because the styling of the message depends very heavily on the intended use of it. Also, in defining your goal clearly, you create the space to develop accurate ways of measuring the success of your podcast. For example, you would not want to measure the success of a sales-oriented podcast solely by the number of downloads or subscribers you get to the podcast. Rather, you would want to set up a way of measuring how many new sales were generated by the podcast.

To review, there are several ways in which you can include podcasting in your business strategy.

Internal communications

Podcasts can serve as valuable tools for internal communications, from training to human resources to messages from the CEO. When producing a podcast for internal purposes, your audience is your own staff. The type of message you convey can range from something motivational for driving sales to something more informative keeping employees current and up to date on policies and procedures. Progressive steps have been taken to offer monthly email and print newsletters into audio podcasts that your employees can download and listen to while they are commuting to work or have downtime at their desk. The information can be conveyed in a more informal, familiar way since your staff is already familiar with the brand and the corporate image. Podcasts also help breakdown traditional communication barriers that exist within a corporation between departments and traditional structure by allowing for easier communication and dialog between these areas.

Branding, marketing, and advertising

Podcasts are also useful tools for branding and marketing purposes. The ability of podcasts to reach niche markets is a huge asset to any marketing strategy, creating opportunities to increase brand awareness or redefine your business's influence on the industry. The applications of podcasting in the marketing arena are still being explored and new ways to deploy this technology are still emerging. Advertising is another venue in which podcasting is becoming a viable medium. Using podcasts for marketing, branding, or advertising purposes allows for a greater degree of flexibility in strategy. This is because producing podcasts is a low cost, minimal risk venture. Your podcast talent can try out a variety of personalities to find which best fits with your market; the styling can be formal, informal, or even entertaining. Creating or utilizing an existing podcast allows you to try out different tactics or test new campaigns with little repercussions, particularly when you consider ROI vs. the costs and risks involved.

Education

If your interests run more toward education and outreach, podcasts can also be used by your business. Educating and informing your audience serves to establish greater credibility for your business in your particular industry. What's more is that, in sharing this information through a podcast, you are developing an audience that is in tune with your business, one who will likely turn to you when they have questions or need a product or service that pertains the information you are providing. Outreach communications are typically produced in a more formal tone since they are offering information, usually from experts. In these types of podcasts, the content dictates the formality of the delivery. Interviews are typically more formal than just having your podcast personality run the show. Still, podcasting with the intention to inform and reach out to new markets is very useful.

Public relations

Many corporations are also beginning to use podcasts in conjunction with their public relations agenda. Because podcasts reach directly into your target audience, they remove the necessity of utilizing traditional media in certain communications. This means you are publishing directly to your target market, whereas with traditional media you are often left to hope that your press release is picked up. In the case of your own podcast you can also extend your message well beyond the written word. Furthermore, you control the message in its entirety, from the presentation to the audience, to the content and details of the message. Podcasts as a medium for public relations allows for a consistency in corporate communications to your market, one that can be constructed to parallel marketing initiatives and advertising campaigns.

Measuring Success

Measuring success in any industry can be challenging. Certain things are easy to measure and rate as successes or failures. For instance, the sales of a new product will either be very high, very low, or an average performer. Other business attributes are more ambiguous and thus harder to measure. Many businesses are still questioning how to measure the success of advertising and marketing campaigns, or the effectiveness of a press release and other communications. There are often many factors that need to be considered when evaluating these initiatives, and the same applies to podcasting.

What works for measuring one means of communication will not always apply to another. Consider an advertising campaign vs. a press event. To measure the success of the advertisement, you would somehow need to track how many sales or inquiries were made because of this advertisement. This can be a very hard key performance indicator (KPI) to track, largely because unless you directly ask each customer why they have purchased your product you cannot assume that sales are directly linked to your advertisement. In contrast, a press event cannot be measured by the same KPI. Sales are not the objective of a press event, which is about getting your product or company into mainstream media. Of course, the event may affect other KPIs you are measuring, but the heart of the event is to generate press coverage.

Podcasting is no different. Measuring the success of your podcast is going to depend heavily on what your objective is in creating it. The best means for tracking podcasts have still not been agreed upon in the field. Some podcasters believe it is best to track the number of times their podcast has been downloaded. Other businesses argue that it is important to look at the number of times the podcast has been completely downloaded, as opposed to just partially listened to. There are many other ways to track podcasts, and nearly everyone is trying something different. Unique solutions to podcast measurement are still in development and being tested. The important thing to keep in mind is your objective, and how you can go about measuring success in that way.

Setting Realistic Goals and Measurements

As with any new initiative, it is important to maintain realistic goals and develop the best tools for measurement when starting your podcast. Keep in mind that, in most situations, you will be starting your podcast from scratch with no audience, so you will have to build your base of listeners/ viewers. It is unlikely that you will have over 1000 downloads after your first podcast is posted; it takes time to form an audience. Of course there are always exceptions to the rule, but in general, it can take a minimum of 6 months before you have a noteworthy audience. And in those initial few months, there is a lot of other marketing and promotion related work to do that we will cover in a later chapter. For this reason, you should not set goals for large numbers of downloads when you first begin your initiative. Understand that there will be a certain degree of trial and error as you begin to develop your audience, with some podcasts being very successful and others not as much. As your podcast matures and evolves with stronger content and better-defined format, it will begin to gather a larger audience.

The first step in setting your goals, after you have researched your podcast and are ready to begin, is to develop a timeline. You need to clearly understand the time required to complete the steps of production and establish clear deadlines for information gathering, content formatting, and actual recording, editing, and publishing time. In the beginning, you should allow for slightly more time to develop each component as the production and timing will be new to your organization. The length of time it will take for you to actually produce your podcast will depend on the length of the podcast and the amount of research actually required to create the content. Right now, it usually takes me about 2½ hours from start to finish to produce roughly 30 minutes of content.

I want to stress again that once your podcast has been published to the Web, you should not expect an explosion of activity with record-breaking numbers of downloads. It will take time for your podcast to gain any critical mass and for a solid subscriber base to form. There is marketing to do, directories to submit to, press releases and blog posts to write, etc. If you have 100 downloads on your first podcast, you are off to an incredible start. My latest podcast, return on investment (ROI) Radio (www.roiradio. com), was just a neophyte back in October 2006, and is only now, 1 year later, just starting to gain a loyal and respectable subscriber base.

Keep your goals realistic and attainable. Setting goals too high will create frustration. It takes time for a podcast to reach a substantial audience.

GREG'S TIP

Goals for the development of your subscriber base need to be kept realistic. The most popular podcasts out there right now have a huge number of subscribers, but this is after years of producing content that has an audience. For instance, NPR has an extremely large subscriber base for their podcasts, but they have been broadcasting their programs and developing an audience for these podcasts for years as a standard terrestrial radio program. If you project that you will have 500 000 subscribers to your podcast in a year's time, you are more than likely setting yourself up for failure. Subscribers and downloads alone are not the only way to gauge the success of your podcast (see Figure 4.2).

Define Success

When determining how you will measure the success of your podcast, you must not limit yourself to looking at RSS subscribers and downloads. There

FIGURE 4.2
The vast majority is only recently starting to consume podcasts; in earlier years podcast production and consumption was largely localized to the innovators of the technology. *Source*: Bridge Ratings (www.bridgeratings.com) "Podcast User Survey" conducted in February 2007.

are a wide variety of metrics that can be utilized to measure the success of your podcast. Many services exist now that specialize in tracking your podcast, such as Podtrac, & Feedburner and many others. There are ways to build tracking mechanisms into your podcast by offering specific information that will direct listeners to a particular site that you can monitor. The most common metrics right now are still RSS subscribers and downloads, but they are not everything.

Some examples of measurements you may consider are monthly traffic, search engine rankings, number of posts about your podcast, or different rankings like Technorati (www.technorati.com) which measures the number of blogs linking to your site (see Figure 4.3) or Alexa (www.alexa.com) which offers an estimate of traffic. Sales are another metric that

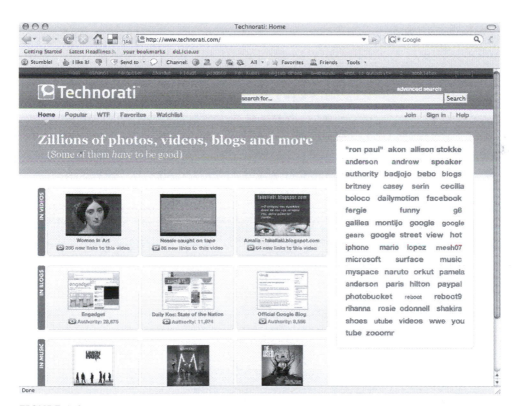

FIGURE 4.3

Technorati ranks Web sites and podcasts according to the number of blogs that link to them. *Source*: Technorati.com.

may be employed, or the amount of resulting press coverage—the metrics all depend on your goal. These metrics are all useful in determining the value of your podcast. If you are looking to establish the success of your podcast based on how much it is worth, you can also examine income history and trends for your production. There is another category of metrics that apply to podcasting—those that measure engagement.

Engagement metrics follow the activity of your listeners. These tools measure success by tracking the number of user comments per post, or the average length of stay on your Web site. Because it can be difficult to measure things like brand awareness and outreach, these metrics can offer help in determining if your podcast is supporting these goals. Further measurements consider different statistics on visitor actions on your Web site. It is possible to track email subscribers, other downloads, or whether your visitors are clicking ad links or links to other pages for more information. These kinds of KPIs are more useful in determining the core value and success of your podcast based on content and traffic drivers rather than the hard numbers of RSS subscribers and podcast downloads.

Christopher Penn, founder and producer of the Financial Aid Podcast (www.financialaidpodcast.com), is an example of someone who has developed a different way of measuring the success of his podcast beyond downloads. On his daily podcast, Penn offers valuable information to students looking for student loans and scholarships to aid them in funding their education. Penn offers links to affiliated loan Web sites that are another arm of his company, and the more traffic he can send to these sites the more successful he will be. To track the success of his podcast, Penn does not depend solely on RSS subscribers, the number of downloads, or the number of listens his podcasts have received (although these are useful metrics in this particular instance). Rather, he offers information in his content that direct students to his affiliated loan Web sites. Because the information directing people to these sites is available only through his podcasts, Penn is able to evaluate the success rate of his podcasts by the number of loans he processes through these other Web sites.

CASE STUDY
FINANCIAL AID PODCAST

Who They Are?

Financial Aid Podcast is a production of the Student Loan Network. The company offers loans for students pursing undergraduate and graduate degrees, as well as loan consolidation programs.

Purpose of Podcasting

The podcasts found on FinanicalAidPodcast.com are intended to educate listeners on various financial aid options for student loans and drive traffic to affiliated loan Web sites and increase the number of loans that go through.

Approach

CTO Christopher Penn initially began recording technical, financial information to MP3 format for internal purposes in 2005. After downloading other podcasts for his own personal use, Penn began posting his own recordings offering tips and financial advice to students seeking loans. The information available through the podcasts offers links to his affiliated loan sites, where the students may submit loan applications.

Results

In 2006, the podcasts generated $20 million in additional loans through affiliated Web sites. Those who visited these Web sites were only able to learn about them through the podcast. The company did $2 billion in loans that same year.

Benefits

Increased revenue for very little costs, a microphone, some audio software, and 45 minutes of Penn's time each workday.

The example put forth by Financial Aid Podcast shows that a little ingenuity and creativity can be very useful in defining the tools of measurement that will represent the success of your podcast. As you are deciding upon your metrics, keep reflecting on the goal of your podcast and build from there. If you are unclear in what you are trying to achieve through your production, you will be unable to successfully develop a means of measuring its success. Success can mean very different things depending on your objective.

For instance, assume your podcast is designed to increase traffic to your business's Web site. You have set a goal that you wish to receive an additional 1000 hits per week. If after 1 week of posting the podcast you have not hit 1000 additional visits to your Web site, it does not mean that the podcast has been ineffective. So long as the traffic has increased somewhat significantly, it shows the potential for continued development. Again, it takes time to build a subscriber base, so to measure success solely based on this metric may give you a faulty view of the true value of your podcast.

The success of your podcast directly correlates to its ability to achieve your goal. A podcast that is designed to increase sales that instead merely generates greater Web traffic, while it may be useful, has failed to serve its intended purpose. Whether or not you choose to maintain the podcast in its current format after that depends on several factors. While the podcast may not have delivered the results you wanted initially, it may have created several residual effects that have benefited your business. Or, you may be able to uncover what is lacking in your podcast that is failing to achieve your given goal. Regardless, to scrap the efforts if your first attempt is not a homerun could mean that other benefits of the podcast have been overlooked, or that a key piece of the production is missing the consumer market. Uncovering what's not working can be just as beneficial as having a star podcast right at the start.

Success is measured by the attainment of a goal. Without a clear goal, you cannot measure success. You must remember to be patient when launching your podcast, as the medium is still young and the audience is expanding. Additionally, your audience is not the general public, but rather a specific group of individuals who are often quite knowledgeable on the topic you are covering. Being able to reach out to these groups and inform them or convert traffic to sales can be challenging, but successfully accomplishing this task will yield benefits for your business.

Different Organizations, Different ROI

I mentioned Christopher Penn and his Financial Aid Podcast. His business is in loans; therefore a successful ROI for him for his podcasts would be in relation to the loans generated vs. the expense and time put into the podcast. So long as the cost of his podcast production efforts does not exceed the amount of loans being generated, Penn is enjoying a positive ROI. Given that last year he was able to generate over $20 million in loans on his affiliated Web sites, while producing his podcast cost only his time, plus the one-time purchase of a microphone and some audio software, his ROI is excellent. The percentage of sales created by his podcast globally through his business is not much when compared to the $2 billion in loans the business did as a whole, but considering the cost–benefit analysis of the podcast, it was a very profitable medium to utilize. Throughout this section I have reiterated the cost effectiveness of podcasting, since it is a relatively inexpensive medium and nearly anyone interested in creating a podcast may do so. But ROI is not always linked to monetary measurements, since different organizations have different goals and objectives in engaging in podcasting.

For example, non-profit organizations are not necessarily podcasting to raise money, but to raise awareness. Certainly if they can garner greater financial backing from podcasting, it would not be a negative thing, but most are not setting out to podcast with that particular objective in mind. Rather, non-profits are seeking to inform the public about particular issues or concerns, in hopes of inciting action, gaining support, or creating dialog. In such situations, ROI is not linked to how much money is being brought in vs. what is going out, but instead how much interest and engagement is being generated or how much action is being taken. We will discuss these topics in greater detail later in the book.

Similarly, as we have already examined the different uses of podcasting in a corporate setting, your ROI means different things based on what you are using the podcasts for. A podcast designed for training could be considered worthwhile if after listening to the podcast employees performed better at the task covered in the training program, or gave excellent feedback on the content provided in the podcast. Producing the podcast should not cost an exorbitant amount of money, particularly in the grand scheme of corporate budgeting (regardless of the size of your business). So when examining the ROI of your podcast, the cost–benefit relationship is less likely to be considered in terms of money, but rather productivity, information dissemination, or the overall effectiveness of the podcast in achieving its goal.

Lessons Learned

- Overcoming the traditional media mindset within your organization can be challenging, but can be accomplished with the gradual introduction of new media into your corporate communications.

- Your core internal podcasting team should include several components, regardless of the team size:
  - talent/host,
  - media and communications knowledge,
  - technical expertise,
  - expertise on the subject matter.

- Defining how you wish to be perceived within the market will affect the objectives and styling of your podcast.

- Know your audience. Conducting market research for your podcast includes studying the success of existing podcasts on similar subject matter, competitor productions, blog research, etc. The more you know about your audience, the stronger your production will be.

- Having a clearly defined goal for your podcast (i.e., lead generation, increased sales, greater brand recognition, etc.) allows you to define your metrics for success.

- Keep your goals realistic. Your podcast probably will not be an overnight success, but instead will likely require a few months to develop a strong number of listens per podcast.

Planning Your Podcast

Ryan Irelan

So, you're ready to start podcasting? Great! Before you buy a bunch of audio gear, some expensive software, and dedicate or hire staff or a production company to produce your podcast, you should do some serious planning. This chapter breaks down the podcast planning decisions you will need to be prepared for the exciting undertaking of producing and publishing your business podcast.

You have all the details you need about how podcasting can have a positive impact on your business, including some great success stories. But before you jump right in, there are some decisions to be made and this chapter will guide you along on everything you need to consider when planning your podcast. It's important to take the time now to think through how your podcast will be structured and the format you want to use. Do you want to do an interview style podcast? A roundtable discussion? Live presentations of your new product announcements? A mix of formats?

Another decision to make is publishing frequency. How often do you want to publish a new podcast episode? Weekly? Monthly? Deciding this now will help you set goals, budgets, and expectations for what comes next.

It will also assist in scheduling how often you need to produce content and help you determine if you can produce content in advance to save on production costs and time.

Equally as important is deciding how you want your company or organization to come across on the podcast. What will your image be? What will be the voice of your company? How will your organization be represented? This includes the choices of picking the people behind the microphone and defining and engaging your target audience. I'll include a few examples of podcasts that excel in certain formats and talk about why what they do works so well.

All of this planning is designed to help you establish a solid foundation for your podcast and give you all of the tools you need to make a successful business podcast—one that engages, grows, and retains your listenership.

Defining the Voice of Your Company or Organization

Now is the time to decide what your podcast will say about you as a company and how you will be perceived by your audience. Before you record one second of audio or plan out a single topic for an episode, you should think about how your company will be represented in the podcast. You want to define your voice. Defining your voice is important for a variety of reasons.

Consistently Connect with Your Audience in a Genuine Way

You'll see the same thread woven throughout this chapter and some others. Consistency is a key to podcasting successfully. It is important to establish a voice that will connect with your audience the same way from the first podcast to the one hundredth.

For example, if you run an outdoor outfitter company and you're using your podcast to market to outdoors adventure seekers, then your voice may be that of the fun and exciting company that is adventurous and enjoys a thrill. This is not only a genuine representation of what the company does (and the products and services you sell), but also connects with your audience who is of the same mindset. An outdoor adventure company wouldn't have a podcast that is slow in pace, with unexcited speakers and mundane topics. Instead it would be a fast-paced-heart racing, podcast that covers information in a fun and exciting way. The music would be up-tempo and inspiring. The voice talent would be genuinely excited about the topic of the podcast. By the same token, you don't expect that your audience will be physically unfit and not interested in thrill seeking. Ensure that your company is positively and accurately portrayed to the public.

You work hard to maintain a positive public image and keep your customers happy and satisfied. You want to extend that to your podcast, making it a natural extension of your other corporate communication efforts. Having control in the beginning over how your podcast will portray your company is very important to ensure that your company is positively and accurately represented to the public.

Make More Informed Decisions About What Kind of Podcast You Want and What Topics You Want to Cover

Knowing now what your podcast voice will be will make all of the decisions you make later (podcast format, hiring talent, choosing topics, frequency of publishing) a lot easier, because you'll be armed with the high-level knowledge of how your podcast should act as an extension of the public face of your company.

These decisions include what podcast format you use, whether or not you should hire talent to host your podcast or use someone in-house, what topics will you cover in your podcast and, finally, how often you should publish a new episode.

For example, the Disneyland Resort wanted to offer a glimpse inside the events and "magical moments" at their resort. They commissioned the Official Disneyland Resort Podcast, which is produced monthly with content that ranges from their introduction of rock music into the roller coaster rides to interviews of celebrities attending official Disneyland events (see Figure 5.1).

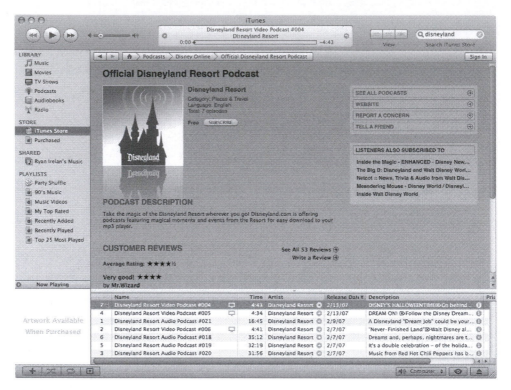

FIGURE 5.1

The Official Disneyland Resort podcast as it appears in iTunes.

If you go over to the Official Disneyland Resort podcast in iTunes and
have a listen to one of their episodes, you'll immediately notice that the
podcast sounds like Disneyland. The podcast also portrays Disneyland as
a fun place where there is exciting things happening all over. It is consistent with their other media efforts and feels like a natural extension of
the Disneyland Resort experience: fun, family-friendly, upbeat, and exciting. Because of this consistency, it connects with the Disneyland Resort
audience—families of all ages that travel to Disneyland for vacation. It
connects them to Disneyland in a way they're used to.

Finally, the production quality of the Disneyland Podcast is excellent.
Disneyland spent time and money to make sure they put out a podcast
that is in keeping with how they produce everything else in their resort.

Disneyland is known for well-executed and polished experiences. This podcast is no different.

Steps to Defining Your Voice

The path to defining the voice of your podcast should be fairly clear by now. There is no magic formula, and it's only three simple steps:

1. What is your current company image? Who are you?
2. Who is your target audience? Who are your customers?
3. Put 1 and 2 together and come up with a voice and angle that represents both accurately.

After you decide what the voice of your podcast is, then keep it in the back of your mind while you progress through the rest of this chapter and begin the planning process of your podcast.

Who Is Representing Your Company on the Podcast?

Now that you have a good idea of what you want your podcast to say about you as a company, I want you to consider how that applies to the people you have host your podcast.

Use company employee as host

If you take the route of using someone (or multiple people) internally as the host of your podcast, consider the following things when choosing who would best represent your company.

Voice quality: The person need not be professional voiceover artists, but he or she should have a voice that is engaging and clear.

Personality: Because you'll only be hearing the voice, it's important that the podcast host has a vibrant personality and is likeable. You don't want to risk boring your listeners or losing the voice you defined.

Additionally, you should pick someone who is

- knowledgeable about the company and its products or services and
- genuinely enthusiastic about what your company does.

But not necessarily someone who is

- the most senior person in your company,
- someone from sales, or
- a public relations employee.

The greatest advantage of using your own people is that there is a better chance the podcast will be more genuine, and that the person will have the personal insight and experience of your organization to bring to the podcast. It's also a nice way to offer employees a different type of task where they express their dedication and enthusiasm for what your company does.

Outsource professional talent

I'll cover the whole process of outsourcing your podcast production in the next chapter. But as far as defining the voice of your podcast is concerned, you should look for someone that

- has experience,
- has a good voice quality, and
- is able to represent your podcast in a way that is in keeping with your public image and defined voice.

Taking the time now to define the voice of your company will allow you to set how you want to be perceived by your audience of current and potential customers. Now that you know what your podcast voice will be, you can begin planning the rest of your production with that in mind and be on your way to publishing a podcast that makes you and your company proud.

The Format of Your Show

The next step in planning your podcast is to decide on the format. What's a format? It is the structure and set up of your podcast. It's how you present your content and message to your listeners. Deciding on a format is important because it allows you to plan and organize your content. Having a consistent format allows your listeners to predict what kind of show they're going to listen to when they download the latest episode.

Making your podcast structure predictable with a format will also assist (but is not the only factor) with audience growth and retention. Your podcast will have a reputation for being a certain format, and that will make it easier to bring on new listeners and retain your current subscriber base. Imagine, if you will, that you tuned into your favorite talk radio show and suddenly the host wasn't interviewing guests and giving editorial remarks, but instead was playing her favorite jazz songs for the entire hour. This would be jarring for you and the entire audience. You were expecting the same talk format that the show had previously. You can bet that this show would lose a lot of listeners, who aren't interested in jazz music but want to hear the opinion of the host and the guests on the topic of the day.

Deciding on a format is also a tremendous asset when it comes to production. Having a format makes it easier to produce your podcast episode after episode. You are able to create and set a production workflow where you know the audio segments that need recording and the people you will need for the production. There are no surprises during the production of each new episode, and you're not constantly reinventing the wheel.

Various Types of Podcast Formats

Before you decide on what format your podcast should take, lets walk through a few different types of formats. This isn't a comprehensive list of every possible format, but instead a small collection of the most popular ones.

As we walk through these formats, I'll share some examples of well-done business podcasts that should help you better conceptualize how you can incorporate a format into your own company's podcast. I've also included the URLs of the podcasts, so you can visit the Web sites and listen to a few episodes to get a good idea of how they're using podcasting in their business and how the format sounds. With all that said, let's jump into the formats.

Single Host Talk

Are you an individual small business owner? Are you in a large organization and experimenting with podcasting in your marketing department and don't have a lot of people or resources to dedicate to it? If the answer to either of these questions is yes, then the Single Host Talk format is probably a good option for your podcast.

This format is probably one of the most popular among new podcasters, because it requires no additional personnel. You can podcast when you want and how you want. The entire show is yours. There is also the benefit that the technology behind the podcast could be less elaborate and less expensive because you will only need one microphone and a simple recording setup.

Now, this may be a tougher podcast to pull of consistently because it can quickly become monotonous and boring. But that doesn't mean it can't be done well. The Single Host Talk format can work nicely if you establish an outline of topics that you want to present and then stick to them. This approach can make this format an excellent informational podcast for industry news, opinion pieces, and announcements.

No matter the size of your organization, because of the relatively ease of entry for this format, the Single Host Talk podcast is a great starting point for your first foray into podcasting. If, after some experimentation, you decide to pursue podcasting more vigorously, you can always move to another format. See Multiple Host Talk and Roundtable Discussion formats below, which are a great way to improve on this format.

Ingredients for a successful Single Host Talk podcast
- Well thought-out and interesting topics.
- A professional-sounding host who is able to present topics in a way that is lively and able to maintain the listener's attention.

A fine example of a Single Host Talk podcast comes from a rather surprising source. Initially, you may not consider law firms when thinking of business podcasting, but law firms are businesses and they spend a lot of time and money on marketing efforts. From Yellow Pages ads to Web sites to web logs, law firms are always looking for the extra edge in marketing to gain new clients. Podcasting has been treated no differently and there are already dozens and dozens of podcasts out there from lawyers and law firms.

One such firm is Stark & Stark of New Jersey. In July 2005 the law firm entered into the podcasting fold with its first episode of the New Jersey Legal Update (see Figure 5.2). The New Jersey Legal Update is a weekly podcast (published every Friday) that covers the most important court decisions of the previous week. Each episode features a different host for the 5–10 minute podcast from one of their law firm practice groups. The host will briefly cover the cases settled that week. Having different hosts for each episode is a great way to not only offer various people at your company the opportunity to participate in the podcast, but it also gives listeners a new voice to experience, which creates a more interesting and enjoyable podcast.

You can learn more about the Stark & Stark New Jersey Legal Update podcast by visiting www.njlawblog.com/cat-podcasts.html.

Multiple Host Talk

Very much like the Single Host Talk, this format offers more variety with different voices and personalities. The material presented can be exactly the same as in the Single Host Talk format, but with just more variety for the listener by adding one or more additional hosts.

Interview

A staple of the podcasting phenomenon is the interview—podcasters interviewing other podcasters, important members of their industry, or someone else of notoriety. It's a practical and informative format in traditional radio, and it is just as practical in the podcasting medium.

FIGURE 5.2

The New Jersey Legal Update podcast is a weekly production of the Stark & Stark law firm in New Jersey.

The Interview format is a great way to share useful information with your listeners. This could include interviews with a product manager about a new product announcement, other experts in your field, or satisfied customers and clients.

Unlike the first two formats, interviews require the pre-production work of securing an interviewee and preparing questions to ask. There is also the additional technology requirement of how to record the interview. Is the interview over the phone? In person? Either way, you'll need to think through the technology implications of this format. This will be discussed in greater detail in the podcast production book in this series.

FIGURE 5.3
Psyched Up is a fine example of a podcast that uses the interview format.

Ingredients of a successful interview podcast
- Use interesting and relevant guests.
- The host should have a general knowledge of topic being covered. This will allow her to ask insightful questions, which draw out information that will be useful for the listener.
- The technology to record phone conversation or second microphone for an "in-studio" interview.

For instance, Psyched Up is a podcast from the Suffolk County (New York) Psychological Association (SCPA). The SCPA is a professional association that advocates psychology in Suffolk County through education.

This podcast is in the interview format (Figure 5.3), with a host and a guest, who is usually on the phone. Each episode of Psyched Up has one broad topic on which the guest is an expert.

You can learn more about Psyched Up by visiting their podcast Web site: scpa.podomatic.com.

Roundtable discussion

There is nothing better than an informational conversation about a topic among a group of qualified experts. The roundtable discussion is a popular format for not only radio and television, but also podcasting. If the topic is controversial or has different sides, you'll want to represent all major viewpoints, so as to keep the discussion vibrant, interesting, and appealing to a wide audience.

A roundtable discussion is not a multi-person interview. Not everyone gets equal time to give an answer. Instead a roundtable discussion podcast should be as lively and spontaneous as a dinner conversation among friends. One topic is picked and the participants should cordially discuss that topic. However, you will definitely want to have one person as the moderator who will ensure the discussion stays on topic.

Ingredients for a successful roundtable discussion podcast
- A panel of guests who are knowledgeable on the topic at hand.
- The technical setup to handle recording multiple phone lines or "in-studio" recording of multiple people.

As highlighted in Chapter 3, Ortho-McNeil Neurologics Inc., a large pharmaceutical company, in conjunction with National Headache Awareness Week, published a short podcast series that discussed migraines, migraine treatments, news and information, as well as symptoms and triggers. This public awareness effort by Ortho-McNeil consisted of three podcast episodes.

All of the episodes were done in the roundtable discussion format (see Figure 5.4). There was a host who had prepared topics and questions for discussion and a small panel of doctors and experts who discussed the latest information on migraines. These episodes were all done over the phone, including the host. This is definitely a viable method to assemble a

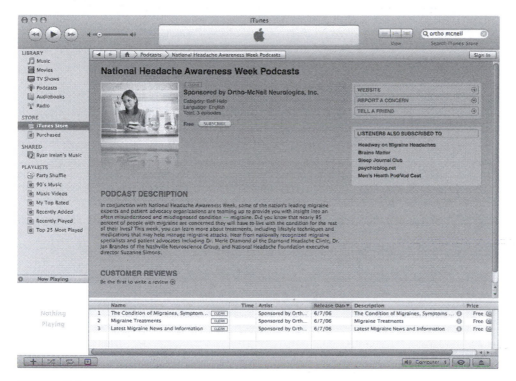

FIGURE 5.4

All episodes of Ortho-McNeil Neurologics' migraine podcast series are in the roundtable format.

virtual roundtable discussion when all of the participants are at different locations.

Sound-seeing tour

A sound-seeing tour podcast is an audio tour that records the ambient sounds of the podcast host's environment. The host acts as the tour guide, offering description and commentary of what is going on around her.

It could be a tour of a city, an event or any place that could make an interesting podcast and keep a listener's attention. It could also be a tour of an industry conference or your company's event.

This format has the benefit of giving the listener an inside look (or listen) to the event you're covering. Try offering something of extra value to the sound-seeing tour, like an exclusive interview with a key person, a backstage look at the event preparations, or an exclusive announcement.

The sound-seeing tour is also an authentic way to cover your company events. When done well it will be perceived as open, unscripted, and honest.

Ingredients of a successful sound-seeing tour
- A large event or location with a lot of ambient noise and goings-on.
- A stereo microphone to capture all of the sounds of the event.
- A host that can navigate an event and ad lib well.
- An inside look at the event or interview with a key person involved in the event.

An excellent example of a sound-seeing tour is the Pontiac Summer Solstice podcast. In June 2005 Pontiac put on a large impromptu summer solstice party to celebrate the launch of their new car, the Pontiac Solstice (see Figure 5.5). This event included a concert with multiple bands, a VIP party and an impromptu event in Times Square, New York City. In this example, Pontiac was using the podcast as a way to market and publicize their large marketing effort in New York City.

The podcast host (in this case, this book's author, Greg Cangialosi) walked around the streets of Times Square and interviewed bands, celebrities and passers-by. Also included was an explanation of the event happenings. The sounds of Times Square and the Pontiac event made for an immersive experience for the podcast listener. When you listen to the podcast, you'll notice that it has a very loose and relaxed feel. This works very well in the sound-seeing format and especially well with a podcast that is covering a rock "n" roll marketing event for Pontiac's Solstice sports car.

Read more and listen to the podcast at http://fastlane.gmblogs.com/archives/2005/06/pontiac_summer.html.

See the "Can a podcast have multiple formats?" section below for more information about the GM podcasts.

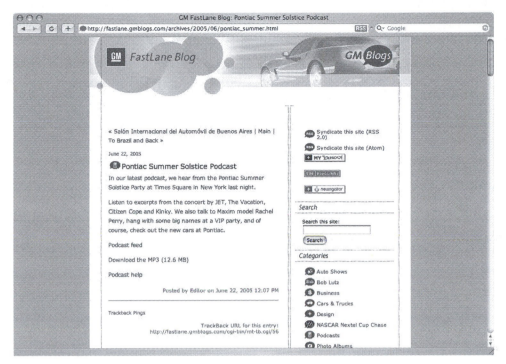

FIGURE 5.5
Greg Cangialosi hosted a sound-seeing tour of the June 2005 Pontiac Solstice launch in Times Square.

Newspiece

Another method of sharing company or industry events and news is to produce a podcast that reports on those events in a news-like fashion. This format can offer a unique way for listeners to get industry or company information.

A newspiece podcast can be created by sending out someone to report (the "reporter") on an industry or company event. This reporter will interview important people, get general reaction and describe the environment. After the initial gathering of interviews and information is complete, the podcast would then be edited down into a compact news report-style audio package. The reporter would narrate with interview snippets interspersed.

Ingredients of a successful newspiece podcast
- Experienced news reporter.
- Industry event or news that is of interest to listeners.
- Editing of raw audio recording into polished newspiece package.

Educational piece

The educational piece is actually more of a hybrid format. It can come in many basic formats—interview, roundtable discussion, or single host. What makes it a format unto itself is that the overall goal is to educate the listening audience. This type of podcast is more of a public service than anything else, and it's a great way to use your company's knowledge and public position to share useful and practical information with the public. The Education Piece format could be made into a podcast on any topic that your organization may be involved in either as a business or a community member.

One the best examples of a educational podcast is Whirlpool's podcast series called American Family (see Figure 5.6). Starting in July 2005 (less than a year after podcasting began!) Whirlpool began publishing a weekly podcast episode on a variety of topics that matter to American families. Podcast topics range from adoption and foster care to pregnancy and premature birth. Each episode is hosted by one person who usually interviews an expert in the field of discussion.

To learn more about the Whirlpool American Family Podcast or to subscribe to the podcast feed, visit www.whirlpool.com/family.

Quiz show

Looking for a different way to make a podcast? This format is certainly different. A podcast quiz show is a unique way to present content to the audience through a series of questions and answers.

To create a quiz show podcast, assemble a small panel of participants who will attempt to answer a variety of questions that fall under one topic. You should have a host who is responsible for moderating the podcast and asking the questions.

FIGURE 5.6

The American Family podcast promotes Whirlpool's products indirectly via its educational format.

This format does require a significant investment of time in creating the questions and securing panel participants. The technical requirements are the same as those for the roundtable discussion format. If all the participants are in the same room, you'll need one microphone per guest and a mixer to hook them all together into a single audio signal that can then be recorded.

A well-produced quiz show podcast could be an entertaining way to engage you customers and the public at large.

Ingredients of a successful quiz show
- Well-written quiz questions that are informational and entertaining.
- Audio setup for recording multiple people at once.

Live presentation

The live presentation format is a good option if your company regularly does live product announcements, company news, or keynote speeches. Did your CEO give a speech to a large conference recently? Did the marketing team recently unveil a new product or service? Any live events can be easily recorded and podcast by plugging into the event sound system or setting up a microphone in the room. Plugging into the event sound system will give you the best audio quality, but will require you obtain permission from the venue and, in some cases, the sound production company responsible for the event. Setting up a microphone in the room to record the event is the alternative method to recording a live presentation or speech.

What you should avoid with this format is podcasting every announcement or presentation. You will want to make sure that the live speeches or announcements you podcast are of interest to your target audience (see the section in this chapter on defining your voice).

The Live Presentation format is a great way to reuse live presentations or speeches and get those live events out to a larger audience.

Ingredients for a successful live presentation podcast
- Good quality recording of the live event.
- Presentations, events, and speeches that are relevant and of interest to your target audience.

Can a podcast have multiple formats?

Yes.

I know that at the beginning of this section, I made clear that one of the reasons of choosing a format and sticking to it is a good thing is because it creates consistency and that in turn is a great way to gain and retain listeners. And that's still true, but let me give you one example where this works really well.

In January 2005, giant US carmaker General Motors started a blog called Fastlane. Its goal is to cover all of the product announcements and information from the GM line of cars and trucks. This includes design, engineering, unveilings, and other information that hard core "car geeks" are interested in. The next month, GM launched the first podcast as part of the GM Fastlane blog.

Because of this variety of information and because we're talking about automobiles, which need to be seen to be admired for their design, it is no surprise that the GM Fastlane blog offered podcasts using a variety of formats. And in this case it works well.

Since their first podcast in February 2005, GM has published almost three dozen episodes using the interview format, sound-seeing tour, and a series of video podcasts that highlight GM car and truck models. In this case the multiple format works well. It allows GM to cover their products in a way that maximizes the experience for their blog readers and podcast listeners. And, ultimately, that's what matters.

Visit the Fastlane blog: http://fastlane.gmblogs.com/.

Building a Podcast in Segments

When you are planning your podcast content, you should think about it in segments. At the very least you should look at your podcast as having three main parts: introduction, main content, sign-off. Your podcast may have more pieces to it—maybe you have a sponsorship message you need to insert or a promotion of an event or announcement about a new product or service. Any of these would also be segments in the podcast. What you want to avoid is having too many short segments. Building a podcast from dozens of small pieces of content can make your podcast feel choppy and even make it difficult to listen to.

Every podcast is created from three basic building blocks:

1 Introduction
2 Content
3 Sign-off

Depending on the type of podcast you're producing, these building blocks can grow and become more defined. For example, here's a sample structure of a podcast using the roundtable discussion format:

- Introduction music/announcement of podcast name.
- Host welcome to listeners.
- Host introduction of discussion topic.
- Host introduction of roundtable guests.
- Topic discussion.
- Host wrap-up and thank you to guests.
- Host announces URL and email address for more information.
- Host sign-off.
- Podcast exit music.

I broke down a lot of the host parts of the podcast into separate bullets, so they would be more defined and clear. The first three host segments will sound like one segment to the listener, but they are three distinct items that the host must cover at the beginning of each podcast.

The main content of the podcast in the example above is the "Topic Discussion" segment. This segment will take up the majority of the podcast—about 95 percent—and the rest of the segments are there to transition into and out of the main content and also to provide the listener with context and more information about the podcast and the guests.

RYAN'S TIP You will notice that podcast formats and structure do resemble traditional radio shows. This isn't by accident. When podcasting first started, many involved were traditional broadcasters and looked to radio as an example when creating their own podcasts.

When planning your podcast, list out the segments that you will need to bring it all together and use that segment list as your outline for production tasks and the creation of any content needed for the podcast. You will want to keep the structure almost the same for each podcast episode, so it is predictable and the audience knows what to expect each time, especially if you have segment that proves particularly popular.

Podcast Length

This is one question that I hear a lot when talking to people interested in podcasting or just starting out with their first podcast. The conversation goes something like this:

"Hey, I'm starting a new podcast about good dental habits. How long do you think it should be?"

I respond, "Well, how much do you have to say?"

I know that looks like a curt response and I know I'm answering a question with a question, but it's an honest answer. There's a simple lesson here. Don't create an arbitrary length for your podcast. The amount of content you cover shouldn't be determined by some pre-determined length. Instead, it should be determined by how much you have to say.

However, there are limits. You shouldn't publish a 3-hour podcast every week. You would have a hard time getting anyone to listen to the entire thing and eventually your audience would dissipate (if you ever gained one at all). Generally, shorter-length podcasts are more successful than longer ones. A sweet spot for podcast length is somewhere around 15–20 minutes, although a podcast of just a few minutes could be just as informative and gain a large audience.

Use this information as a guideline when creating your podcast. There are no rules. If you keep your target audience in mind and create content that they will enjoy at a length that is reasonable, you will be headed in the right direction.

Podcast Production Decisions

With the major decisions about format, structure, and length out of the way, you'll want to focus on some big picture production decisions.

This isn't about which microphone cable you should use or anything of the sort. This section will be about getting your podcast produced regularly and how to maintain the momentum.

By making these decisions in the planning phase, you can more accurately predict what kind of resources you'll need for production, file storage for your podcast episodes, and the amount of time you and your team will have to dedicate to make the podcast happen.

How Often Should You Publish?

Choosing a publishing schedule is important for two reasons. First, it defines your commitment to podcasting and helps you set the production requirements and timelines. Second, it sets the expectations of your listenership. Let's go through this in more detail.

Impact of publishing schedule on production

With everything you've read so far in this chapter on planning your podcast, choosing how often you publish will decide how many resources you need to dedicate to production. Obviously, if you decide to publish a daily podcast, it's going to require a lot more man-hours each week to get that podcast out the door than it would if you only publish once a week. It would be even less if you decided to publish once a month. And that should certainly be weighed when you're making a publishing schedule.

How long will it take to produce a podcast?

The horribly dissatisfying answer to this question is: it depends.

In the next chapter I'll cover everything about the podcast production process in detail, and I'll talk about whether or not you want to create the podcast in-house or contract out production to a podcast production company or consultant. Until you make that decision, let's assume you'll be creating all of your podcasts in-house.

Not including the amount of time it takes to research a topic, schedule guests (if any), and write any prepared content or questions, you should plan on the actual production (setting up equipment, recording, basic editing, and publishing) of your podcast to take about three times the length of the podcast. So, if your podcast is 30-minutes long, expect production to take about 1½ hours. This doesn't include extensive editing. If you're working on a sound-seeing tour, for example, that requires you to edit together dozens of short audio clips, you can expect the editing to take about five times longer than the show length. These numbers aren't exact science, but you should use them as a guide to help you gauge how much time to budget for your production time.

Setting the expectations of your listeners

While the internal reasons for publishing frequency are important, don't forget about your audience! They, too, should be considered when formulating your production schedule. As with almost everything else I've mentioned in this chapter, always produce your podcast with your audience in mind. Deciding on a publishing frequency is no different.

Put yourself in a listener's position. How many podcast episodes could you really have time to listen to in a month? Two? Three? Four? Thirty? There are some podcasts that are published daily, but these days that is more of the exception than the rule. With so much media and information online and offline, the average person only has so much time to spend listening to podcasts. You should feel free to set a publishing schedule that makes sense for your audience and your organization, but my general advice would be to not publish more than once a week and at least once a month. If you publish too often (especially if your podcast is longer than 10 minutes), you'll risk overloading your audience with too much content. If you publish too infrequently, it will be difficult to build a relationship with your audience, because you only come around occasionally and they're more than likely to forget about you and, even worse,unsubscribe from your podcast.

Consistency: retain and grow your listenership

I have one favorite television show and I will schedule my time around its weekly broadcast to be sure I see it. It comes on every Thursday, without fail.

As a dedicated follower of the show, I can rely on a new episode (or at least a repeat) every week. If you create compelling and interesting content and publish consistently your listeners will think the same about your podcast.

Your subscribed listeners count on you to publish a podcast on the schedule you establish—whether it is daily, weekly, or monthly. Imagine a television show that was broadcasted sporadically. I'd bet that it would have a small viewership that would be just as undedicated to watching it as they perceive the show producers are with creating it.

What to do? Publish regularly and follow your schedule. Let your audience know your publishing schedule and then stick to it. If you need to adjust the schedule then make an announcement about it on your weblog or Web site. It's a simple courtesy that can go a long way in retaining listeners and encouraging them to spread the word about your podcast. Respect your listeners and, in return, they'll show that same respect and dedication to your podcast efforts.

Recording in Advance: Getting Ahead of Schedule

Once you get started podcasting and have a few episodes under your belt, you'll begin to realize that one of the greatest challenges is to stay current with your podcast. In the last section I talked about consistency and that you should try to publish new podcast episodes on a predictable and set schedule. Keeping that schedule seems like a simple task, but with all of the planning, production, and post-production involved in each episode, it might take a lot of work to produce each and every episode of your podcast. Great content takes time to create!

The method I recommend you use to keep on schedule is to produce podcast episodes in advance. Producing in advance will always ensure that you have a show in the hopper that you can publish.

How far in advance?

If you publish your podcast weekly, I'd suggest you produce four episodes ahead of time, so that you're always one month ahead. This not only gives you peace of mind about meeting your publishing schedule, but also allows you to easily manage any production issues that arise. For example, if your only microphone is broken or ruined, by being a month ahead you have more time to manage a replacement without affecting your publishing schedule. You still have to produce the same amount of podcasts to stay ahead of schedule, but with the extra cushion of time it's easier to rearrange the production schedule to make up for lost time due the broken microphone.

An exception to the rule: current events podcasts

The one genre of podcasting that this method of producing podcasts in advance doesn't work in is for current events podcasts. If your podcast covers a news item or the latest happenings in an industry, you probably won't have the luxury of producing full episodes 1 month in advance. However, not all is lost. If only part of your podcast consists of current events, then you should record and edit everything else ahead of time and add in the news items at the last minute.

> **If your podcast topic and format permits, publish as far out as you possibly can. It's a good rule of thumb to be 3–4 episodes out so you can ensure consistency in publishing.** RYAN'S TIP

Avoiding Pitfalls

As you begin the process of planning and producing your podcast, there will be a lot of challenges along the way. Most will be exciting and hopefully a result of intense interest in your podcast. However, there are some big pitfalls that you want to avoid.

Emphasizing Quantity Over Quality

In the last section I talked about how you should produce podcasts ahead of your publishing schedule, so you can keep on schedule and easily deal with any bumps in the road. While this is important, podcast episodes shouldn't be shoved out the door if they're not ready just to meet a schedule. Don't publish episodes that aren't up to your highest standards of content and production quality. You risk alienating your audience and damaging your reputation as a quality podcaster.

Creating an Infomercial Podcast

On the Internet, and especially in the social media revolution, there is a very low tolerance for companies that produce content that is overly commercial. Podcasts that are nothing more than infomercials for a company's products will not only not be listened to, but also possibly scorned. This could cause you and your company embarrassment.

When conceptualizing and producing your product, you should keep in mind that you want to try to bring something of value to the table, something that is worth the listener's time. Commercials are everywhere and people will not subscribe to commercials.

Publishing Too Often

If you have the fortunate position of being able to create quality podcast episodes at fast pace, then you might be tempted to push them all out as quickly as possible. Doing that may overload your audience, who is usually listening to more than just your podcast. Instead of publishing too much at one time, stick to your publishing schedule and push out only one episode at a time.

Not Valuing Production Quality

There is no expectation that your podcasts will be produced in a state-of-the-art studio and sound as good as a professionally mixed and mastered music album. But there is the expectation that your podcasts won't be inaudible or difficult to listen to. This includes things like distorted audio or volume that is too low. Your and every podcaster's goal should be that your podcast has the highest production quality possible depending on your budget and format.

Lessons Learned

- Define your voice. Before you begin production or brainstorm on content for your podcast, you should think about how you want your company to be represented.

- Decide on a show format. Choosing a format is an important early step so you can plan content and production.

- Make your podcast as long as you want, but be sure you have something to say. Don't fill your podcast with anything but quality content.

- Be consistent. Choose a publishing schedule and stick to it. Your audience counts on you to publish regularly.

Pre-production Decisions

Ryan Irelan

In the last chapter, I walked through all of the major considerations you'll face when planning your podcast. These ranged from defining your voice and choosing who will represent your company on the podcast to what format you want to use. Those decisions, along with ones about publishing schedule and how to avoid common pitfalls, will help you be prepared for the next step. That next step is getting ready for the production of your podcast.

The good thing about this step is that you only have to do it once. After setting your goals and deciding on production and budget, you can then concentrate on creating content and publishing it. Everything after this is all about producing individual episodes since your big project decisions will have been made.

There are only a few items to cover before you set off to produce your podcast, but they are very important; the decisions will impact your production quality and the amount of money you spend on your podcasting efforts. The decisions fall into two primary categories:

- *Production*: As mentioned in Chapter 4, every organization must ask the question "Should we produce our podcast in-house and with our own employees and equipment, or hire out a podcast production company to do all of the heavy lifting?" There's also the option of only contracting out a portion of the podcast production. I'll give you the full rundown on all aspects of producing it yourself or doing part of it in conjunction with a production company.

- *Setting a Budget*: It's the question everyone asks: "How much will it cost to do my podcast?" The answer is a resounding "It depends." While I can tell you approximately what audio hardware will cost, I can't say what companies will charge for their production services. I will explain a few different production scenarios and some example budgets to help you gauge what scope of work you can expect for your budget. This will include three different budgets for contracting out the work and for doing it yourself in-house.

Production Decisions

There are three ways you can go with your podcast production. You can outsource the entire thing to a production company, plan and produce the podcast in-house using your own resources, or go with a hybrid solution where you outsource only the tasks that you cannot efficiently do internally. Of course, there are also budgetary reasons for choosing one or another. We'll talk more about budgets at the end of the chapter, but for now you should read through and get an idea of what each option has to offer and where your organization fits in.

Outsourcing Your Podcast Production

The term "outsourcing" is a loaded one, but in the context of podcasting it simply means to contract out all of the production duties for your podcast. By outsourcing the podcast production, you free your company to continue to focus on the business at hand, similar to the way companies contract out the creation of television commercials to production companies.

Even though podcasting is fairly new, there is no shortage of qualified professionals to help you produce your podcast. Many of the professionals that are now offering podcast production services are in fact audio and video production companies who are simply offering a new service. I mention this because it is important to have faith in the people and industry doing the work for you. Shortly, I'll talk about what you need to consider when choosing professional services for your podcast, but for now here's a look at what these production companies can offer.

Types of services

- *Content creation*: Creating your scripts and podcast content ideas. This would usually fall under a complete podcasting package that requires little or no work on the part of the client.

- *Studio recording*: Some types of podcasts, like roundtable discussions or interviews (see Chapter 5) are best recorded in a studio environment where the best audio quality possible can be achieved.

- *On-site recording*: A podcast that covers special events or interviews that cannot take place in a studio are done on-site. On-site recording requires different equipment and approach than recording in a studio. Usually, on-site recording requires travel and lodging for the production team.

- *Audio elements* (*intro, outro*): Your podcast will include different chunks of audio that will be reused for every episode. These typically include an introduction ("intro") and a piece of audio played at the end of your podcast ("outro").

- *Royalty-free music*: Royalty-free music is generally instrumental music that can be used in commercial audio and video recordings without paying any royalty to the creator. The only cost involved is for the initial purchase of the audio recording. Royalty-free music generally comes in bulk on CDs or DVDs, or as downloads from Internet Web sites that specialize in that type of music.

- *Voice-overs*: Voice-overs are a technique that usually employs anonymous voice talent to announce information in an audio or video recording. Voice-overs are typically done in podcasts for the "intros" and "outros" or any announcement-type audio segment.

- *Post-production editing*: A simple podcast will consist of three main parts—intro, content, and outro. During the recording of your podcast, you will typically record only the content section. It is in post-production editing that all three components are put together to create the final podcast episode. For more complex podcasts, post-production editing can be quite involved, especially if the source audio is of poor quality.

- *Really simple syndication (RSS) feed creation*: Your podcast is just an audio file until it has an RSS feed. You can read more about RSS feeds in the last chapter of this section. Podcast professionals can assist in creating an RSS feed for you to distribute your podcast.

- *Podcast marketing*: How to get your podcast out in the public. Best practices for good marketing and how to not embarrass yourself or your company.

- *Directory submission*: As with Web sites, it is important to submit your podcast to some select podcast directories. This service is typically part of a full production package from a podcasting professional.

- *Web site creation and hosting*: Podcasting professionals can set you up with a new Web site or blog and hosting. You can read more about all three in Chapter 8.

- *Custom podcast workflows*: A podcast workflow is all of the steps necessary to produce and publish your podcast. More involved podcasts may require custom tools or consulting to establish the most efficient workflow.

- *Hourly consulting*: For companies that are just looking to bounce off information and ideas of experienced podcast professional.

Advantages and disadvantages of outsourcing your podcast

Completely outsourcing all of your podcasting needs has one important advantage: it allows you to focus on your business and allows professionals to handle the production. You will not need to worry about audio hardware and software, or learning the mechanics behind podcasting. You can turn it all over to the podcasting company and simply be involved enough to give them the information they need to produce a quality podcast for your company.

The downside is that producing a quality podcast can be expensive. Later on in this chapter, we'll see a few scenarios. Every podcast consultant will have different prices, but you should expect to spend well to get the best podcast production.

In-House Production

You can also produce your podcast entirely in-house. What I mean by this is that your company would be responsible for devising a plan, writing content, hosting, recording audio, doing the post-production work, and publishing. This would include all of the types of services listed above. For companies that already have employees with these skills, in-house production is a good fit. It allows your employees to be part of something new and participate in the podcast. In-house podcasting offers great freedom and flexibility, but with all of that comes a lot of responsibility and work.

There's also the potential financial benefit. Producing in-house can save a lot of money and drastically reduce your budget requirements. With in-house production, your budget will consist mostly of funds to purchase and maintain the audio equipment for your podcast and any web hosting you might need to secure (see Chapter 8 for more on web hosting).

Hybrid Production

It would be a safe bet to say that this last option, the hybrid, is the most popular. What is it? Basically, hybrid means that you do the production work you can manage and then hire out the rest. Typically, your company would do the recording of the main podcast content and then hire some-one to do the editing and post-production work. But this could also mean that you just contract out of the voice-over work for your podcast "intros" and "outros." The degrees of hybrid arrangements can vary depending on your needs.

The downside to using the hybrid approach is that your organization is responsible for ensuring that a high-quality audio show is delivered to your subscribers. If you're audio engineers, that's not a problem. However, if there are no audiophiles among you, this could prove a daunting and difficult task. It's not impossible to pull off, but this is just a fair warning that there is more to producing high-quality audio than just hitting the record button.

Choosing Professional Services

There isn't much difference in hiring a podcast professional to consult on and produce your podcast than from contracting out any other type of work, but there are some things you should consider and ask a potential podcast consultant or contractor.

Sorting the Good from the Bad

Check the company's qualifications and get some references from their previous clients. You should also request samples of any previous audio or podcast work. Listen to these samples and decide if you like how they sound and if they will work with your company, voice, and message. Since podcasting is fairly new (about 3 years old at the time of publication), some production companies may not have a large podcast portfolio to present to you. That's to be expected. I would request more information about their background and years in business. Some companies have a long history of audio production (either the company or its principals) but have only recently branched out into podcasting. Their audio production skills are probably solid. Use the information from this book to judge whether they understand the podcasting medium and can lead a successful podcast effort on your behalf.

What to Expect

Hiring a podcast production company or a consultant is very similar to hiring someone to design and develop a new Web site for your company. You will need to explain to a prospective consultant or production company your vision and motivation for doing a podcast. Fill them in on all of the ideas that came out of the brainstorming you did after reading the earlier chapters of this book. What's the voice of your company? Who is your audience? What are your goals?

Additionally, you will want to have a rough idea of your budget for the project. This is important because it helps the consultant gauge whether your production wishes and your budget match and, if they don't, what can be done to bring them more in line with one another.

Every company has its own project workflow, but here's an example of the process of working with a podcasting company or consultant.

Step One: Project evaluation and information gathering

In a face-to-face meeting or conference call, the podcast consultant or production company will learn more about your project, your goals, and your budget. It will be their goal to gather as much information from you as possible, which will enable them to deliver an accurate and appropriate proposal for your podcast (both in terms of scope, timeframe, and cost).

Step Two: Proposal of services and costs

Using the information gathered from step one, the consultant will then come back to you with a written proposal that details the project scope and the cost. Any outstanding items should be clarified and added to the proposal.

Step Three: Sign contract and make initial payment

If both you and the consultant are in agreement, a contract is signed. Normally, 50 percent of the cost of the contract will be due at the outset. This can vary from consultant to consultant, with some choosing to bill upon delivery of the final product or even breaking up payment into smaller chunks based on milestones. This is particularly useful for large projects that span a longer period of time.

Step Four: Consulting and production work

All of the work stated in the contract happens in this step. For projects that are revolving—that is, a contract to produce two podcasts every month—this and the next step will be recurring.

Step Five: Completion of production deliverables

After completion of consulting and production, the consultant will deliver to you the final project deliverables. This can mean many things; the consultant could publish your podcast to your Web site and create the RSS feed or just simply deliver you an MP3 audio file that you then publish and market yourself. The deliverable is dependent on the scope of the project that was determined in step two.

Setting a Budget

Similar to other projects you undertake in your business, setting a budget sits high on the list of priorities. In the case of producing a podcast, setting a budget is important for a number of reasons:

- It assists you in establishing what kind of podcast service you need and can afford.

- It allows a podcast consultant to gauge project scope and prepare an accurate plan for producing and marketing your podcast.

- It establishes what kind of podcast you produce based on the formats discussed in the last chapter. If you have a low budget, then doing on-location recording that requires air travel and lodging is probably out of the picture.

RYAN'S TIP

If you decide to do an in-house or hybrid production, you'll need to consider not only the costs of professional podcast services but also any audio hardware and software that you might need to purchase. Keep these items in mind when creating your budget.

Outsource Budget Considerations

If you decide to outsource the entire production of your podcast, here are some examples of what you can expect in terms of services. These are very general and the goal is to give you an idea of what types of services would fall under each level. Not every podcast professional will offer all these services or necessarily categorize them as I have here.

Basic service, low budget

- Basic consulting on podcast direction
- Recommendation of tools and hosting
- Assistance on first podcast episode and limited support thereafter
- Delivery of "intro" and "outro" audio for use in podcast

Plus service, moderate budget

- Single episode production
- Extensive consulting
- Recommendations for and securing of tools and hosting
- On-site recording and production
- Customized production workflow

- Basic post-production work
- Setup of hosting and any needed software to publish your podcast

Full service, high budget

- Extensive consulting
- Multiple episode production
- Recommendations and securing of tools and hosting
- On-site recording and production
- Customized production workflow
- Extensive post-production editing
- Secure and hire voice and host talent
- Design and develop Web site or blog for podcast

In-House Budget Considerations

If you plan to produce your podcast completely in-house, your budget will mainly consist of hardware and software purchases. There may be some money required for hosting and marketing, but the bulk will be to purchase the necessary audio equipment. For more details on recording and editing and sample hardware setups see Chapter 7. Here are a couple of the items you'll need to purchase to do in-house production:

- audio recording hardware—microphones, microphone stands, cables, mixers, etc.
- recording/editing software.

Lessons Learned

- Choosing your production method will have a direct impact on your podcast budget.

- Producing your podcast completely in-house will allow you to do your podcast for less money but without the benefit of a podcast professional's involvement.

- A popular solution is the hybrid production where some of production work is framed out by a podcasting consultant and the rest is done in-house. This allows you to do what you're capable of and the rest is handled by podcast professionals.

SECTION 3: PRODUCING THE PODCAST: PRODUCTION, DELIVERY AND LEGAL ISSUES

Podcast Production

Ryan Irelan

The production of your podcast is the practical application of all the planning you have done up to this point. You've decided on format and a budget. Hopefully, you've also assembled a team of people inside or outside of your company to make the podcast happen. These people will handle the technical details of what goes into producing the podcast, but I want to highlight the major parts of podcast production so you will be better prepared to make any necessary decisions along the way.

Production Decisions

The decisions you will need to make at this point will be directly influenced by those you made in previous chapters. For example, if you chose a sound-seeing tour as your podcast format, you will then want to focus on setting up a mobile recording rig and not on building a small podcast studio. It will also influence the kind of microphones you purchase, the hardware you record with, and the type of software you use to edit the audio into a final published podcast.

Additionally, the type of production you've chosen (in-house, outsource, or hybrid) will also impact production decisions. If you're doing all of the production in-house (and not on location) then you'll want to build a mini studio or at least dedicate a small space to recording and editing your podcast. What should this small space be? Well, you'll want to find a location that is quiet, air-conditioned, and secure. Microphones can be very sensitive, and while some background noise can be removed during editing, it's important to find a location to record that is as quiet as possible. Try to find somewhere that is devoid of excessive street noise, computer noise, chatting co-workers, or ringing telephones. All of these items will distract the listener. Finding an air-conditioned location will most likely not be difficult. Audio equipment and computers will produce heat and can get warm, so proper ventilation and cooling is necessary. Finally, you want the location secure. Your monetary investment in audio hardware, software, and microphones may be very significant. Protect it by locking it up when not in use.

Don't forget about editing! Ideally, you'll have an editing workstation set up (it can be the same one you use for recording) that includes a powerful computer, proper editing software, headphones, speakers, and Internet access. These items will allow you to listen to your podcast on both headphones and speakers. Using headphones and speakers gives you two good listening references, allowing you to listen to the podcast the ways your listeners would.

If you're only doing part of the production, then you'll simply need to purchase the needed hardware and furnish the necessary spaces. Obviously, if you're outsourcing the entire production, you don't need to do anything, since the podcast production company will take care of all of that for you.

So, let's get started. In this chapter we'll talk about the different facets of podcast production, including hardware, software, sample podcasting rigs, and basic run-down of the recording process. This won't be a highly technical explanation, but instead an overview that gives you the information and tools needed to make informed decisions concerning the production of your podcast.

Recording Hardware

The first place to start is with the hardware. The recording hardware will probably be the most expensive part of your podcasting investment (except your time, of course), and it's important to take enough time to plan what you need. If you're not familiar with audio hardware, this may seem overwhelming. But there's nothing to worry about. I'm not going to show you how to create a complicated recording setup or test your knowledge of electrical engineering. This chapter will also not be a look at the finer points of audio production hardware. Instead, this section will give you a high-level overview of what audio hardware is available to use for your podcast and where you can purchase it. Additionally, we'll review a few sample podcast recording rigs that range in cost and expertise.

Do Microphones Matter?

The short answer is yes, microphones do matter, and usually you get what you pay for. A quality microphone will make it easier to produce a great-sounding podcast, because the audio quality will be better and you'll spend less time trying to edit and tweak the audio to compensate for a poor quality microphone. But that doesn't necessarily mean that you need to go out and buy the most expensive microphone available. As with the rest of your podcast setup, your budget and format will be the two major factors in deciding what kind of microphone you need.

How do we choose?

The general rule of thumb when planning a podcast studio or mobile rig is to purchase the best microphone or microphones you can within your budget. There's not really a set amount that you should or shouldn't spend on a microphone. If your total project budget is only a few hundred dollars, then you won't purchase the most expensive microphones (because they're all well over $300), but instead get something that is a smaller percentage of your budget but is nonetheless a quality microphone for the price. There are dozens of decent-quality microphones that are around $100. Any one of these microphones would be perfect for the budget-conscious podcaster.

Another consideration when choosing microphones for your podcast is your podcast format. As you've noticed by now, we keep coming back to the format. It really does affect many of the decisions you make downstream, so hopefully you have it nailed down already.

I'm going to use the roundtable discussion as an example again. If you plan to do a roundtable discussion podcast that takes place in a studio or conference room, then you should consider studio microphones. The microphones are built for indoor studio use and do not tolerate any type of weather, moisture, wind, or rough handling. These mics will be labeled as studio microphones (see Table 7.1). You'll want to use these in an indoor, climate-controlled environment. They provide excellent sound quality, but need to be handled with care.

For podcast formats that take place outside the studio, there are many microphones that are rugged and perform well under tougher conditions. While these microphones can't be abused (you should always care for your equipment, especially microphones), they can handle a whole lot more than the more fragile studio microphones.

So, the goal is to match a microphone to your podcast format and budget. There are plenty of microphones to choose from, so this should not be a problem.

TABLE 7.1 Microphones Worth Buying

Name	Type	Connection	Price (US$)
Audio Technica AT2020	Condenser	XLR	100
Audio Technica AT3035	Condenser	XLR	199
Rode Microphones Podcaster	Dynamic	USB	229
Sennheiser MD46	Dynamic	XLR	250
Shure SH55	Dynamic	XLR	250
Heil PR-30	Dynamic	XLR	300
Shure SM7B	Dynamic	XLR	400
Electrovoice RE20	Dynamic	XLR	400

Microphones you can rely on

No matter your budget or format, there's always a decent microphone out there. Will the more costly microphones sound better? Yes, they will. But with some good planning and a little testing, you can make even a low cost mic sound good enough to use on your podcast. Conversely, you can also make a great microphone sound poor, if you don't know what you're doing (and that's why, if you don't, you'll want to hire a podcast professional to assist with production).

Here is a list of microphones that are reliable and mostly affordable. They also have different applications—some are for studio and some are meant for outdoor or location use. The prices listed are approximate, in US dollars and may have changed by the time you are reading this. Refer to the list of hardware outlets for current pricing.

Recording Hardware

The most reliable way to record your podcast audio is using a dedicated piece of recording hardware. Recording hardware are stand-along devices that serve one task only: to record what is said into the microphone. These units are often more expensive than audio recording software, but offer distinct advantages to podcasters (see Table 7.2).

TABLE 7.2 Recording Hardware Worth Buying

Name	Price (US$)
Marantz PMD660	500
Fostex FR2-LE	600
Marantz PMD670	700
Edirol R-4	1200
Fostex FR-2	1300
Edirol R4-Pro	2000
Sound devices 722	2500

Recording directly to hardware is better for two simple reasons: noise and ease of use. Computers are noisy. They have a lot of moving parts: fans, hard drives, and optical drives. All three can affect your audio either through ambient noise that is transferred through the air or electrical noise that is transferred through your power cables. Both can also be very difficult to isolate and remove.

With recording hardware, recording your podcast is as simple as plugging in the microphone and hitting record. There is no software to download, install, and configure. Most recording hardware is portable and can also be used for on-location recording.

Podcasting Rigs

The hardware you use to record and edit your podcast should be tailored to your budget, technical requirements, and needs. I would recommend you look at the Podcast Academy PodcastRigs™: http://podcastacademy. com/pcr-index/

If you're unsure of what equipment to buy, you may want to hire a podcast professional to help you make wise choices with your budget. By hiring a professional you will ensure that you're spending money on the right equipment.

Where to Buy Hardware

Depending on where you live, some of the microphones and audio hardware mentioned in this chapter won't be readily available nearby. You'll most likely need to find a reputable audio store in your area or use one of the handful of quality online merchants. If you do decide to buy online, it may be worth finding a local store where you can test out the equipment and get a hands-on look first.

Table 7.3 is not a comprehensive list of merchants nor should it be taken as an endorsement of them. It is provided as a starter list to help you research, price, and purchase the audio hardware you need.

TABLE 7.3 Where to Buy Audio Gear

Merchant	Web site
BSW Professional Audio Gear	www.bswusa.com
Musician's Friend	www.musiciansfriend.com
Amazon.com	www.amazon.com
Sam Ash Music	www.samash.com

Recording Software

Back in the old days, audio was recorded onto magnetic tape. In professional studios, the tape was stored on large reels, usually 2-in thick. The bulk, weight, and price of not only the tape but also the recording machines made it difficult for amateurs to record and edit high-quality audio. Thankfully, that's no longer the case. With the widespread use of computers in audio recording over the last 20 years and the increased quality and lower cost of audio recording software, you can now record and edit high-quality audio right on your home computer. Even better, with the right gear, you can record high-quality digital audio on the go with a good laptop.

There are plenty of options when it comes to choosing audio recording software for your podcast. Prices range from free to thousands of dollars. All of the software mentioned here will do the basics—some better than others—but there's definitely a software that will fit every budget and need. Some of the software packages listed will offer a free trial. While evaluating what you'll need, you should take advantage of the free trials to learn more about the software and test it out for yourself.

Some of the upper-tier products will not have free trials. If you're in the market for those products, you probably already know enough to make the purchase or are working with a podcasting professional, who will help you evaluate the best product for you. Ultimately, the right software product is the one that works for you and your podcast.

TABLE 7.4 Free Recording/Editing Software

Name	Platform	URL	Notes
Audacity	Windows, Mac OS X, Linux	audacity.sourceforge.net	Completely free, open-source software
GarageBand	Mac OS X	www.apple.com/garageband	Free with purchase of new Apple computer, otherwise it's part of the $79 iLife software suite

RYAN'S TIP

When making the decision to purchase audio recording software, it is important to take note of the system requirements listed with the software. Most modern recording software will need a computer of substantial speed and memory (RAM). Be sure your computer meets at least the minimum requirements. Not doing so could cause the software not to function reliably and cause a horrible experience recording and editing your podcast.

A Quick Look at Audacity

Audacity is a free, open-source audio recording and editing application (see Table 7.4). It is available for Windows, Mac OS X, and Linux. Because it is free and cross-platform, Audacity is a popular tool among beginning podcasters and those on a tight budget. It can do all of the basic functions that you would need when recording and editing audio, but it does have some limitations. For example, the user interface is less than polished and can be difficult to navigate. Also, in order to save your podcast as an MP3 file, you will need to install an extra bit of software called the LAME MP3 Library.

In the main window of Audacity, you can record and edit your podcast (see Figure 7.1). Audacity will allow you to do multiple tracks and then combine them at the end into one stereo or mono track. This track can then be exported as an MP3 file (see Tables 7.5 and 7.6).

You can tweak and alter your audio tracks using one of the default effects listed in the Effect menu (see Figure 7.2). One common effect you

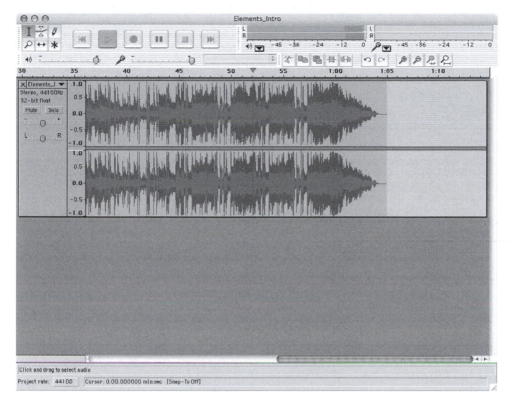

FIGURE 7.1
Main recording and editing window in Audacity.

would use when producing your podcast is the compressor, which will take your audio and smooth out the peaks and valleys of volume, so it's more uniform and easier for your audience to listen to.

When you select the compressor, a small window appears where you can adjust the settings for the desired amount of compression on your audio track (see Figure 7.3).

A Quick Look at Sony Sound Forge

Sound Forge is a single-track editing and recording application (see Figure 7.4). Unlike Bias Peak LE or Sound Studio, Sound Forge cannot do multiple tracks. This may be a disadvantage for some—in a sound-seeing tour, for instance, it would allow you to add a voice-over in the studio on top of a track you recorded on location—but it is still a powerful editing

TABLE 7.5 Prosumer Recording/Editing Software

Name	Platform	URL	Notes	Price
Adobe Soundbooth (beta)	Windows/ Mac OS X (Intel only)	labs.adobe.com/ soundbooth	A simplified version of Adobe Audition (see below), which is aimed at non-audiophiles	Currently free while in beta. $199 upon release
Audio Hijack Pro	Mac OS X	www.rogueamoeba.com/ audiohijackpro	Records audio from a variety of system sources, very flexible, but no editing capabilities	$32
Fission	Mac OS X	www.rogueamoeba.com/ fission	Audio editing of MP3 files	$32
Sound Studio	Mac OS X	www.freeverse.com/ soundstudio	A powerful, yet simple to use audio recording and editing application	$79.95
Bias Peak LE	Mac OS X	www.bias-inc.com/ products/peakLe5	Limited version of Peak Pro (see below)	$129
Sony Sound Forge	Windows	www.sonycreativesoftware.com	Full-featured audio recording and editing software	$299

TABLE 7.6 Professional Recording/Editing Software

Name	Platform	URL	Notes	Price (US$)
DSP Quattro	Mac OS 8, 9, X	www.i3net.it/Products/ dspQuattro	Audio editing, recording, and mastering	149
Pro Tools M-Powered	Mac OS X	www.digidesign.com	Lite version of the professional Pro Tools package with special support for M-Audio devices	299
Adobe Audition	Windows	www.adobe.com/ audition	Recording, editing, and mastering software	349
Bias Peak Pro	Mac OS X	www.bias-inc.com/ products/peakPro5	Professional tool for audio editing and mastering	599
Soundtrack Pro	Mac OS X	www.apple.com/ soundtrackpro	Part of final cut studio	1299

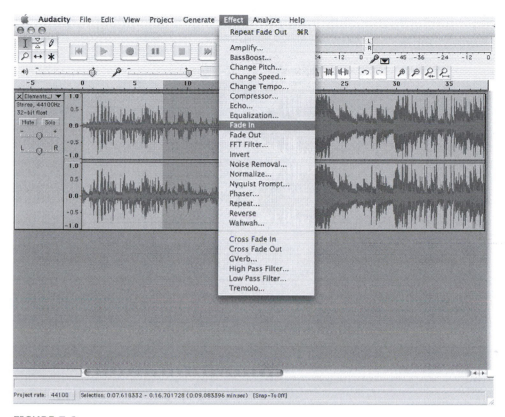

FIGURE 7.2
The Effect menu in Audacity.

application. It has tools that let you do batch processes (perform the same task on a number of files at once), scripting, and dozens of effects that could come in handy when producing a high volume of podcasts.

A Quick Look at BIAS Peak Pro

BIAS Peak Pro is a high-end recording, editing, and mastering software application (see Figure 7.5). It is in the upper range in terms of functionality and cost (see Figure 7.6).

In the main window of BIAS Peak Pro you have all of the tools you need to record, edit, and process your audio file. This includes the option to use plug-ins. BIAS offers its own set of plug-ins, which are powerful tools to enhance your audio file.

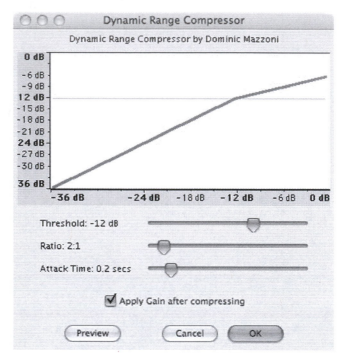

FIGURE 7.3

Dynamic compressor in Audacity.

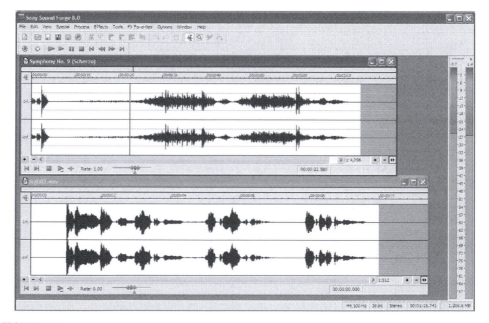

FIGURE 7.4

Main window in Sony Sound Forge.

FIGURE 7.5
Main window in BIAS Peak.

FIGURE 7.6
Batch processor window in BIAS Peak.

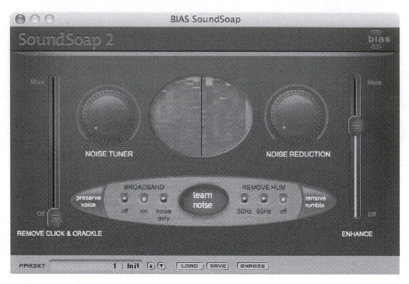

Soundsoap, a BIAS plug-in that cleans up your audio.

Using the Soundsoap plug-in you can easily remove unwanted noise from the audio file and enhance it, making the audio sound richer and fuller.

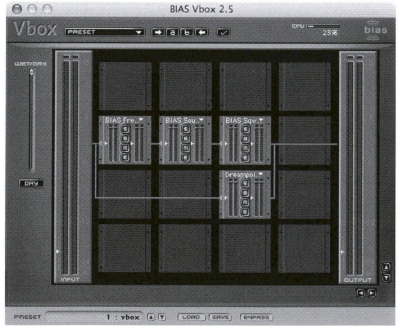

Vbox, a BIAS plug-in that allows you to chain multiple-effects plug-ins together.

BIAS Vbox is a multi-effects control environment for plug-ins. Essentially, it allows you to run multiple plug-ins simultaneously and in almost unlimited configurations. You can route the audio through the plug-ins in any order.

One piece of useful functionality for podcast recording and editing is the batch processing, which is great for automating (and speeding up!) any post-production work on your podcast.

BIAS Peak Pro 6 promises to be even more useful to podcasters. It isn't due to be released until Q3 2007, but the new version will include functionality to author and upload your podcasts right from within Peak. To learn more about the new version of Peak, visit their website: http://bias-inc.com/products/peakPro6/

The Recording Process

Since this isn't a technical book, I'm not going to bore you with detailed instructions on how to record your podcast. Instead, I want to give you an overview of the recording process by answering some common questions. The goal is that these answers will help you better prepare for your podcast, as well as make it easier to communicate with the technical people involved in your project.

The recording phase of producing your podcast is the act of getting in front of microphone, pushing (or clicking) the record button, and then recording the primary content for your podcast. If you're doing an interview podcast, you'd sit down with your guest and do the back and forth with questions and answers. Removing unwanted audio and inserting an "intro" and "outro" is part of the editing phase. At this point you should be concentrating only on recording the raw content.

What Is Proper Microphone Technique?

For starters, don't eat the microphone. They're sensitive, and you don't need to touch your mouth to the screen. Not only will it give your audio excessive low-end sounds (called the proximity effect), but the moisture from your mouth could damage the microphone. Everyone speaks at a different volume and with varying tone, so there's no set distance you should be from the microphone. Start at about 6 in away and then talk into the microphone and listen to yourself through a pair of headphones. Record the audio and listen back on speakers and with headphones. When you find the sweet spot—the distance at which your voice sounds good—note it and always speak into the microphone from that distance.

RYAN'S TIP

In the audio world, the proximity effect occurs when a person speaks into a microphone at a very close range, causing the mic to exaggerate bass or low-end frequencies. This is also called "eating the mic."

To help prevent unwanted pops and other mouth noises, use a pop filter or windscreen. One perfect way to ruin your recording is to have intermittent explosive pops and "s" sounds (called sibillance) obscure the audio and distract the listener. If you've ever listened to an amateur audio recording, you know what I'm referring to. A pop filter for a studio microphone will serve two important purposes. First, it will help eliminate the pops from your recording; second, it will keep speakers at the proper distance from the microphone (see the first point in this section). If you're recording on the go, on location, or with a mobile rig and handheld microphone, you'll want to consider a windscreen for your mic. A windscreen is simply a foam covering that slips over the mic head (the mesh part you speak into). The windscreen will help eliminate mouth noises like pops, but also any light wind.

Recording Your Format

In Chapter 5, we talked about the various formats and some of the technical implications of each one. The recording phase is where you will begin to see these implications. The technical specifics of recording your podcast will vary depending on the format you're using. A simple one-person podcast is much simpler to record than a sound-seeing tour that takes the listener through the busy streets of downtown Chicago or New York city.

We are going to use the roundtable discussion format as an example. It is an example of a format that requires a good bit of hardware and configuration. We won't get into the details here, as this is just to show what one format takes to record.

If you're doing a roundtable discussion with a host and three guests, you'll need the following equipment:

- four microphones,
- four pop filters,
- four microphone cables,
- four microphone stands,
- four pairs of headphones (not required but very helpful),
- one audio mixing board to connect them all together, and
- table and chairs for everyone to sit comfortably.

As you can see, the roundtable discussion format requires a lot of hardware. This doesn't include a recording device (usually a computer with recording software) or any other gear you might need to enhance the sound (compressors or some of the other items we discuss later in this chapter). When considering your podcasting hardware purchases, list out all of the items you'll need in order to produce your chosen format.

How long will it take to record?

It depends. If you're doing a roundtable discussion, the recording will only be as long as the discussion. But there's more to it than that. You also want to plan time for any pre-recording setup, like running cables for microphones, testing, or any unforeseen problems. In the beginning, the recording phase will take you longer; as you do more podcasts, you will learn to streamline your workflow and get things done faster.

Is it OK to mess up?

Not only is it OK, but you're sure to do it. Even the best announcers, voice talent, and actors mess up frequently. If you do mess up in a way that will confuse listeners or otherwise make the podcast unappealing, you can easily edit out that content during the editing phase. However, you do want your podcast to sound natural and authentic, so you don't want to edit long pauses, pronunciation errors, or minor stutters.

What's different about mobile recording?

If your podcast format requires that you record on location, then there are a few things you should consider:

- Use a mobile podcast rig. Earlier in this chapter, I listed a URL that leads to more information about the different types of podcast rigs. If you're going to do mobile production, be sure to get the proper gear, and the mobile rig listed at that site provides an excellent example. That will ensure that you're not carrying around bulky studio recording hardware that isn't built to be transported and exposed to bad weather and humidity.

- Plan and scope out your recording location in advance. Knowing ahead of time where you're going to be recording will help you better plan the time you need to get the job done, as well as prepare you for any potential problems. Going onsite before production will allow you to measure ambient noise and other distractions. For example, if there is a massive construction project going on nearby that will make it difficult to record listenable audio, you will want to make alternative plans for a location or with your recording style. Additionally, you'll know if you'll be recording inside or outside and what options you have in the case of inclement weather. You want to be aware of this so you can protect your expensive audio hardware!

Editing

After you record your podcast there is one more step left to make it a polished audio show: *editing*. I'm going to talk about editing as a broad description of anything you do to alter the original recorded audio. This could range from removing portions of the audio to enhancing it using compression or equalization to outputting the final file that your sub-scribers will download. Editing is the process whereby you take an unpol-ished and raw recording and turn it into a polished podcast that accurately represents your company and conveys your message.

During the editing phase you will be able to craft the audio into a well-structured and professional-sounding podcast. Editing is important because it removes unnecessary and distracting audio, evens out peaks and val-leys in audio volume, and completes the podcast by inserting "intros" and "outros."

> **If you flub a few words during recording, stop what you're saying and wait about 5 seconds. After the 5 seconds have passed, resume what you were saying, including the words you misspoke. These extra seconds of silence will make it easier for you to edit out the mistake later.** RYAN'S TIP

Too Much of a Good Thing

One trap that new podcasters fall into is to over-edit their podcasts to the point where they no longer sound natural and are difficult to listen to. This is caused by too much editing and in a way too much post-processing—adding of effects, compression, equalization, or other audio enhancing tweaks to the audio of the podcast. Also, too much compres-sion will make your podcast sound flat. This is especially apparent when post-processing audio of the human voice. The distance between a great-sounding voice track and one that sounds unnatural and over-processed is very small. Always use restraint when post-processing your podcast audio. The new audio hardware and software are great toys, but there is too much of a good thing!

> **Don't edit your podcast in isolation. After listening to the same audio over and over, your ears will fatigue and it will be difficult to judge what sounds good and what doesn't. For that reason, I recommend you always have others listen to the podcast during and after editing.** RYAN'S TIP

How Long Should it Take to Edit?

The amount of time it takes to edit your podcast will depend on a few variables:

- the length of your podcast;
- your podcast format; and
- your software and hardware setup.

If your podcast is a 15-minute roundtable discussion that requires only that you edit in the "intro" and "outro" music, the time spent editing will be minimal. Once you do a few podcasts, you could easily complete editing in twice the length of the podcast, so plan for 30 minutes. For a more involved podcast like a 30-minute sound-seeing tour that is comprised of a half-dozen interviews and commentary, you should plan to spend more time editing the pieces together into a coherent audio package. You should expect to spend three to four times the length of the podcast in the edit phase. None of these numbers are hard science, but just an estimate so you can better plan and budget your time. The more podcast episodes you produce, the more comfortable you become with your hardware and software setup, and therefore the quicker you'll be able to edit your podcast.

Example Editing Tasks

To give you a better idea of what is involved with editing your podcast, without going into step-by-step detail, here is a list of some popular tasks performed during the editing process.

Removing outtakes

There's no escaping the reality that you'll make mistakes during the recording of your podcast—Words horribly misspoken, excruciatingly long pauses, technical difficulties, or content that simply doesn't fit or belong in the final podcast. Removing these outtakes is the main task when editing your podcast.

Removing/Reducing noise

Professional recording studios spend a lot of money to ensure that the recording space is free of noise, including that from heating and air conditioning, electrical noise, and outside sounds. Since most of you will not have the luxury of building a state-of-art studio, you may find yourself needing to remove or reduce noise in your podcast. This is usually accomplished using what is called a noise gate. Simply put, a noise gate only allows sounds to pass through that are above a certain volume threshold. Sounds that do not rise above that threshold are not allowed to pass through the noise gate and are therefore not recorded.

Double-ender

A double-ender is a recording technique that allows two (or more) people in different locations to do a podcast and sound like they're all in the same studio together. In order to pull off a double-ender, every participant needs a quality microphone and the ability to record their voice digitally. There also has to be a way for all participants to communicate during the conversation. This is usually done using some type of telephony service, whether it be internet-based (Skype, www.skype.com is one example) or a traditional landline. After the recording, every participant sends their audio file to the editor and then all the tracks are synced up to form the final podcast. If everyone starts their recording at the same time, syncing up all the participant tracks is actually quite simple. The end result is an audio recording where everyone sounds like they were sitting in the same studio talking to each other. A great effect!

Adding "intros" and "outros"

A very common editing task is the insertion of "intro" audio at the beginning of the podcast episode and the "outro" audio at the end. You can hear this on almost every podcast. This is an easy edit to make, because it is just a matter of inserting the audio into the recording—something that someone with little editing experience can pick up quickly.

Adding a "music bed"

A "music bed" is a track of music that plays beneath a more prominent audio track, usually a voice-over of some type. During a segment of your podcast you may want to have some music in the background to create a mood or set the scene for the podcast. This background music is a music bed.

Level compression

Not to be confused with file compression (converting a file into a smaller size), level compression takes your audio recording and makes it more uniform so that the loudest portions are quieter and the quietest portions are louder. This gives the audio file a predictable dynamic range. The person or people speaking can talk normally and not be concerned with controlling the volume of their voice. This then allows the speakers full expression and speaking volume without altering the overall audio level (which could potentially cause distortion of the audio signal). (Note that compression can be applied in most of the recording software listed earlier.)

RYAN'S TIP

Audio editing isn't like editing a press release or other written document. It isn't feasible to try to edit out individual phrases or words. There is a definite limit to which audio editing can be done and still sound pleasing and natural to the ear.

Sweeten Your Audio with The Levelator™

Sometimes your audio files sound a little off or you have a problem with one person in a recorded phone conversation being louder than someone else. There are certain situations like these that are difficult to tackle with manual editing.

GigaVox Media released a simple software tool, The Levelator™ (Mac/Windows/Linux), that is easy to use audio enhancing software. In fact, all it requires is that you drag the audio file you want to process onto the application and The Levelator™ does all of the heavy lifting. Using a special algorithm,

The Levelator™ adjusts the audio in your file so that conversations between multiple people sound more even and your audio file comes out sounding better. It's like magic.

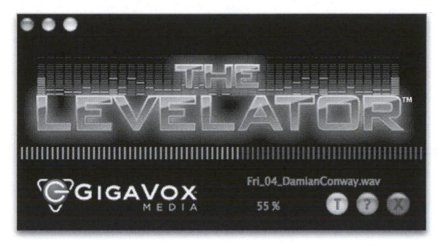

The Levelator™ as it looks when running on your computer. Simply drag your audio file onto the window and The Levelator™ will process it and output a processed file.

The Final File

After you complete your editing, it's time to output the final audio file that will be distributed via your podcast feed to subscribers. This can't be just any kind of audio file. It needs to be a consumable audio file, one that subscribers can easily download (a manageable file size) and listen to (in a predictable supported file format).

There are a couple of ways you can go with audio files, but the one way that is sure to be 99 percent compatible with your current and future podcast listeners. The most popular way to format a podcast audio file is as an MP3. MP3 stands for MPEG-1 layer 3. It is a compressed, lossy format (i.e., there is some sound degradation compared to the original recording, but not so much that most listeners will care) that boasts a small file size with good audio quality. MP3 audio files end in the extension .mp3. If we have an MP3 file called "my_podcast," it would look like this: my_podcast.mp3.

You can also distribute your podcast as an "enhanced" audio file. An "enhanced" audio file is one that has accompanying data like images or URLs. You can place these extra data at strategic points in the audio file, so as to correspond with the audio content. "Enhanced" audio is currently only available in the m4a/b formats and only supported by Apple, Inc. hardware and software. This means that if you distribute a podcast with "enhanced" audio it will only be playable in Apple iTunes and on Apple iPods. This is a great second option for your listeners, but you do not want to distribute your podcast only in "enhanced" format. Stick with the popular and almost universal MP3 format as the audio format of choice for distributing your podcast.

Encoding your MP3: size and quality

The final MP3 file that you deliver will have to be encoded from your original edited file. Normally, you can do this straight from your editing software. Most programs allow you to export as MP3. I won't get into the technical details, but suffice to know that how you encode your file will have a huge impact on the audio quality, file size, and the amount of bandwidth you consume distributing that file to your subscribers. Table 7.7 provides some general guidelines, and you should review it with your podcast professional or the technical person in your team. Please note that this assumes that your podcast consists mostly of voice and only a little music.

For a table with greater detail including the amount of disk space needed for storage, please refer to http://www.libsyn.com/rec_size_chart.html

TABLE 7.7 MP3 File Size and Quality Table

Quality	File Size/ 7-minute Podcast	Encoding Settings
High	6.7 MB	128 kbps stereo
Medium	3.4 MB	64 kbps stereo
Low	1.7 MB	32 kbps stereo

Metadata

Your podcast is now recorded and edited into a nice package of audio information and compressed into an MP3 file. All of the content is there, but there is one last step before you make it public. You want to make sure your podcast is as user- and machine-friendly as possible. This final step is a very important one because it determines how people see your podcast on their computers or MP3 players. This is where metadata comes in.

What is metadata? In this situation metadata is the information stored inside the MP3 that describes what it is. This includes information like podcast title, author, episode title, genre (in this case it would be "Podcast"), and more (see Figure 7.7). Including this metadata is important in order to keep current listeners informed about your podcast episodes and attract new listeners that come across your podcast. Why's that?

Think of metadata as the ID for your podcast. Everything a listener needs to know about the podcast will be contained in this metadata. And, most importantly, this metadata travels with the MP3 file, no matter where it goes and how it is transferred. When the podcast is played on a computer or a portable audio player (like Apple's iPod), this information is displayed. This helps listeners identify the podcast as well as learn where they can find more information.

To see this for yourself, go online and find an interesting podcast and then download it to your computer. Open this podcast in your media player (I use Apple iTunes). In the display area of the media player you'll see the podcast name and information. This are all pulled from the metadata that is inside the MP3 file. Cool, no?

FIGURE 7.7
Podcast metadata displayed during playback in iTunes.

Different Types of Metadata

When talking about metadata in MP3s, you'll hear it commonly referred to as ID3 tags. ID3 tags is a technical name for the specification that determines the structure and underlying technology for MP3 metadata. You don't have to know anything except that you need to be sure you insert metadata into every podcast file you publish. Later on I'll show you how to do this. With the right software (which you probably already have) it's a very simple task.

There are several different types of data that you can enter and save in each MP3 file. Table 7.8 lists those that you'll need to fill out for your podcast.

In the example below, I'm inserting podcast metadata using Apple's iTunes music software. This is one of the more popular media applications

TABLE 7.8 ID3 Tags Relevant to Podcasts

Name	Description	Example Data
Name or title	This field will contain the name of your podcast episode. This should be a descriptive name that says what the episode is about	Finding Your Favorite Acme Product Online
Artist	Here you will enter your name or the name of the company that is producing the podcast	Acme Inc.
Year	Enter the year that you produced the podcast episode	2007
Album	In this space type in the name of the podcast. This is different than the "Name" or "Title" above. That contains the episode name, while this contains the podcast name	Acme Corporate Podcast
Comments	Include information about the podcast, a URL for more information, and optionally an email address for listeners to use to contact you. Some podcasters also include episode information in this space, like topics covered and Web sites or products mentioned	Get in touch by calling us at 800-555-555 or sending an email to info@ example.com
Genre	The proper genre to put here is "Podcast." Putting any other genre in this space will only confuse your listeners	Podcast

on both Mac and Windows. It can handle not only the encoding of your MP3 file, but you can also use it to add or edit your podcast metadata.

To add metadata to your podcast file, simply right-click on the file in iTunes and choose Info (see Figure 7.8). A window will open that will contain information about your podcast file. Click the Info tab and you will see several fields.

Using the guidelines in Table 7.8 begin filling out the form. When you're done, click OK to save the information to your podcast file. If you don't click OK, the information will not be saved.

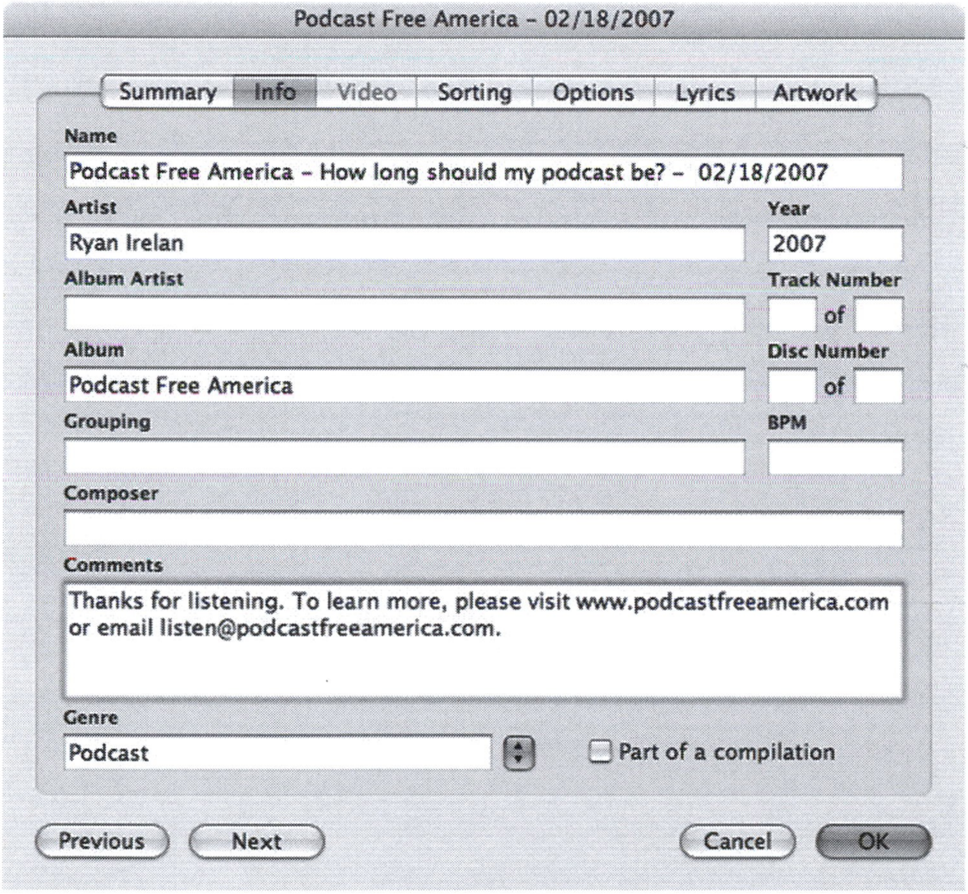

FIGURE 7.8
Adding metadata to your podcast file in iTunes.

Artwork for your podcast

Another piece of metadata that is important to include is the "album art-work" or, in the case of a podcast, the podcast artwork (see Figure 7.9). Think of this as a way to extend your visual brand to your podcast.

I would suggest having a special graphic created just for your podcast. It doesn't have to be of print quality—although you might want to go ahead and do that for collateral materials—but can instead be a web-quality image.

Using software like iTunes, it's very simple to add an image to your podcast. Control-click on the episode and then choose "Get Info." A window will appear. Select the last tab, "Artwork." Click the Add button and then select the image that you want to use. Once you've selected the image, click OK so it will save.

FIGURE 7.9
Adding album art to your podcast file.

Once you add metadata and an image, your podcast is now set to be listed in directories (like the iTunes Store shown in Figure 7.10) and distributed to your subscribers.

> **RYAN'S TIP**
>
> Many portable media players, like newer versions of Apple's iPod, will display the album artwork on the iPod screen while it is being played. This is another important reason to include album artwork with your podcast audio file.

The Business Reasons for Good Metadata

Over the course of this section, I've alluded to most of the business reasons for ensuring you include good metadata with each and every podcast episode you publish. But for good measure, I want to list here exactly why publishing good metadata with your podcast is a great business decision.

FIGURE 7.10

How your album art will appear in the iTunes Store, one of the most popular place to find and subscribe to podcasts.

- It makes it easier for listeners to understand what your podcast is about and what topics are being covered. This is a great service to your listeners and it keeps them subscribed and listening.

- Including your contact information or Web site in the Comments section of the metadata will allow new listeners to learn more about your company and products.

- Using your company name and branding in your podcast image (album artwork) will extend your company branding into the podcast space.

Lessons Learned

- The production process of your podcast is the practical application of almost all of the planning you've done up to this point. This is the phase where your decisions come to life.

- Purchase audio hardware and software with your budget and podcast format in mind. If you have doubts about what is needed, consult a podcasting professional.

- Editing is the process that takes your raw audio and turns it into a nicely packaged audio show. Too much editing can negatively impact the quality of your podcast.

- Adding good metadata to every podcast episode is not only a worthy service to your listeners, but also a great business decision.

Preparing to Publish Your Podcast

Ryan Irelan

Congratulations! You are now in the homestretch of creating your podcast and one step closer to publishing it for the world to download and listen to! Having gone from the early steps of learning about social media and the podcasting revolution, to understanding how you and your company can interact with your customers through innovative use of technology, all the way to making the important decisions about creating your podcast, you are now almost ready to make it all a reality. You are ready for the final decisions that will make sure all of that hard work isn't for naught.

It is also important that you have a home for your podcast online, a place where visitors can always go to subscribe or learn more. In this location you can list every podcast episode and the show notes. This allows visitors to quickly scan episode topics and click on any links discussed or referred to in the episode.

In this chapter, I'll cover the important topics of how to tune your Web site (or blog) for your podcast, so that you maximize its exposure to your Web site visitors and encourage them to subscribe and listen. Every podcast episode should have some accompanying text, called show notes, on your Web site or blog. I'll cover what show notes are, where they should go, what they should look like, and why they matter. And, yes, they do matter. There's also the important topic of how your podcast will be delivered and where the podcast files will be hosted. Because podcasts can be large audio files, you'll want to plan ahead and have solid file hosting in place, in the event that your podcast sees tremendous popularity. Additionally, your podcast hosting needs to be reliable and a good fit for the kind of traffic you expect your podcast to get.

Now that you have an overview, let's get started.

Show Notes

Show notes are a condensed text version of a podcast episode. Show notes are not a written transcript of the podcast, although some podcasters do offer transcriptions as an extra service to their listeners. Good show notes accompany every podcast episode and serve two distinct purposes:

1. They provide your listeners with links and information on topics mentioned in the podcast episode.
2. They offer a way for search engines to index your podcast using the keywords listed in your show notes.

Let's break each one down.

Serving Your Current Listeners

One of the greatest benefits of podcasting for the listener is that she can listen to audio content while on the go. Whether in the car, on a bike ride, a walk on the beach, or commuting on the subway, she can take my audio content with her and listen to it on her time. While this model is flexible for the listener, it also leaves her almost always disconnected from the Internet, unable to look at Web sites referred to in the podcast, or look up other information that was discussed or presented during the episode. So how can a listener get this information while stationed at a computer before or after listening to the podcast? Show notes offer a solution, where a listener just needs to visit the podcast Web site or weblog and read the episode show notes to get to relevant links and information.

In addition to offering regular listeners notes and links from your podcast episodes, the show notes will also offer Web site visitors an overview of the podcast episode so they can see if the topics discussed are of interest to them. A brief summary of your podcast's content can be very enticing and may close the deal on a download.

Search Engine Optimization to Gain New Listeners

Search engines like Google index text, not audio. As of right now there are a few tools available to search audio content, like Everyzing (www.everyzing.com), but these are emerging technologies just taking hold in the marketplace. The best way for helping new listeners to find you through search engines, is that you offer a text representation of your podcast. You want to be sure your show notes are full of relative and descriptive keywords. Put yourself in the position of a potential listener and think of the keywords you would use to search for information on that topic.

As an example, if Bob's Power Tool podcast has an episode that talks about the latest circular saw from a company called Acme Power Saws, Bob would want to be sure the show notes mention circular saws, the company Acme Power Saws, and any other keywords about power saws that are relevant to the conversation or discussion that took place on the podcast.

In the next section of the book there will be extensive discussion around the importance of search engines and how to optimize your rankings using show notes and transcriptions.

How to Create Effective Show Notes

In addition to the two topics covered above, there are some other things you can do to create effective show notes. What makes a show note effective? Effective show notes offer your listeners' information about your podcast in text and encourage new listeners to subscribe to your podcast feed.

- *Include them with every episode*: Every episode of your podcast should have related show notes. Coming back to a theme of the production section of this book, consistency is important. Your subscribers will come to expect the show notes and even rely on them for links and information about your podcast.

- *Include URLs to sites*: If your podcast episode discusses or mentions Web sites, be sure to include links to those Web sites in your show notes. Many people will be listening to your podcast away from their computer and will not be able to visit the Web site right as you mention it.

- *Use timestamps*: If your podcast episodes run longer than 10 minutes, you should consider using timestamps in your show notes. A timestamp is simply an hour and minute listing. This makes it easier for listeners to skip to any content they find particularly interesting, as well as making it easier to reference content later on.

Show Notes Example—TwiT Podcast

TWiT (This Week in Tech, www.twit.tv), hosted by technology personality Leo LaPorte, is a weekly podcast on all things technology. On each episode he discusses a variety of topics and mentions numerous Web sites. In order to keep listeners informed on the topics discussed, every episode has its own show notes on the TWiT.tv Web site.

The show notes are organized as a simple bullet list with each topic covered getting its own bullet (see Figure 8.1). You'll notice that the notes are littered with links to other Web sites that were discussed or offer more information for the listener.

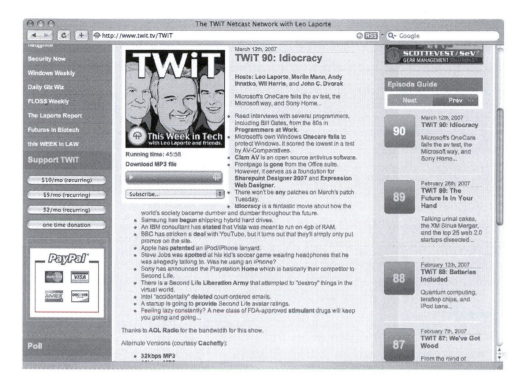

FIGURE 8.1

The TwiT podcast lists show notes as bullet points for every episode.

Tuning Your Web Site for Your Podcast

Now that you have your podcast produced and ready to unleash to the world, you need a place to put it. There will be a lot of information covered in Chapter 11 on this topic, but for now let's cover the basics.

Your podcast needs a home. Listeners will want to visit the Web site to find out more about you, your company, and your podcast, including the shownotes discussed in the last section. Visitors will also come to listen to or download older podcast episodes and to look for a way to contact you and read the show notes from your latest podcast episode.

For people that visit your Web site and aren't currently subscribed to your podcast or don't even know anything about it, you want to highlight how to learn more, a way to listen to episodes, and how to subscribe. Having your podcast properly integrated into your Web site will have the positive side effect of converting casual Web site visitors into podcast listeners and subscribers.

Web Site or Blog?

Where should you house your podcast? Today you have two options to consider (and a possible third that we'll discuss later). You can give your podcast a home on your current Web site or you can create a blog dedicated exclusively to your podcast updates, news, and information. Let's consider both of these in more detail.

Using your Web site

The key benefit of using your own Web site to house your podcast is that you draw on existing traffic to the site. Regular visitors or customers will see that you've added a podcast and, hopefully, subscribe or listen to it. But because of design and layout constraints, it may not be easy to just drop in information about your podcast. Here are a couple of ways to easily integrate your new podcast into an existing Web site:

- Highlight the podcast on the front page of the site (see Figures 8.2 and 8.3). Using a sidebar or other prominently visible portion of the page, highlight your podcast and link to a page that contains details about it, like how to subscribe, past episodes, and contact information. This can be presented as a box in the sidebar, at the top of the page, or, a less desirable option, at the footer of the page. If you have a person or team that designs and develops your Web site, you can work with them to come up with the best location for information about your podcast.

- Create a page on your Web site for your podcast. With the podcast link and information in place on the front page of your Web site, now

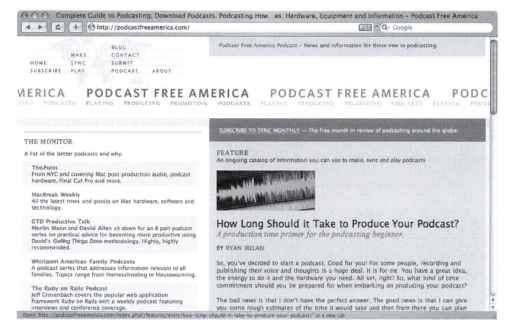

FIGURE 8.2

On the Podcast Free America site the podcast is called out in two areas on the front page. There is a prominently placed box at the top of the page that describes and links to the podcast. There is also a link to the podcast page in the page navigation.

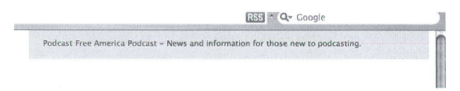

FIGURE 8.3

The box on the front page of the Podcast Free America that highlights the podcast and links to the podcast page.

you need to create the page that those links will lead to (see, e.g., Figure 8.4). This page should contain the following information:

- podcast title
- host name
- brief explanation about the podcast

FIGURE 8.4
This is the page that the links from Figure 8.2 lead to. Listed is all of the basic information about the podcast, including the last five episodes with links to download the podcast audio file.

- link to subscribe to the podcast feed
- email or contact form so listeners can get in touch
- list of most recent podcast episodes, with link to audio file (optional).

Using a blog

You don't have to use your Web site as the place to host your podcast. The most popular way is to use a blog (better known today simply as a blog). If you don't already know, a blog is a regularly updated Web site that lists updates (called "entries" or "posts") in reverse chronological order, so the latest entry appears at the top of the page. Blogs lend themselves to podcasts because they're easy to update, include the really simple syndication (RSS) feed functionality, and can be set up fairly quickly. Additionally, blogs automatically archive past content by date, so your visitors have a

TABLE 8.1 Popular Blog Software

Software Name	URL	Cost	Notes
Movable type	www.sixapart.com	$149+	Clean user interface, very popular
WordPress	www.wordpress.org	Free	No cost, lacks quality user interface
TextPattern	www.textpattern.com	Free	More complex to setup and use, very powerful
ExpressionEngine	www.expressionengine.com	$250	Powerful, customizable, and extensible

simple way to go back in time and listen to past episodes. You have a couple of options when deciding to set up a blog.

Host Your Own

Hosting your own blog means that you install software to run the blog on your own server or web hosting account. This will allow you maximum flexibility to customize the blog and make it fit into your current Web site look and feel. Additionally, you will be able to place your blog in a subdirectory or on a subdomain of your Web site domain (e.g., mypodcast.mycompanyname.com). Table 8.1 lists the four most popular blog software tools.

Wordpress is a very popular blogging tool among podcasters. It is a free application and very simple to set up on your own web server or web hosting account. Additionally, all of the plugins you need to get started podcasting are available. You can learn more at codex.wordpress.org/Podcating

Use a Hosted Service

If you don't want to or don't have the capability to host your own blog, there are a few quality services that will host it for you (Table 8.2). One tradeoff of using hosted services is that there are limitations to customization of your blog.

TABLE 8.2 Hosted Blog Services

Software Name	URL	Cost	Notes
Blogger	www.blogger.com	Free	Nice interface, popular, easy to get started, difficult to customize
TypePad	www.typepad.com	$5–15+/month	Simple to use and set up, difficult to customize
WordPress	www.wordpress.com	Free	Similar to the self-hosted version above, difficult to customize

One thing to keep in mind is that some of the hosted services will not allow you to use a full custom domain name for your blog (e.g., mybizblog.com). Unlike hosting your own blog, some services will not allow you to extend your Web site domain to your blog. Instead you will be required to use a subdomain. Using WordPress.com as example, this would be myblogname.wordpress.com. This is a disadvantage because your company and podcast branding will not be present in the domain. That said, WordPress also comes as a non-hosted version that you can download and install on your own server using your own domain.

A hybrid solution

What I'm calling the hybrid solution is a combination of Web site and blog. If you have an existing high-traffic Web site, this may be the best solution. The idea here is to leverage all of the power of a blog—easy to use, built-in RSS functionality, and automatic archives—but make it an extension of your Web site. To do this you would design the blog to look similar to your Web site and the use a subdomain as its location (e.g., mypodcast.mydomain.com). You still want to highlight your podcast on the front page of your site and link to the blog.

No matter whether you choose to use your existing Web site, a blog, or the hybrid solution, you always want your Web site visitors in mind. It is

FIGURE 8.5

An example of an inline audio player on a Web site. This allows visitors to easily preview the podcast before downloading or subscribing to the podcast feed.

important to make their experience of accessing, listening, and subscribing to your podcast as simple as possible. Here are some things to consider:

- Offer an inline player that lets a visitor listen to your podcast in the web browser without having to download any files (see Figure 8.5). This can be one player for each podcast episode or one player that contains all recent episodes.

- Make the podcast feed available on every page and with every podcast episode. Many listeners will check out your podcast, but you will want to make it easy for them to subscribe. For this reason, you should make the podcast feed as readily available as possible.

Hosting and Content Delivery Networks

Your podcast isn't a podcast until you have a way to deliver it to your listeners. Later on in the book I'll talk about using RSS as the delivery mechanism for your podcast, but before you can deliver the podcast file you need a place to host it. A host is a service that physically stores your files on a server and makes them available for download on the Web.

Choosing a Web Host

If you already have a Web site then you probably already have a web host. It might be that your company hosts its own Web sites. Either way, you have a place to store files and make them available to the public for download. You could host your podcast on this web host, but don't act too fast. It could cost you a lot of money.

There are hundreds of web hosts out there and many are good, but some are bad. It's beyond the scope of this book to list and review hosts, although I would suggest asking a friend, colleague, or business partner for recommendations. To view a large table of hosts, costs, and features, visit http://www.okaytoplay.com/wiki/Podcast_Hosting.

RYAN'S TIP

> **Bandwidth is the amount of data that can be transferred in a specified amount of time (usually monthly). It is measured in megabits per second (mbps) and limited by hosts in gigabytes (GB) (1000 MB) per month.**

Most web hosts have specific limits when it comes to bandwidth, the amount of data that can be transferred in a given time period. While the limits a host might have in place are plenty for running just web pages, hosting and serving audio files can run through bandwidth allotments quickly. It is important to carefully project your needs so as to avoid getting stuck with an expensive bandwidth bill. As an example, if you have a podcast that runs 10 minutes and is about 5 MB in file size, it only takes

1000 people download it for 5 GB of bandwidth to be consumed. Most basic tier hosts offer around 1–3 GB per month. Overages for bandwidth are priced similarly to overages on your cellphone minutes—very steeply. So, in order to avoid that situation altogether, it's important to plan ahead and be sure you're on the hosting plan that will work best with your podcasting aspirations and goals.

But there are other ways to deliver to your podcasts. Using a web host is probably the most popular way for podcasts with average-sized audiences, but if your podcast has a large audience (or the potential for one), you may want to consider services that are dedicated to delivering media files at higher download rates and with redundancy and speed.

Content Delivery Networks

Content delivery networks (CDNs) are companies that have a series of web servers strategically located in order to quickly deliver the same content to anyone with internet access worldwide. Initially, it's not required that you host your files on a major CDN, unless you are a large corporation that needs a powerful global infrastructure for all of your web properties and content. For podcasting, this means that audio files won't be delivered from just one server in one location, but instead from multiple servers in multiple locations. What's the advantage of this? Speed, reliability, and cost. Because a CDN has so many servers in different locations, costs to deliver content can be controlled by serving content from locations that are closer to where the content is being requested.

A CDN consists of a large series of web servers that are strategically placed across the Internet. The CDN operates between the podcast files that live on your server and the subscribers who download them. Each time you update your server with a new podcast, the CDN retrieves it and uploads it to all of the CDN delivery servers. Because the CDN servers are spread out across the world, this allows your files to be delivered to your subscribers from the closest server to them. A list of some of the more popular CDNs can be found in Table 8.3.

TABLE 8.3 Popular CDNs

Name	URL
Akamai	www.akamai.com
Limelight	www.limelightnetworks.com
Peer 1 RapidEdge	www.rapidedgecdn.com
CacheFly	www.cachefly.com
Amazon S3	aws.amazon.com/s3
VitalStream	www.vitalstream.com
NaviSite	www.navisite.com
Libsyn Pro	www.libsynpro.com

Podcast Hosting Services

TABLE 8.4 Podcast Hosting Services

Name	URL
Libsyn	www.libsyn.com
Hipcast	www.hipcast.com

Unlike CDNs, podcast hosting services are not designed to offer enterprise-level content delivery. They are aimed at medium-traffic podcasts that require more than just the simple hosting you get with your web host but fall short of the requirements that warrant using a CDN. These podcasting hosting services (see Table 8.4) will not only host your podcast files, but also create the podcast feed. These services are aimed at the cost-conscious user and not recommended for high-traffic podcasts.

Lessons Learned

- Show notes are an important service to your subscribers, as well as a tool to gain new ones through search engine optimization.

- Give your podcast a home. Whether it's on your current company site or on a standalone blog, your podcast should have its own space.

- Thinking ahead about how you will host and deliver your podcast will save you money and ensure your listeners can always access your episodes.

Legal Issues

Colette Vogele

Like all media and advertising content produced within an organization, podcasting presents some important legal issues for the organization to consider and resolve. These issues can be viewed as falling into four broad categories: (1) clearing rights for images, text, and sounds appearing in the podcast (like copyright, rights of publicity, and trademark rights); (2) protecting the podcast content from being infringed (except in those instances when you *want* it to be ripped, remixed, and virally spread across the Internet); (3) media law issues (like avoiding defamation); and (4) general Internet business issues (like terms of service (TOS) and general contract rules over the Internet).

Interestingly, many of these issues are not necessarily unique to podcasting, or even unique to online media and advertising. As other parts of this book explain, the business of podcasting presents a truly new and revolutionary approach to distributing content. It permits the business to reach a niche audience or a broad audience with relatively low barriers to them. The business can engage its employees, partners, clients, and customers more directly and even have an interactive and meaningful dialog with them. While distributing content to reach internal groups or external customers is nothing new (think of printed flyers, direct mailers, news-letters, etc.), and distributing content over the Internet is not particu-larly earth shattering these days either (think of Web sites and electronic newsletters), what *is* new is the interactive nature of podcasts and other social media. That interactivity raises some unique issues that your legal department—or attorney for hire—should consider, and which are described further in this chapter.

Early thinking about each of the legal topics addressed here can help to keep your production process running on time and minimize the risk of unexpected legal costs down the road. We will address each of these four categories in this chapter, but first we have two important notes to remember when approaching the law and legal issues in your organization.

The Care and Feeding of the Legal Department

It is not uncommon for the legal department in an organization to be the last to learn of the trailblazing ideas coming out of the marketing or com-munications group. When these new ideas are revealed to the legal depart-ment, the wheels that were once spinning quickly over in marketing may come to a screeching halt. The "blessing" the marketing department thought would come in a couple of hours ends up taking weeks or even months to secure. "What on earth could be causing this delay?" one might ask.

Unfortunately, because the legal department is often not engaged in early discussions about new initiatives involving blogs, podcasts, or other social media, it may learn very late in the process about copyrights that need to be cleared (which can take months), or it may be faced with broader legal considerations of significant liability to the organization (like whether com-ments on the proposed blog should be moderated). With a changing legal landscape related to electronic contracting, copyright and implied licensing, online defamation, and other issues, the law department is in a challenging position when it comes to opining quickly on a new Web-based initiative.

Moreover, because podcasting makes it possible to become a content pro-ducer when the organization has never done so before, the law department may not have expertise in reviewing content licenses, clearing rights, or considering liabilities associated with interactive media. All this is to say that the attorneys for the business may need some time to digest the legal ramifications of a new initiative before green-lighting a particular project. And, let's face it, lawyers are not typically disposed to a "ready-fire-aim" approach. Thus, to avoid the problem of an unexpected delay in the production process, it's essential to both find an advocate in the legal department who will understand the internal enthusiasm about these new Web 2.0 tools and then provide that individual with the information and time needed to assess the risks and champion the legal issues for the company.

WARNING

Please note some of the limitations of this chapter. First, it discusses only US-based legal questions. The laws of other jurisdictions may be applicable to your podcasting venture, and you should consider seeking information about those jurisdictions as well. Second, this chapter provides general information about legal topics, but it is not a complete discussion of all legal issues that arise in relation to podcasting, nor is it a substitute for obtaining competent legal advice. Using this book does not create an attorney–client relationship. The authors and publisher make no warranties about the general legal information provided in this chapter and disclaim liability for damages resulting from its use to the fullest extent permitted by the applicable law. Third, please also note that this chapter attempts to provide an overview of how the law is likely to treat many of the issues that arise in relation to podcasting. Bear in mind that this chapter does not necessarily advocate for how the law should treat podcasting, only what the law is likely to be currently.

Many of the topics covered in this chapter are also detailed in the *Podcasting Legal Guide: Rules for the Revolution* (2006), a practical guide developed by Colette Vogele and Mia Garlick through the fellowship program at Stanford Law School's Center for Internet & Society, Creative Commons, and the Berkman Center Clinical Program in Cyberlaw at Harvard Law School. The *Podcasting Legal Guide* can be found on line at http://wiki.creativecommons.org/Welcome_To_The_Podcasting_Legal_Guide.

Creative Commons Canada also recently published the *Podcasting Legal Guide For Canada: Northern Rules For The Revolution*, which is an adaptation of the original US guide and highlights some of the major differences between US and Canadian law in the new media space. The Canadian guide can be found on line at http://www.creativecommons.ca/blog/wp-content/uploads/2007/06/podcastinglegalguide-forcanada.html.

Clearing Copyrights for Images, Text, and Sounds Appearing in a Podcast

When creating a podcast for the corporation or small business, it is important to make sure that all necessary rights and permissions are secured for the material included in the podcast. This is relatively easy if the corporation creates or already owns all of the materials included in the podcast. But these issues become progressively more complex the more you include material created by third parties. This section provides a brief overview of copyright basics, explains the most common instances when permission is *not* needed, and then describes how to get permission when required.

Copyright Basics

Copyright law applies to creative and expressive works. This includes most of the things that are found in a podcast—e.g., any images and sounds in the podcast, any scripts created for the podcast, the printed transcript of the podcast, the content of an interview, the design of the Web site where the content is hosted, and any musical works and sound recordings incorporated into the podcast.

What does copyright law protect?

Under current US copyright law, copyright attaches automatically to every creative and expressive work once that work has been "fixed in a tangible medium of expression" (that is just legalese meaning the moment the expression is captured in any reproducible format). For example, words, sounds, or images captured on a digital video or audio recorder, images captured on film, sounds created through a computer program, images drawn on an artist's canvas, and even a sketch on a restaurant napkin, all receive copyright protection under US law. The US Copyright Office's Web site (www.copyright.gov) provides a good description of the scope of copyrighted works in Circular Number 1, "Copyright Office Basics."

What are a copyright owner's basic rights?

Under U.S. copyright law, the owner of a work that is protected receives a number of important exclusive rights to control certain activities in relation to the work. For example, a copyright owner of an original podcast can control whether another person **makes material "copies" (or "phonorecords")** of the podcast, creates a "derivative work" by making changes to the existing podcast (e.g., creating a mash-up of sounds or images from the podcast with those of another podcast, or by adding advertising to the podcast), distributes the podcast to the public in the form of material "copies" or "phonorecords", or **performs publicly** "by digital audio transmission" the sound recording of the podcast. If the podcast includes a muscial work, images, or a video, then the owner also has the right to control whether another person **publicly displays or performs** the video podcast or individual images from the video podcast. Consequently, under the current U.S. legal structure, any person other than the copyright owner who wishes to do any of these protected acts must secure permission from the copyright owner before doing so, unless an exception or exclusion applies, like making a fair use which is discussed further below.

The terms "copy" and "phonorecord" are specifically defined by the Copyright Act as "material objects" in which a work is fixed. A healthy debate exists among scholars, copyright attorneys, and judges regarding whether disseminating content over the internet can be considered a "distribution" of a "copy" of a copyrighted work, since it is questionable whether a "material object", is in fact transferred. This is a critical point that remains unsettled by the courts, and the views of stakeholders can easily differ on the interpretation of these terms.

WARNING

Who owns the creative content?

Typically, the person (or persons) who initially creates the work is the legal "author" of the work. Ownership ordinarily rests with the author in the first instance. However, in the context of a business, and if the work is made by an employee "within the scope of his/her employment," the Copyright Act directs that ownership rests with the business. In fact, under US law, the business is considered the legal "author" of the work. Works created in a business are called "works made for hire" (or simply "works for hire").

WARNING

Remember that the default "author" under US copyright law of a work for hire is not the creator of the work but rather the party/business who hired out the work. The fact that the business—rather than the person who actually created the work—is considered the "author" is fairly unique to US copyright law, and in many other jurisdictions the opposite rule applies.

Under the Copyright Act, a work for hire also includes a work that is "specially ordered or commissioned" for certain limited uses (e.g., as a contribution to a collection, as a motion picture or "other" audiovisual work), but *only if* there is a written contract that is signed by the creator of the work that expressly states that the work is considered a "work made for hire." (For more information, see the Copyright Office Circular Number 9, available at www.copyright.gov, which addresses works made for hire.)

Because of these special ownership rules, there are at least two best practices to employ for the business podcaster. First, if the podcast is produced internally by the business's employees, the Copyright Act provides that ownership of the copyright lies with the business. Nevertheless, it may be prudent to have employees sign short transfer agreements relating to their creative work for the organization. This avoids any possible ambiguity about whether the work was within the "scope of the employment" and who the proper owner of the work is.

COLETTE'S TIP

Secure copyright interests from employees or contractors through written agreements to avoid ambiguities in the understanding of who owns what, and especially if the work is created in whole or in part outside of the US.

Second, if the business hires an outside consultant to create or produce the podcast series, ambiguities may arise as to who owns the content. The language of the Copyright Act suggests that for "audio visual works"— which would include video podcasts—the business will be the default owner. But it does not appear that an audio podcast would receive the same default interpretation. Therefore, unless the business agrees that the consultant shall be the owner of the content, to avoid any doubt as to ownership, it is a best practice to obtain signed agreements from all non-employees involved in the podcasting project transferring rights and ownership interests to the business.

When a written agreement is absent, if there is a dispute over ownership, a court will apply a number of very fact-intensive questions to determine ownership of a work. Litigation over such issues is bound to be a very expensive proposition, especially when compared to the cost associated with negotiating these rights up front with the podcast consultant. It is also good business practice to have that discussion with the consultant up front, so that expectations are clearly defined at the outset of the project.

Another ownership issue that arises in the business/corporate setting relates to ownership of very old materials in the business's archives. As noted earlier in this book, one approach to podcasting content by the corporation is to take previously recorded materials in the business's archives and post them as podcasts. This older material may or may not be owned by the corporation, depending on when it was produced and under what circumstances it was developed. For example, materials dating from decades ago that a corporation may have never considered for public distribution may today be uncovered and utilized for a historical podcast about the corporation or the industry. Confirmation of the material's ownership may be necessary before including the material in a podcast. (Interestingly, many older corporate materials may have fallen into the public domain because the materials were not properly registered or their copyright registrations were not properly renewed.)

Is it necessary to register a copyright?

As in the world of text blogging, a common question arises about how and when to register podcasts for copyright. While registration is optional and works in the US are copyright protected from the moment they are "fixed," registration offers many benefits and is a prerequisite for bringing an infringement action (for a US work) and for certain remedies in the event of infringement. Further, if registration is made within 3 months after the first publication of a work, remedies for infringement will apply even if the registration has not yet issued from the Copyright Office. Registering a work within 3 months after the first publication also permits awards of statutory damages (ranging from $750 to $150 000 per infringement) and attorneys' fees if the copyright is successfully enforced.

COLETTE'S TIP

The Copyright Office's Web site offers simple step-by-step instructions for submitting copyright registration applications. See "How To Register" at www.copyright.gov.

One approach to registration is to submit each podcast for registration separately. This may prove practically cumbersome if podcasts are produced daily or on a frequent schedule. Another approach is to collect a series of podcasts and submit them periodically under a single registration (e.g., monthly or quarterly). There is no clear right or wrong answer to this dilemma, but if there is a chance that the corporation may seek to enforce the copyright in a podcast, waiting beyond 3 months may have a negative effect on the remedies available for infringement. For example, statutory damages and attorneys' fees are not available for infringements prior to the registration date, if the registration application is not submitted within the first 3 months after the podcast is published. In the world of viral media, this could prove problematic. For example, if a copyrighted podcast (or portion of a podcast) is posted without permission to a viral video distribution site (like YouTube) prior to the registration but after the 3-month window is passed, statutory damages and attorneys' fees for infringement after the initial publication of the podcast and before the effective date of the registration will not be permitted. Accordingly, if enforcement of the copyright in a podcast is anticipated, registration within 3 months of first publication would be wise.

What are the risks if permission is not cleared?

The legal and financial risks of rolling the dice and hoping that an uncleared use of someone else's content flies under the radar of the copyright owner are significant, to say the least.

Direct infringement

Briefly, using copyright-protected content without permission may lead to liability for direct infringement. To prove direct infringement, a plaintiff must show ownership of a copyrighted work and copying by the defendant. Direct copyright infringement is a "strict liability" tort. This means that once the plaintiff proves ownership and copying, the plaintiff is entitled to a remedy (provided no defenses to copyright, like fair use, are available). The plaintiff does not need to prove the defendant had any intent or knowledge of the infringement. Therefore, as a defendant, relying on an argument that you did not in fact know the work was protected, or that you had no intent to infringe the copyright in question, does not negate your liability (though it may weigh in defendant's favor when damages are assessed).

> **WARNING**
>
> Providing attribution or credit to the author of a work that is copied will not alone clear the user of liability for copyright infringement. Likewise, including an upfront disclaimer that denies association between the user and the owner of the copyrighted material does not necessarily protect the podcaster from liability (though it may help if there is a trademark-related dispute.

Indirect infringement

Moreover, in addition to direct infringement, use of copyright-protected content without permission could lead to contributory, vicarious, and inducement theories of liability. (These theories are sometimes refereed to as "indirect infringement" or "secondary liability.") Contributory infringement means that the defendant causes or materially contributes to the infringement by a third party with knowledge of the infringing activity. Vicarious liability means that the defendant maintained the right and ability to supervise the infringing activity and had a financial interest in those infringing activities. And the newest theory (added to the copyright owner's rights in 2005 under the MGM vs. Grokster Supreme Court decision) is inducement, which means that the defendant's conduct involved affirmative steps directed at fostering infringement by others, and the defendant intended to promote copyright infringement.

Once a party is found to be liable under one or more of these theories of direct or indirect infringement, the remedies for copyright infringement can include an injunction (an order forcing the defendant to stop or take some remedial action), an award of statutory damages (ranging from $750 to $150 000 per infringement), or an award of actual damages (like the copyright owner's lost profits or a reasonable royalty rate). As a matter of course, a successful copyright plaintiff will also be awarded the costs to litigate the case and its "reasonable" attorneys' fees. All of these remedies to the copyright owner can add up to a significant monetary award and should discourage infringing uses of copyrighted content.

When should permission be sought?

As a general rule, unless the podcast creator is confident that the use of another's copyright-protected material falls within the fair use parameters, permission should be sought. There is no firm "rule" about how much of a work may or may not be copied to avoid infringement concerns. For example, it does not matter if an entire article is read aloud without changing it or if the producer changes it a lot and simply bases the podcast loosely on the text—either way, a business cannot avoid copyright issues by, for example, changing the work 10 percent or 20 percent. Once the work is used, either in verbatim or altered format, copyright law is implicated.

WARNING There is no "bright-line" rule to establish how much of a copyrighted work may be used before the use becomes infringing.

Consequently, the corporate podcast producer (and the legal department) needs to think about copyright issues before incorporating any materials into the podcast. In general, this means (1) identifying the copyright owner and (2) seeking permission to include the material in a podcast. The copyright owner may be identified by checking for a copyright notice on the work. Notice is usually in the form "© [year] [name]." For works created in the US, you can also search the Copyright Office's register, which is available at www.copyright.gov. (For more information about investigating the copyright status of a work, check out the Copyright Office's Circular 22, available at the same site.) Moreover, for works licensed through Creative Commons licenses (see discussion below), the copyright owner is often easy to identify because these licenses require attribution and/or a link to the original licensor (copyright owner).

The Most Common Instances When Permission Is *Not* Needed

While much of the content created by others that may appear in a podcast is protected by copyright, certain things are not. In addition, there are circumstances where permission is not required. This section describes these instances.

COLETTE'S
TIP

> You won't need to get permission when (1) you own the work, (2) the work or information you are copying is not protected by copyright, (3) the copyright term in the work you are copying from has expired, (4) the work is in the public domain, or (5) you are making a "fair use" of the work.

The business owns the copyright in the work

Initially, of course, the easiest way to avoid needing to obtain permission for the content of the podcast is to create the content from scratch, making it original to the business and not "borrowed" from another author. This means that the music, lyrics, video images, artwork, photographs, texts, and other content included in the podcast are newly created and not copied from (or closely modeled after) another source. If this is the case, then permission is not required to clear the content, because the corporation/business already owns the rights.

COLETTE'S
TIP

> Reminder: To the extent the business hires consultants to do the work, as noted above, having work-for-hire contracts in place will avoid doubt as to ownership and licensing issues.

The work being copied is not protectible by copyright

Certain content is not subject to copyright law in the first place, and therefore permission to incorporate the unprotectible content is unnecessary. Generally speaking, these unprotectible works fall into the following categories.

Facts, ideas, and theories; slogans, short phrases, and titles

Although an entire textual work may be protected by copyright, there are elements of that work that may not be subject to the exclusive rights of the copyright owner.

As a general principle of copyright law, copyright does not extend to facts or ideas; rather, it only protects the creative expression of a fact or idea. As a result, for example, you can discuss the ideas and theories that are discussed in an article, an editorial, or other opinion piece without ever asking the permission of the author or publisher.

Also, titles and short phrases or slogans will generally not be protected by copyright because these items lack the necessary spark of creativity and so can typically be used without special permission.

WARNING
If you engage in particularly harsh criticism of a theory or of an author, you may want to think about defamation laws. Also, for titles, short phrases, or slogans, you should consider trademark law because these items may receive trademark protection. Both defamation and trademark laws are discussed later in this chapter.

Finally, the Copyright Act expressly excludes any "idea, procedure, process, system, method of operation, concept, principle, or discovery regardless of form in which it is described, explained, illustrated, or embodied" from protection. This rule means, for example, that a podcaster may include a discussion of factual events reported in a newspaper or on a blog—such as facts about historical or current events—without obtaining permission from the copyright owner of the newspaper. It also means the podcaster can describe and discuss a new economic theory or business system in the podcast, because theories and systems do not generally receive copyright protection. Even recipes (the mere list of ingredients and instructions for combining the ingredients to achieve an end product) are seen as "a system, process, or method of operation."

COLETTE'S TIP

While an idea is not protected under copyright, the expression of an idea (e.g., the way a particular author has described or characterized the idea) typically is protected. This concept is called the "idea-expression distinction," and though it sounds somewhat simple, its application is one of the more complex concepts in US copyright law.

Many materials created by the US government are not protected by US copyright law

Works that are created by a US government employee or officer, as part of their official duties, are not protected by copyright. Similarly, federal and state statutes and judicial opinions are not protected by copyright. However, this extends only to federal officials and employees, which means that works created by state and local officials are usually copyright protected and, similarly, material created by private persons who are commissioned by the US government to prepare a work may be protected by copyright.

When incorporating government works into your podcast, you should also consider including in any copyright notice that accompanies the podcast a statement that identifies which portions of the podcast are protected by copyright and which are US government works. This is important because it allows others to know which works they can freely use, and it removes the ability, if the podcaster later needs to file litigation against someone for infringement, for that person to argue that they did not have proper notice of the copyrighted status of the work.

Expiration of the term of copyright

Under US Copyright law, the copyright for all works will eventually expire and the work will fall into the public domain. For any works whose copyright has expired, the work is in the public domain and the owner's permission is no longer needed.

Duration of the copyright in a particular work is one of the more difficult issues to sort out. This is due in part to the fact that the law has progressively extended the term of copyright since the passage of the first Copyright Act (back in 1791) when duration was only 14 years (and, by the way, only applied to books, charts, and maps!). Today, the term is equivalent to the life of the author plus 70 years, or, for corporate works (e.g., works for hire) the term expires either 95 years from its first publication or 120 years from its creation (whichever is shorter). While calculating the duration of a given work may require significant analysis, a few initial guideposts can help determine duration for many works:

- It is relatively safe to assume a work will be in the public domain if the work was published prior to 1923.

- If the work is unpublished, then it will be in the public domain if the natural author was deceased before 1936, or, if it is a work for hire/ corporate work, it was created before 1886.

- For any works published after 1978, the term of copyright is life of the author plus 70 years, or for a work for hire/corporate work, the shorter of 95 years from its first publication or 120 years from its creation.

- For works created between 1923 and 1978, duration is very complicated. This is in part because the term of copyright has been repeatedly extended, and renewal requirements were in existence for some time. Many works created in this time period have fallen into the public domain because the copyright was never renewed.

COLETTE'S TIP

To research questions related to copyright duration, an excellent and handy starting point for calculating duration is Peter B. Hirtle's table entitled "Copyright Term and the Public Domain in the United States," available at http://www.copyright. cornell.edu/training/Hirtle_Public_Domain.htm.

These guideposts are just that: markers for consideration. You can learn more about duration and renewal requirements from the Copyright Office's Circulars 15 and 15a, available at www.copyright.gov. If a question of whether a work is still protected by copyright comes up, it should be properly researched before assuming the work is in the public domain. The Copyright Office provides some research services in this regard, as can an attorney familiar with copyright duration.

Dedication to public domain

A work may also be in the public domain because an author or copyright owner has dedicated the work to the public domain, for example, by using the Creative Commons Public Domain Dedication (http://creativecommons. org/licenses/publicdomain/), or another form of open source licensing. Works in this category need no special permission prior to use. The entire work could conceivably be copied, sold, or given away without obtaining permission from the author or the original copyright owner.

There is an important wrinkle when using public domain works. Sometimes works that have fallen into the public domain may be incorporated into another work that is copyright protected. When this happens, although the public domain portions remain unprotected by copyright, the author's new expressive content into which the public domain work is incorporated may be protected by copyright. For example, as a general rule, slavish photographs of public domain works such as the *Mona Lisa* are not considered to attract copyright protection because they are designed to replicate the original public domain work as much as possible. However, an artistic photograph of a sculpture, even a public domain sculpture, may be protected by copyright because of the skill and creativity involved in setting up the shot.

COLETTE'S TIP

Another example of this wrinkle is when a book has fallen into the public domain. Although the text of a public domain work is no longer protected, an image of a recently published edition of the book may implicate the publisher's copyright in the layout and formatting of that text, the cover art, etc. To use an image of the newly published edition of the book in the podcast, the publisher's consent should be obtained (unless the use is considered a "fair use").

Fair use

Of course, some uses of otherwise copyright-protected material may be considered "fair" under the Copyright Act, in which case the Act states that such use is "not an infringement." Fair use is a heavily fact-specific inquiry that typically applies to works that are created for "purposes such as criticism, comment, news reporting, teaching…, scholarship, or research." In analyzing a question of fair use, a court balances at least four statutorily defined factors: (1) the purpose and character of the use (e.g., whether the use is "transformative" and whether the use is commerical); (2) the nature of the copyrighted work; (3) the amount and substantiality of the portion used in relation to the copyrighted work as a whole; and (4) the effect of the use upon the potential market for or value of the copyrighted work.

Today, many new resources are being developed regarding the importance of fair use as a mechanism for protecting an individual's freedom of speech in the First Amendment. For example, Stanford Law School's Center for Internet & Society recently established the Fair Use Project which provides "legal support to a range of projects designed to clarify, and extend, the boundaries of 'fair use' in order to enhance creative freedom." (Learn more at cyberlaw.stanford.edu/)

Since businesses/corporations are primarily for-profit entities, the fact-specific application of what constitutes a "fair use" under the Copyright Act will likely be narrower because "commercial speech" is not typically allowed the same level of First Amendment protection as other forms of speech (like political speech). Recent judicial holdings, however, appear to be signaling a shift in how fair use is determined when an allegedly infringing work is commercial. For example, the US Supreme Court found in 1994 that 2 Live Crew's rendition of Roy Orbison's song "Pretty Woman" was a non-infringing, transformative, fair use of the song even though it was plainly commercial in nature. Nevertheless, the financial resources and personal wherewithal required to mount a lengthy copyright defense (even in the most defensible situations) is often not where a business will want to place its time and resources.

Ultimately (and unfortunately), in a close case of fair use under the current state of US law, it may make greater business sense to expend some reasonable resources to obtain either permission for use of a copyrighted work rather than relying on the fair use defense alone or an opinion of counsel regarding the "fair use" so as to help minimize the exposure to damages if the business is later sued over the use.

> **COLETTE'S TIP**
>
> Libraries, archives, and educational organizations have many special exceptions to copyright liability that are not addressed in this book. For such uses, special attention should be paid to Sections 108 and 110 of the Copyright Act, as well as the broader protections under fair use, Section 107.

How to Get Permission When Legally Required

There is both bad news and good news when it comes to licensing content for a particular podcast. The bad news is that clearing copyright for music or video is not typically a simple task, and for someone new to it, it may seem like an unnecessarily complicated proposition. But the good news is that there exist a few great tools for finding easily licensable content for use in a podcast. We will first discuss some key terms used in the world of content licensing, then some of these tools, and lastly turn to the how-tos of licensing other content.

Key licensing terminologies

Licensing lawyers often throw around terms without realizing that their meaning, significance, or importance is not always obvious. While all parts of the license contract should be carefully reviewed, pay special attention to these terms in any form of a license that is considered for the podcast.

Exclusive vs. nonexclusive Rights

When a license includes "exclusive" rights, it means that the person receiving the license is the *only* person being given the rights to use the content by that owner under those terms. A "nonexclusive" license means that the owner may license the exact same content in the same way to other parties (and to as many parties as she/he wishes). Naturally, exclusive licenses are typically more valuable, and a licensor will seek more compensation for such a license, because they are then excluded from further licensing of that content.

COLETTE'S TIP

Under US Copyright Law, exclusive copyright licenses must be in writing to be effective.

One practical issue for a business considering whether to license content exclusively or non-exclusively has to do with whether the brand of the business is going to be defined in any manner by the content being licensed. For example, if the business would like to license the intro/outro music for an interview podcast, the question to ask is whether is it important to the business's brand identity that this music be associated *only* with that one brand? If so, sticking with an exclusive license allows the business to control its brand identity. Another example may have to do with artwork. If the album artwork or design work for the podcast is licensed from an artist outside the organization, the business should query whether the artwork will be associated with the business like a logo or other piece of branded content. If so, it would make sense to obtain an exclusive license for the artwork.

Time-limited rights
A copyright license can be time-limited or can be unlimited in time (meaning it can last for the duration of the copyright in question). For example, a theatrical play is ordinarily licensed to be performed on specific dates, and once those dates have passed, the theater in question is not permitted to continue performing the play. In the online world of podcasting, however, time limitations in a copyright license have a different impact. A podcast, once released, may live for a long time in an archive and listeners may download (e.g., copy) the podcast long after its initial release. Thus, it is important to pay close attention to whether the rights obtained through a license are limited in time—e.g., limited to use for a number of months, years, or even perhaps a specific number of episodes—or whether

the rights are granted "in perpetuity" or as "perpetual rights" (meaning, no time limitation). Time-limited rights can pose a problem for a podcast archive, because if the right to certain content expires, it may become difficult to extract that content out of the podcast archive without the expense of significant time and resources.

Geographic-limited rights

Copyright licenses can also be divided by region. For example, the play in the previous example may be licensed for a specific theater or in a particular region. Placing geographic limits on the license for a work to be included in a podcast, however, does not make much sense. This is because a podcast is by its nature intended to be distributed over the Internet, which is a global network. Ordinary geographic boundaries do not exist on the Internet, and thus, as a general rule, a license for content to be used in a podcast should include a "worldwide" right.

Warranted vs. unwarranted rights

When licensing content, the person receiving the license may seek certain warranties from the copyright owner. These warranties typically include that the content is original to the content owner, or that if the content is not original, the owner warrants that she or he has obtained all necessary rights to license the content. For licenses that are commercial in nature where the person receiving the license is paying for the rights obtained, these sorts of warranties are typically provided by the licensor. For content that is licensed freely through Creative Commons licenses (discussed below), however, all warranties of this kind are disclaimed. Content obtained through other "podsafe" channels may or may not include these sorts of warranties, and each license should be considered specifically for this issue.

Sub-licensable rights

An important but sometimes overlooked right to consider when seeking a copyright license is whether the rights obtained are sub-licensable. This simply means that once the content is incorporated into the podcast, the podcaster has the right to then sub-license that podcast. For example, if music is licensed from The ABC Band to the XYZ Shoe Corporation for use as intro/outro music in the podcast series XYZ is creating, the license needs to include a sub-licensable right for XYZ to then distribute its podcast to its listeners who need the right to copy the podcast to their computers and personal media players (iPods). XYZ may also want to license parts of their podcast for advertising purposes or for an anthology CD/DVD. Without maintaining a complete sub-licensable right, some of these later uses of the podcast series may not be permitted under the license without going back to the copyright owner and seeking a further license.

"Podsafe" content

In the world of podcasting, the term "podsafe" is used to describe content for which some or all of the rights are already granted, so that negotiation of separate permissions is unnecessary.

For example, music services like IODA's Promonet (www.iodalliance.com) and the record company Magnatune (www.magnatune.com) offer pre-cleared musical tracks for promotional use or through very simple licensing tools available on these service's Web sites. Creative Commons (www.creative-commons.org) is another organization providing solutions in the pre-cleared content space. While Creative Commons does not itself license content, it provides musicians, authors, composers, videographers, photographers, writers, or other content producers with form licenses through which they can make their content available. It will be clear that a piece of media is licensed through a Creative Commons license because it will likely contain one of the logos shown in Figures 9.1.

COLETTE'S TIP

Use the search tools available at Creative Commons Web site to find Creative Commons-licensed media anywhere on the Web. Currently, these specialized search engines are offered by Google, Yahoo!, Blip.tv, flickr, Owl music search, and SpinXpress, and all are available from a single link at the Creative Commons Web site: http://search.creativecommons.org/. The Firefox Web browser also offers a plug-in tool to help locate Creative Commons licensed materials on the Web (see http://wiki.creativecommons.org/Firefox_and_CC_Search).

FIGURE 9.1

Examples of logos that indicate a creative commons license.

While these new licensing tools are an important step toward permitting content to proliferate around Web 2.0, it is important to pay very close attention to the rights that are licensed or acquired through any of these tools. In fact, as with any license, this is where it pays to "sweat the small stuff" and read the license document, paying special attention to the licensing terminology noted above. Depending on the needs of the podcaster, these tools can provide great efficiency when creating excellent business podcasts.

Traditional licenses

A traditional license is in writing and specifically clears each of the rights the owner grants to the party for using the content. This depends in part on what sort of work is being licensed (e.g., a written text/literary work, a song/sound recording, or images), and whether the work is being used in an audio or video context.

Written texts

Written texts are the simplest to license. They require a license to reproduce, distribute, and perform or display publicly. Typically the ownership of the copyright in a text is a single person (the author) or entity (the publisher). Publisher contact information is typically not difficult to find, though with large publishing houses it may take some time to get a response to your request for permission. Locating an individual author, on the other hand, may require some investigation. If the work has been registered with the copyright office, records are available online at www.copyright.gov and they include the author's contact information.

Table 9.1 Rights That Must Be Cleared for Musical Works, and from Whom the Right May Be Cleared

	Performance right	Reproduction right	Distribution	Performance by digital audio transmission
Sound recording	Copyright owner directly (usually record company)	Copyright owner directly (usually record company)	Copyright owner directly (usually record company)	Copyright owner directly or Sound Exchange
Underlying musical work/composition	ASCAP, BMI, SESAC or directly from artist	Harry Fox Agency, or Section 115 compulsory license	Harry Fox Agency, or Section 115 compulsory license	N/A

Musical works

Licensing gets measurably more complex for music and audiovisual works. For music, you need to obtain the specific rights for two separate kinds of works—the underlying musical work (i.e., the written lyrics or musical composition) and the sound recording (i.e., the work as performed by particular recording artist). Table 9.1 provides a shorthand analysis of different kinds of licenses for musical works; the text that follows goes into greater detail.

LICENSE FOR REPRODUCING AND DISTRIBUTING THE MUSICAL WORKS The license to reproduce and distribute copies of the musical work may often be obtained from the Harry Fox Agency (www.harryfox.com/public/index.jsp); most uses of other people's copyrighted music in podcasts will require that you obtain such a license. To determine whether a particular song selected for a podcast is available from the Harry Fox Agency, search the Harry Fox Agency's "Songfile" database (www.harryfox.com/public/songfile.jsp).

COLETTE'S TIP

When searching the Harry Fox Agency's database, search both on the title of the song you want over the author/songwriter's name. The reason for this is that the singer who performs a song is often not the author/songwriter. By searching on title, you will be more likely to find the title you intend to find.

The current rates for licensing from the Harry Fox Agency are posted on its Web site. As of this printing, the price is 9.1 cents per song per download for songs up to 5 minutes. If the song is longer than 5 minutes, the rate per download is 1.75 cents times the number of minutes (or fraction thereof). In either case, the payment due is this rate times the total number of downloads. So, a podcast including one song of less than 5 minutes in length downloaded by 1000 users, for example, would result in fees of $91 ($.091 × 1000). A podcast that is 6 minutes and 18 seconds long downloaded 500 times would cost $61.25 (7 minutes × $.0175 × 500). Licenses from the Harry Fox Agency are available at www.harryfox.com/public/licenseeServicesDigital.jsp.

There is also a per-song "processing fee" of $8 to $10. More details of these costs are found in Harry Fox Agency's FAQ, available at www.harryfox.com/songfile/faq.html#faq1. If you want to distribute more than 2500 digital downloads of the work, you need to contact Harry Fox Agency and set up an "HFA Licensee Account" (for more information, see www.harryfox.com/songfile/faq.html#faq3).

Alternatively, podcasters can obtain licenses similar to the rights available from the Harry Fox Agency by following the procedures of Section 115 of the Copyright Act. This license is known as a "compulsory license" and requires notifying either the music publisher or the Copyright Office (if the publisher cannot be located) for every musical work desired. Information on notifying the Copyright Office is available from a "Checklist" at www.copyright.gov/carp/m-200.pdf. The usage fees are the same for the compulsory license as for a license with the Harry Fox Agency.

The license obtained from the Harry Fox Agency or through the Section 115 compulsory license process covers only the right to reproduce and distribute copies of a musical work and does not cover the right to perform publicly the musical work or the right to reproduce, distribute copies of, or perform the sound recording.

LICENSES FOR PUBLIC PERFORMANCE OF MUSICAL WORKS There are three main performing rights organizations (PROs) in the US—ASCAP, BMI, and SESAC—who own and license the public performance rights for the majority of commercially available musical works. ASCAP (http://www.ascap.com/weblicense/release5.0.pdf), BMI (http://www.bmi.com/forms/licensing/internet.pdf), and SESAC (http://www.sesac.com/licensing/internetLicensing.asp) each offers general Web site or Internet licenses.

Whether to obtain a public performance license for a podcast that is *solely* being offered as a downloaded file is up to the podcaster at this point. In a recent case involving ASCAP, a District Court in New York opined in March 2007 that a "download" is a reproduction and not a "performance," and therefore no performance royalty is required. This opinion, however, may be appealed by ASCAP. If you are highly risk-averse, it may still be prudent to clear the performance right through one of the PROs.

The current rate schedules and licensing information for the ASCAP, BMI, and SESAC licenses are available from their Web sites (www.ascap.com, www.bmi.com, www.sesac.com). Separate licenses from each organization may be necessary, because each organization holds the rights to a different set of musical works.

Once licenses are obtained from Harry Fox for the reproduction and distribution of copies of the composition, and (if elected) from ASCAP, BMI, or SESAC for the performance of a composition, the podcaster can legally podcast its own renditions of those compositions. However, if the podcaster wishes to include copyrighted sound recordings made by others (e.g., a song copied off a legally acquired CD or copied from a legal download), then it is necessary to obtain a license for reproduction and public performance (by a digital audio transmission) of those sound recordings, which is discussed next.

LICENSES FOR REPRODUCTION, DISTRIBUTION, AND PUBLIC PERFORMANCE (BY DIGITAL AUDIO TRANSMISSION) OF SOUND RECORDINGS The person or entity who owns the copyright in a sound recording also enjoys the exclusive right to publicly perform that sound recording by means of digital audio transmission. The Copyright Act defines "digital transmission" very broadly (any "transmission in whole or in part in a digital or other non-analog format"). If a podcast contains a copyrighted sound recording on an interactive basis (i.e., the user can select and download the podcast), then that may be regarded as a digital audio transmission. Ordinarily, to secure a license for that use, the user must approach the copyright holder of the sound recording directly.

All of the rights to a sound recording are usually owned by the record company that produces the sound recording. Unfortunately, this may require negotiating separately with multiple record companies for the right to reproduce and distribute their respective sound recordings as part of a podcast. In some sense, dealing directly with the record company that owns the rights to a particular song may ultimately be preferable because the record company likely has the legal power to grant licenses for all the types of rights discussed above—to reproduce and distribute copies of the sound recording and to publicly perform the sound recording (by digital audio transmission).

Music and images

For using music together with images, there are three types of additional licenses that should be considered: synchronization (or "sync") licenses, "master use" licenses, and "videogram" licenses. Like the licenses for reproduction and public digital transmission of sound recordings (see previous section), these licenses do not fall within the mechanical licensing schemes and must be individually negotiated.

> It should be noted that these licenses stem from "traditional" practices in a pre-podcasting and pre-Internet world. As such, they typically pertain to movie releases and television broadcasting, and their specific application to the digital on-line world is not obvious. Because of that, use of standard forms should be tailored carefully for the podcasting situation.

WARNING

SYNC LICENSE The sync license is negotiated with the copyright owner (likely the music publisher) directly. Traditionally, the sync license allows you to "synchronize" a musical work with an audiovisual work, such as a motion picture or television program, and to make copies of the resulting audiovisual work. Also traditionally, these licenses come in only two flavors: a theatrical sync license and a television sync license. This means that under a traditional sync license, a podcaster may only distribute the licensed copies for the specific purpose of either exhibiting the audiovisual work in motion picture theaters or broadcasting the work on television. It is not clear how exactly these sorts of licenses will be applied in the podcasting context, but by analogy, the podcaster may propose that a sync license specifically permitting the podcaster to exhibit the audiovisual work in a podcast (expressly clearing the fact that that distribution is online and via RSS (really simple syndication)) be created to clear those rights directly with the music publisher.

MASTER USE LICENSE The master use license is negotiated with the record company. It applies only if the podcaster wants to use a particular recording of a musical work with a video image that will be heard in a video podcast. Permission for this license must be obtained from the record company to use the "master recording" of the song for inclusion in the video podcast.

VIDEOGRAM LICENSE Traditionally, a videogram (which is shorthand for "video" + "program") license is used to describe a license for programs contained in audiovisual devices—like videotapes, laser discs, or DVDs—primarily intended for sale to the public for in-home use. Whether a podcast is legally considered the same as a videotape, laser disc, or DVD remains unclear and, as noted previously in this Chapter, whether the distribution right of a copyright owner is implicated by disseminating content over the internet is a question open for debate. Nevertheless, assuming for the sake of argument that the podcast is considered the same as one of these forms of distribution, a separate "videogram" license from the music publisher and the record company would be required if the podcaster plans to distribute the podcast to the public (which, of course, is how most podcasts are distributed). The videogram license may be necessary because the music publisher's permission under the traditional sync license may not extend to copies of the podcast that are distributed to the public in forms not included in the sync license. Likewise, the record company's permission under the master use license to use the recording of a song in the podcast may not authorize releasing the podcast for distribution to the public. The important notion here is that the trigger for this license is that the content is made available to the public generally, and not merely for a specific purpose (like theatrical release or television broadcast). In theory, for podcasting, it would make much more sense to have a single specialized license that covers the issues necessary for a sync license and a videogram license in one document. And since all of these rights would be negotiated with the same entity, there is no reason that these rights cannot be cleared in a single negotiation and covered by a single license agreement.

Publicity Rights

In general, publicity rights (sometimes called "personality rights") allow an individual to control how his/her voice, image, or likeness is used for commercial purposes. Publicity rights are governed by state law, which means that the law can differ from state to state, and there is no general federal law that applies to this area. Nearly every state has some form of protection for the "right of publicity" either through a state statute (legal code) or through common law (case precedent) enforceable by the courts.

The laws vary from state to state and sometimes are inconsistent with each other. Some states—like California and New York—have well-developed publicity laws, but even these two state's laws differ somewhat in their application. To state a claim in California, for example, a plaintiff must show three things: that the podcaster knowingly used an individual's name, voice, signature, photograph, or likeness; did so for purposes of advertising or selling, or soliciting the podcast (or any other products or services); and did so without the individual's consent. If the plaintiff proves his/her case, he/she is entitled to payment of damages of at least $750, plus profits from the unauthorized use, and her attorneys' fees and costs. California's publicity law applies even *after* the individual has died (but only for "personalities"—e.g., anyone "whose name, likeness, or voice has commercial value at the time of his/her death"). In other states, the right is enforceable only by living individuals.

Publicity rights are relevant to podcasts created by a business because, in many instances, the podcast will include audio or video interviews or other spoken or visual content depicting employees, customers, and visitors. When transmitting this sort of content, permission from those individuals may be necessary. For example, if the business selects images from a video interview to promote the podcast or a product or service of the business, to solicit advertising, or to make other commercial uses, consent from the individual appearing in the image may be required.

In many states, there are a number of exceptions to the consent requirement. For example, under California's right of publicity statute, First Amendment protections will allow uses of a public figure's name or likeness so long as it is done in a truthful way and does not imply a false endorsement of the podcaster or the podcast by the public figure. Moreover, in California, when the name, voice, signature, photograph, or likeness of an individual is used "in connection with any news, public affairs, or sports broadcast or accounts, or any political campaign," consent is again not required.

These circumstances may arise fairly infrequently in the corporate context, as opposed to a podcast from a traditional news organization or even a citizen journalist, but nevertheless reviewing the exceptions to the publicity right under the relevant state law should be considered when seeking to clear rights of publicity. Interestingly, the language of this section of the California code is deliberately broad, so it is likely to apply equally to bloggers and podcasters as it would to traditional media, though this question has never been tested by California courts.

Further, under the California right of publicity laws, if the employer includes the photograph or likeness of an employee in an advertisement (or other publication) when the employee's image is merely "incidental, and not essential, to the purpose of the publication," a rebuttable presumption is created affecting the "burden of producing evidence that the failure to obtain the consent of the employee was not a knowing use of the employee's photograph or likeness." This shift in the presumption to favor the business can play an important role if a right of publicity matter involving an employee is litigated.

Related to the right of publicity, in California, there is also a tort of misappropriating identity. For example, if the business imitates the voice of a "widely known" professional singer in the podcast, the business needs to be concerned about violating that singer's property interest in her/ his voice. This is the result of a court decision from 1988 involving Bette Midler and Ford Motor Company. In that case, Ford Motor Company used a sound alike singer to sing "Do You Want to Dance" (a song made famous by Midler) for a commercial, after Midler had declined to allow her rendition of the song to be used. The appellate court found that although there were *no* copyright or right of publicity interests in the voice, Ford had nevertheless "appropriated what is not theirs"—Midler's identity. While the case may be somewhat narrow on its facts, the take-home lesson for the corporate pod-caster is simple: if the podcast will imitate the "distinctive voice of a pro-fessional singer" which is "widely known" and if it "deliberately imitates" the voice "in order to sell a product," the corporation may run into legal problems relating to a misappropriation of identity under this holding.

Clearing publicity rights

> **COLETTE'S TIP**
>
> **It is best to ask individuals appearing in a video or audio podcast for their release at the time the content is recorded. Seeking to close up these loose ends after the fact is time consuming and may be overlooked if not handled up front.**

The most effective and legally accepted way to clear publicity rights is through a written document showing affirmative consent of the indi-vidual whose consent is required (and, if consent is from a minor, then proper consent from a guardian). When the voice or images are captured in a live face-to-face meeting, this can be accomplished through a short release form that can be presented by the interviewer or the photogra-pher or videographer. Often, however, in the context of online media and in podcasting in particular, interviews are conducted by telephone over Voice-over-Internet-Protocol (VoIP) systems (like Skype) where handing an agreement to the person whose release is sought is terribly inconvenient. In those situations, the parties may exchange an agreement by email or fax, such that the written signature of the party giving consent is unam-biguous and the identity of that individual giving consent is confirmed.

Whenever an issue arises related to publicity rights, two questions must be immediately assessed: (1) Where did the problem arise? (2) Who or on whose behalf was the consent given. The location of where the problem arises helps determine which state's law will be applied, and determining who gave consent helps to determine whether proper consent was obtained (e.g., whether consent was given by someone of majority age).

Two other methods for seeking to establish consent are also worth noting here. Although neither of these methods has been legally tested, using both together may form the basis for a best practice in instances where obtaining a printed/written signature is, for whatever reason, not possible.

First, for WordPress users, a free tool for obtaining signatures on releases was introduced in January 2007 (see Figure 9.2) by Michael

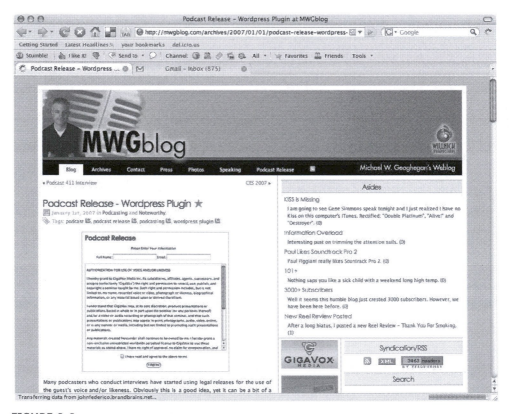

FIGURE 9.2

The WordPress tool for obtaining signatures authorizing the use of voice or likeness.

Geoghegan of Gigavox Media (http://mwgblog.com/archives/2007/01/01/
podcast-release-wordpress-plugin/).

This plug-in tool allows the podcaster to obtain a "click through" release
agreement from an interviewee or other person whose release is required.
The podcaster needs to prepare the language for the release agreement
itself, and this plug-in tool will then permit the recipient (e.g., the
interviewee) to confirm agreement. While this tool solves the problem of
obtaining some form of consent to the use of the image, likeness, voice, or
photograph of the individual, there are legal questions remaining as to the
effectiveness of such consent because confirming the identity of the person giving consent may be difficult.

Second, a podcaster can obtain the interviewee's consent on the audio
or video record. For example, before commencing the interview, ask the
interviewee expressly for her/his consent. Like a deposition—and all lawyers who have taken a deposition know this rule—get each intervie-wee
to express consent audibly, not just with a nod of their head! That part of
the interview, of course, will later be edited out, and should be archived
somewhere securely so it is available, if need be, at a later time.

COLETTE'S TIP

**While neither of these methods has been legally tested, the "click-through
agreement plus on-record consent" approach may be the best practice for podcasters unable to obtain a formal printed/written signature from the interview
subject. If nothing else, it gives the business's attorneys something to rely on in
negotiating a release at a later time.**

Clearing Trademark Rights

Generally, trademark law is designed to protect consumers from being mis-
led or deceived as to the source of goods and services, or the endorsement, sponsorship, or affiliation of one good or service with another. In
other words, trademark law works to ensure that a consumer can rely on
particular branding to equate to certain product features.

While there may be little risk that a business podcaster will use someone else's trademark to associate with its podcast, trademark law can be implicated in what is said and in relation to the podcast in other ways.

Generally speaking, trademarks may be infringed in at least two ways, by direct infringement and by dilution.

Direct infringement occurs when someone else's trademark (often a competitor's trademark) is used in a way that is "likely to cause consumer confusion" as to the source, affiliation, or sponsorship between the trademark owner and the party using the mark. This might occur if a trademark is used to describe the podcast, and the trademark owner thinks that the podcast is sufficiently related to their product or service so that a listener might conclude that the podcast comes from or is endorsed by the trademark owner, when that is not the case.

Dilution can occur if the character of the trademark becomes clouded by an unwanted association, either through tarnishment, which occurs when a famous mark is used to promote a product that is considered offensive (e.g., the mark "GYMBOREE" being used to market an X-rated podcast), or through blurring, which means the use of a famous trademark causes consumers to blur the two companies in their minds (e.g., naming your podcast the "Addidas Hemorrhoid Discussion Group"). In a dilution claim, a trademark owner must prove actual dilution, not merely the likelihood of dilution. Note that dilution does not occur from a "nominative" or informational use of a trademark, such as a critical review or what is known as a "descriptive" use of a trademark (i.e., using the trademark in a sentence to discuss the actual trademark owner or its product). But, under the dilution theory, even if consumers are not at all confused about the source, a trademark owner can have a claim for dilution.

When is permission required?

Generally, permission is unnecessary when making an informational (also called "editorial" or "nominative") use of a trademark. Permission is also unnecessary when making a truthful comparative advertisement (however, comparative ad situations often provoke trademark owners into legal action even when their trademark claims are weak, especially if the statements made are not wholly accurate). But if the podcaster wants to make a commercial use of the trademark, a license will be needed.

All normal trademark rules apply in podcasting just as they do in other forms of print and written advertising (or even text blogs). But in the context of podcasting, the business should think more broadly about how trademarks will appear in the podcast (e.g., as sounds and images). Consideration of whether the use of the mark is purely informational (informing, educating, or expressing opinions protected under the First Amendment) or commercial (like advertising, promotion, or marketing) is also necessary.

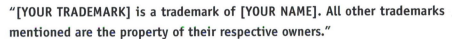

> If a trademark is used in a commercial context in the podcast, it is a good practice to include a reference to registered trademarks of others in the show notes, as well as in the podcast itself. A statement along these lines would suffice:
>
> "[YOUR TRADEMARK] is a trademark of [YOUR NAME]. All other trademarks mentioned are the property of their respective owners."

COLETTE'S TIP

Businesses often post their trademark use policy on their Web sites. While using a disclaimer does not immunize the user or clear the necessary rights to use a particular trademark in a commercial context, it can help to show the good faith of the trademark user.

Protecting the Podcast from Being Infringed

The previous points in this chapter address some of the risks of liability for infringing someone else's rights in copyright, publicity rights, and trademark. Another aspect of the podcast process is deciding whether and under what sorts of restrictions the corporation will distribute its own content, and to what extent it may seek to enforce its copyrights and trademarks.

Copyright Considerations

Obtaining a copyright registration

As noted above, obtaining a copyright registration is a good idea if you anticipate ever needing to enforce it.

Licensing under the traditional "all rights reserved" model

Traditional "all rights reserved" style distribution is the default in most businesses when considering how to distribute content. Under this model, the business would "reserve" all copyright-related rights in the podcast by marking it with the © symbol. While copyright attaches automatically to a work, whether or not it is marked with the "circle c" notation, the traditional way to mark any work as "all rights reserved" is to use the following marking:

© [owner] [year]

Including a statement (verbally and/or visually) in the podcast itself that all rights are reserved is also a good idea. You can also include the "© [owner] [year]" language on your Web site's homepage and on any page where copyrighted podcast content appears. If you include a statement that you "reserve all rights," then you are likely giving people who listen to or watch your podcast a limited, implied license to use and listen to your podcast based solely on the circumstances of how you are making it available.

Licensing under alternative models

There exists a large amount of content being created and distributed in the blogosphere or podosphere under the "some rights reserved" model, typically through a Creative Commons (www.creativecommons.org) or "open source" licensing system. In the Web 2.0 world, businesses centered on social computing or content sharing are exploring the use of "some rights reserved" licensing as a piece of their overall business model.

COLETTE'S TIP

Learn more about "some rights reserved" licensing options through the resources available at the Creative Commons Web site (www.creativecommons.org).

Trademark Considerations

As with other forms of branded content, the trademark associated with a podcast can provide value to the company and also serve as an enforcement tool if others use Web sites that create consumer confusion. Once a term or phrase is used to identify a particular good or service, it is being used as a trademark. Common law rights in trademark begin when the mark is first used to identify the good or service. Registering a trademark with the US Patent and Trademark Office (www.uspto.gov) is, however, an important step to protecting the podcast brand. Several benefits arise from registration (like nationwide notice of the mark, evidence to prove ownership of the mark when it is licensed or when seeking investors, the right to sue for infringement in Federal Court, and evidentiary benefits once the mark is registered for 5 years) and entities who plan to build out a brand relating to the podcast should engage a trademark attorney and take the necessary steps to register the trademark for all the goods and services associated with the podcast.

Defamation and Section 230 of the Communications Decency Act

The law of defamation applies to publications on the Internet with equal force as with offline publications. Its application to a podcast or its associated blog means that just as in public communications in the offline world, businesses should take care to consider issues of defamation in their podcast.

Defamation is a matter of state law, so the laws may vary from state to state on specific definitions and protections. Generally, defamation is when a party communicates publicly (to someone other than the person defamed) a false statement, which is expressly stated or implied to be factual, harmful to another's reputation, and published "with fault" (meaning that the communication was made as a result of negligence—in other words, that a reasonable person would not have published the statement).

COLETTE'S TIP

Defamation is also called "slander" when it is spoken or "libel" when it is in a printed form.

Note that unlike a basic claim of direct copyright infringement where there is strict liability, defamation law requires the plaintiff to show some fault on the part of the defendant. In cases where the defamed person is a public figure, moreover, the plaintiff must prove "actual malice" (not just negligence) on the part of the speaker. This means that the plaintiff must show that the defendant knew of the falsity or published in reckless disregard for the truth.

Some statements are considered *per se* defamatory, meaning that, while context is still relevant, the court will presume the statement is defamatory. For example, a false statement that imputes criminal activity, relates to a person having a "loathsome disease" (historically leprosy, a sexually transmitted disease, or today also including mental illness), is injurious to another in their trade, business, or profession, or imputes to a person impotence or a want of chastity, are considered *per se* defamatory.

Opinions are not subject to defamation law, but it is important to distinguish between true opinions and facts characterized or labeled as an opinion. A court will consider in the specific context of the case whether a "reasonable" person who read or heard the statement would understand the statement as asserting a verifiable fact. A statement asserting a "verifiable fact" is a statement that conveys information that can be proved false.

COLETTE'S TIP

One California court found that calling someone a "dumb ass" is not a statement of verifiable fact, holding that "[i]f the meaning conveyed cannot by its nature be proved false, it cannot support a libel claim" (Vogel vs. Felice).

Other defenses to defamation include proving that the statement is true or that it is privileged. In some states, like California, privileges apply to reports about public proceedings. Also, in California, "accurate and disinterested" reporting about potentially defamatory allegations in public controversies is protected from defamation claims.

Section 230 of the Communications Decency Act

In 1996, as part of a major telecommunications reform act, Congress passed Section 230 of the Communications Decency Act. Section 230(c) provides a broad immunity for "providers" of "interactive computer services" when another person publishes content that may be defamatory. The law simply and specifically states: "No provider or user of an interactive computer service shall be treated as the publisher or speaker of any information provided by another information content provider." It also provides that no claims can be brought (and no liability can be imposed) under any state or local law that is inconsistent with the broad immunity.

> It is also important to note that while Section 230 creates a substantial protection around online speech, it does not apply to federal criminal law, intellectual property law, and electronic communications privacy law.

WARNING

As a podcaster, this section is relevant to the extent the podcast (or its associated blog or other online spaces) includes third-party content that is not created or edited by the podcaster. For example, Section 230 likely applies to the comment space on a blog associated with the podcast (or any Web site space hosted by the podcaster) where third parties may post content. Though this is yet to be legally tested by the courts, to the extent a business allows for comments or other content to be posted by third parties, the business hosting the blog or Web site would most likely be immune from the defamatory statements contained in those posts.

A slightly trickier question relates to whether immunity under Section 230 is possible when the podcaster takes audio comments received on a listener comment line and inserts them into the podcast directly. In theory, this should also be protected under Section 230 assuming the podcaster did not edit the content being brought into the podcast. The more it is like a blog comment, just in audio form, the more likely it would be protected by Section 230. However, like many situations with Internet legal questions, this application of Section 230 has not been tested in any courts.

Even if comments are moderated, information is taken down when the blog owner receives a request, or entire posts are later deleted, the immunity provided in Section 230 still applies.

It is important to note that even if the host of the site where third-party content is posted decides to edit the content or even delete certain posts, the protections from Section 230 may still apply. Section 230(c) expressly protects a provider of an interactive computer service from civil liability, if the provider removes content that it believes in good faith may be "obscene, lewd, lascivious, filthy, excessively violent, harassing, or otherwise objectionable, whether or not such material is constitutionally protected." The courts, however, have not resolved the precise line between when a party moves from being merely a "provider ... of an interactive computer service" (immune) to an "information content provider" (liable), which is an area of the law likely to be further developed in the near future.

General Internet Business Issues

Web Site Terms of Service

Many Web sites include a TOS document that outlines users' obligations to the service and the service's obligations to the user. These are often assented to through a click-wrap agreement or merely posted on the site from the homepage.

Why write a Web site Terms of Service?

The TOS document is a place where a Web site can convey to its audience important information about the service. It can put users clearly on notice of various rights associated with using the service and, depending on how it is written, it can also put users at ease about the rights associated with using the service. Sometimes users expect to see a TOS, which can provide the site with legitimacy. Moreover, though not well tested at this time in the courts, a carefully crafted TOS may include important disclaimers of liability and limitations on damages, as well as establish rules of conduct for users of the site.

What should a Web site Terms of Service include?

Although the specific content of a particular Web site TOS will depend greatly on the goals of the organization, the laws or regulations of the particular industry in which it is engaged, and many other factors, the following is a list of some key provisions that should be considered for inclusion in a TOS document:

- *Acceptance*: Identify how acceptance of the TOS is determined (e.g., by clicking agreement in a certain check box).
- *Description*: Describe the service accurately.
- *Age restrictions*: Include any terms relating to whether the site is limited to certain age groups.
- *Conduct*: Identify any "house rules" for users of the site or service.
- *Licensing/Copyright*: If users may upload content to the site, address issues concerning who owns content that is uploaded to the site.
- *Privacy*: Include how the company handles personal information of its users (this may also be handled in a separate privacy policy).
- *Digital Millennium Copyright Act (DMCA)*: Include the designated agent's name and contact information as required by the DMCA, if relevant to the service. (See the section below on the DMCA for more information.)
- *Indemnity, disclaimers, and limitations of liability*: Include information on any of these issues as relevant to the business or industry in which the site is operating (though, it is worth noting that the legal effectiveness of blanket disclaimers is not fully resolved).
- *Contact information*: Include physical contact information and an email address for users who have questions about the policy.

It should go without saying that, as much as possible, it is best to use plain and simple language in the TOS and avoid as much technical jargon as possible unless it is clearly described in the TOS document. Those users who read the TOS document will be grateful if the document is concise and easy to read, and will be more likely to understand it, which, after all, is the goal when you later want to hold the user accountable to the TOS.

COLETTE'S TIP

Useful tips for making online contracts consumer friendly are available from Americans for Fair Electronic Commerce Transactions (AFFECT) (http://www.fairterms.org/) and from the Electronic Frontier Foundation (http://www.eff.org/wp/eula.php).

Privacy Considerations

Privacy on the Internet is an important issue that is gaining more and more attention. The way a company handles the personally identifiable information collected from its customers triggers legal obligations that must be addressed by businesses with Web sites.

Privacy laws governing Internet sites

Numerous regulations govern privacy on the Internet, and as a result, the business may be *required by law* to post a privacy policy or a privacy statement.

At the Federal level, Congress has enacted several privacy laws, often in industry-specific fields. For example, under the Children's Online Privacy Protection Act (often referred to as "COPPA"), Web sites attracting children must obtain verifiable parental consent before gathering information from children. Financial service companies are required to post a privacy policy that explains specified data security measures under the Gramm–Leach–Bliley Act (GLBA). And medical or insurance Web sites may be required to follow the Health Insurance Portability and Accountability Act (HIPAA), which governs the collection, use, and storage of health-sensitive information.

WARNING Failing to comply with the Internet privacy regulations enacted by Congress can lead to steep fines and other sanctions.

At the state level, in 2003, California enacted the "Online Privacy Protection Act," which requires every Web site either in California or collecting personal information from California consumers to post a privacy policy online.

Considering jurisdictions outside of the US may also be necessary when it comes to privacy considerations. For example, Canada has enacted the Personal Information Protection and Electronic Documents Act, which requires all Canadian industries and organizations to comply with its privacy rules. And sites doing business with the European Union are subject to the European Union's Data Directive, which regulates the collection, use and security of personal information of European Union citizens.

How do privacy concerns arise in podcasting?

If a business asks for users or subscribers of a podcast to log in and provide any personally identifiable information, the need for a privacy policy is triggered. If a podcast includes a newsletter subscription tool, it may find that it is also collecting personally identifiable information of its customers/users. Another way issues arise in this area is when a computer and server within the business that hold any personally identifiable information is compromised either through theft or by copying the data and removing it from the business's control.

> **WARNING**
>
> Physically locking down servers and laptop computers that contain personal information is one of the most fundamental steps a business can take to secure its data. Failing to take this initial step to securing data may give rise to significant legal liabilities.

As noted above, posting a privacy policy may be required by law, so it is important to consider these questions as the podcaster's Web site and business is developed.

Writing a privacy policy

A privacy policy (also called a privacy statement) is an important document that requires significant consideration within the organization about how it handles personally identifiable information about any third parties.

Taking the time to consider all the ways the company treats these materials (both online and offline) is essential to writing a legally sufficient policy. This can require input from many departments within the organization, including the marketing, operations, engineering, and legal departments. It is also essential to consider the policies of other entities that the company contracts with and who may come into contact with the company's customers' private information.

COLETTE'S TIP

The number one, most important aspect of the policy is that it accurately reflects the company's actual practices. A well-crafted privacy policy can engender trust from users of a Web site and provide for consumer confidence in the products related to a podcast.

The Federal Trade Commission (www.ftc.gov) offers a set of guidelines, which come close to an industry standard in providing proper notice through a Web site privacy policy. These guidelines require the following from a privacy policy:

- *Notice*: The Web site should provide full disclosure of what personal information is collected and how it is used.
- *Choice*: Consumers at a Web site should be given choice about how their personal information is used.
- *Access*: Once consumers have disclosed personal information, they should have access to it.
- *Security*: Personal information disclosed to Web sites should be secured to ensure that the information stays private.
- *Redress*: Consumers should have a way to resolve problems that may arise regarding sites' use and disclosure of their personal information.

Here are a few additional best practices:

- Provide an offline contact, meaning a real physical address where parties can write to the privacy manager within the organization.
- Prominently post the privacy policy from the Web site's homepage.

- Use plain language and keep the policy as short as possible.

- For policies that are longer, consider also providing a short summary version of the policy.

- Consider both online and offline uses of personally identifiable information.

- Review the policy frequently, and update it if the business's practices change.

- Lock down servers and laptop computers that hold personal information.

- Limit information that is collected from consumers.

- Be sure to inform the entire company of the policy.

Certification options

An organization called Truste (www.truste.com) offers a privacy statement seal program that approves "consumer-friendly" privacy policies and also provides a way for parties to file privacy complaints.

Truste also provides a helpful white paper entitled "Your On-Line Privacy Policy," available from http://www.truste.org/pdf/WriteAGreatPrivacyPolicy. pdf, which outlines many important considerations about writing and maintaining a good privacy policy. Truste also provides "Model Privacy Disclosures" that can be used as a starting point when drafting the business's privacy policy.

DMCA Policies

Finally, if a business's Web site allows for the posting of third-party content by users, it is important that the business familiarizes itself with the DMCA, and specifically the "safe harbor" from copyright liability for online service providers and the "notice and takedown" procedures for copyright owners whose works have been infringed.

The DMCA's "safe harbor" and "notice and takedown" provisions were enacted in 1998 and are found in Section 512 of the Copyright Act. While subject to much controversy as it relates to online video and music services, for the average podcaster, it may play only a small overall role.

The safe harbor

First, *if* the business includes space on the Web site associated with the podcast where users can post content, then the business should consider adopting an internal policy about how to handle uploaded materials under the DMCA, and following the steps required by the act to be protected by the "safe harbor."

WARNING Only when the business complies with all of the requirements of Section 512, will it be shielded from any liability for copyright infringement if a third party posts infringing content to the business's Web site.

The requirements to obtain the safe harbor are stringent. First, the business must register a designated agent with the Copyright Office (which requires paying $80 and submitting a form) and also make the contact information for its designated agent available through its Web site. Second, the business must not have actual knowledge that the material is infringing, be aware of facts or circumstances from which infringing activity is apparent, or, upon obtaining such knowledge or awareness, the business must act expeditiously to remove or disable access to the infringing content. Third, the business must not receive a "financial benefit directly attributable to the infringing activity, in a case where the business has the right and ability to control such activity." Fourth, upon receiving notice of a claimed infringement (compliant with the "notice and takedown provisions"), the business must "act expeditiously" to remove or disable access to that material. The business would also be protected if, after receiving a counter notification from the alleged infringer, the material is restored to the Web site.

Because of these requirements, businesses often include a "DMCA policy" or "copyright policy" as part of their TOS or as a stand-alone policy.

Notice and takedown

The second way a business podcaster may encounter the DMCA is when the business seeks to have unauthorized and infringing copies of its content removed from other Web sites. The steps for notice and takedown are fairly straightforward but, like the safe harbor provisions, have a number of specific requirements. The notice must be in writing and sent to the DMCA agent of the Web site where the information is wrongfully posted. The notice must include the following details in a single document:

- Identification of the copyrighted work.

- Identification of the material that is infringing the work and that should be removed (including information, like the URL, that will permit the service provider to locate the material).

- Contact information of the complaining party (including address, telephone number, and email address).

- A statement that the complaining party has a "good faith/belief" that the use of the material is not authorized.

- A statement, under penalty of perjury, that the information in the notice letter is accurate and that the party is authorized to act on behalf of the copyright owner.

- A physical or electronic signature of a person authorized to act on behalf of the copyright owner of the allegedly infringed work.

COLETTE'S TIP

When identifying the copyrighted work, include the copyright registration number and/or a copy of the registration certificate to remove any question on the part of the service provider about whether the complaining party actually owns the copyright interest in the work.

Once the proper notice letter is received by the service provider, it will be required to takedown the allegedly infringing content and keep it down for 10 days. It will also typically notify the party who posted the material (if known). A party whose material is wrongfully removed may send a counter notice to the service provider (with an equally detailed list of requirements), in which case, if the service provider reposts the material, it will continue to enjoy the safe harbor.

WARNING ⬤ Be careful not to overzealously police a copyright. One danger of sending takedown notices in instances where the posting is making a fair use, or there is otherwise no infringement, is that the copyright owner may be liable under Section 512(f) for misrepresentation. If found liable under 512(f), the owner may be required to pay damages, including costs and attorneys' fees.

If the notice and takedown process works as it should, using this procedure of the DMCA to remove unauthorized copies of the podcast should be an efficient way to police the copyright in a podcast.

Lessons Learned

· Don't delay considering the legal questions surrounding the podcasting project within the organization.

· Help the legal department by bringing the project to their attention early so that appropriate measures can be taken to minimize risks associated with the podcast project.

· Get familiar with basic principles of copyright law by visiting the US Copyright Office Web site at www.copyright.gov.

· Don't risk infringement. Get permission and clear copyright for content that is not original to the business, still under copyright protection, and does not fall under fair use.

· Prepare and execute contracts that clearly resolve any ambiguities about ownership of content when using independent contractors or employees to create original content for the podcast.

· Clear publicity rights by obtaining a written release at the time the podcast is being recorded.

· Make an informed decision about whether to submit each podcast for copyright registration.

· Consider using podsafe (or pre-cleared) music to enhance the podcast.

· Experiment by licensing some of the business's podcast content through Creative Commons' or "some rights reserved" models of copyright.

· Don't defame people through the podcast.

· Take the time necessary to create thoughtful and well-developed Web site terms of use or TOS documents, a privacy policy, and, if applicable a DMCA/copyright policy.

RSS: The Plumbing Behind the Medium

Ryan Irelan

As the title of this chapter suggests, really simple syndication (RSS)—the technology that allows the syndication and subscription of content on the Internet—is what makes podcasting work. Without RSS, we would still be listening to and watching content in front of our computers and reading it only in our Web browser. Podcasting without RSS is nothing more than online radio all over again.

Online radio has been around for more than 10 years and it requires the listener to be tethered to the computer and connected to the Internet. The audio content is pushed to the listener in real time and, as with terrestrial radio, there is no rewinding to hear something again or fast-forwarding to get past content that doesn't interest you. It is a one-way relationship, with the listener at the mercy of the radio station.

RSS dramatically changed the delivery of content online, especially for audio and video. With RSS as the delivery mechanism, all types of content can now be delivered and then listened to offline at the leisure of the consumer. It might be helpful to think of this as similar to time-shifted radio or television. Just like the digital video recorder you use to record your favorite television shows for watching at a later time, RSS (and some software) enables you to subscribe to and then automatically download new content every time it is published. When you consume that content is up to you. You are in control.

But before we go deeper into the workings of RSS and its work as the delivery mechanism for podcasting, it is appropriate talk about how it was developed and why one particular development in RSS is so important to podcasting and makes the delivery of audio files possible. This won't be a technical overview so much as a historical explanation of how RSS developed and became the tool that we use today to support podcast delivery.

History of RSS and Syndication

Despite all of the success that RSS has had over the last few years, it does have a sordid, complicated, and fractured history. The politics of technology, competing business interests, and old-fashioned human ego all had a hand in making RSS the powerful content delivery technology as it is today. This book is not the place to rehash old battles, so we'll stick to the simple history of the format and how it developed into the powerful medium we have today.

The idea behind RSS isn't terribly new. It has been refined over the last half-dozen years, but the original intent has always been the same—to deliver content directly to the end user.

Early Syndication Formats

An early sign of a syndication format was from a company called PointCast, one of the biggest darlings of the "dot com" boom at the turn of the century. PointCast's model was to push content like news, sports, and weather headlines to users' desktops, eliminating the need to surf the Web (see Figure 10.1).

The "push" model requires no action or input from the end user. The content is gathered from the Internet and then delivered to the desktop. The "poll and pull" model that RSS uses checks every content source the user subscribes to for an update and then pulls down any new content.

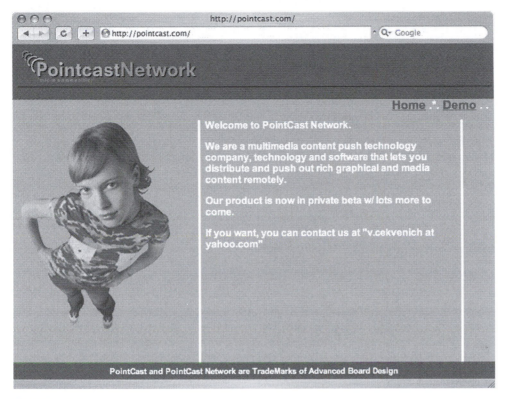

FIGURE 10.1
The PointCast Web site in 1997.

The "push" model fell out of favor and PointCast fell into troubled times as a company that was burning through venture capital cash at a rapid rate. Additionally, PointCast found themselves with competitors and they saw the technology start to swing away from proprietary content channels like theirs and move toward open channels where users had the ability to define the content and the syndication format was open and freely available for anyone to use.

In the first half of 1997 both Microsoft and Netscape submitted syndication formats to the World Wide Web Consortium (W3C). Microsoft submitted the Channel Definition Format (CDF) and Netscape proposed their version called the Meta Content Framework (MCF), which used XML (eXtensible Markup Language). This is significant because in 1997 Dave Winer, a software developer and founder of UserLand Software, developed the scriptingNews syndication format—the predecessor to RSS—which was similar to Microsoft's CDF. Winer's scriptingNews format also used XML.

RYAN'S TIP

The Worldwide Web Consortium (W3C) is a vendor–neutral international governing body for Web standards and is responsible for developing and approving standards, providing specifications, documentation, and guidelines. You can learn more about them at http://www.w3.org

The Birth of RSS

The first version (0.90) of RSS was developed in 1999 by Netscape for their my.netscape.com portal. It allowed them to pull in news headlines for customized user homepages. In an effort to improve upon RSS, Dave Winer rolled out a new version (2.0b1) of his scriptingNews feed format only a few months later. He did this because he wanted to address issues with the 0.90 release by Netscape that limited the content to headlines only. The new scriptingNews format included all of the features of Netscape's RSS 0.90 plus the capability to syndicate more content than just headlines.

In an effort to standardize RSS, Netscape's next version included most features from Winer's scriptingNews and the biggest proponent of RSS at the time, UserLand, adopted Netscape's latest version. Shortly thereafter, Netscape dropped support of RSS completely during the AOL acquisition and restructuring of Netscape.

What followed was a "forking" or split in RSS development. A group called RSS–DEV released their own version of RSS and named it as RSS 1.0. Meanwhile, Dave Winer and UserLand continue to develop their version and released an update (version 0.92). Online discussion and bickering about which format was the one to use was ensued.

RSS 0.92 from UserLand was an important update to RSS and is directly responsible for podcasting because of the addition of the "enclosure"

TABLE 10.1 Different Versions of RSS, Their Authors and Significance

RSS Version	Date	Author	Significance
0.90	March 1999	Netscape	First released version of RSS
0.91	July 1999	Netscape	Integrated features from UserLand's scriptingNews 2.0b1 format
1.0	August 2000	RSS–Dev	First fork of RSS
0.92	December 2000	UserLand	Included optional elements like "enclosure," which paved the way for podcasting
2.0	July 2003	Dave Winer	Similar to 0.92, but with optional elements

element, which allowed a file (in the case of podcasting, an MP3 file) to be referenced in the RSS feed. RSS was now ready to become the plumbing and delivery mechanism behind podcasting. See Table 10.1 for the entire history of RSS.

The RSS Payload

RSS enclosures are the payload of the RSS feed, a way of associating media files to RSS feeds (see Figure 10.2). The files are not actually part of the feed, but instead a URL is specified in the "enclosure" element, which points to the media file on a public Web server. Software that receives the feeds (see more in the last section of this chapter) reads the "enclosure" URL and then downloads the media file to the user's computer. With the right software this becomes an automatic process and requires no action on the part of the user.

The first experiment with automating the download of media files using the enclosure in an RSS feed happened early in 2001 when former MTV VJ Adam Curry and software developer Dave Winer brainstormed a way to get around the poor user experience of watching video online. But it wasn't until late summer of 2004 that podcasting as we know it today was launched.

FIGURE 10.2

A sample podcast feed "enclosure." It has three parts to it: the URL to the audio file, the length in bytes, and the type of file.

RSS Today

All of the history, forking, and multiple versions of RSS is a result of an intense interest and passion for creating a content syndication format that is flexible and able to deliver a lot of different types of content. While there are seven different flavors of RSS, it is recommended to use the latest, RSS 2.0. Most podcasting and syndication software solutions use this version.

As the popularity of blogs grew, so did the popularity of RSS and content syndication. This growth of RSS has extended past blogs, and major media outlets, government agencies, and corporations now use RSS to syndicate content. As of early 2007, there are more than 60 million blogs and an estimated 20 million podcasts.

Visit any of today's major media outlet Web sites, and you are certain to come across an RSS feed that you can use to subscribe to various types of content. Most media organizations have multiple feeds available, which allow you to receive syndicated content for top stories and news by topic (politics, national, weather, technology, etc.).

The *USA Today* Web site has almost 100 different feeds available (see Figure 10.3). CNN.com has more than 20 available. The National Weather Service publishes RSS feeds for every type of severe weather by region, worldwide. This includes text forecasts and audio forecasts delivered as

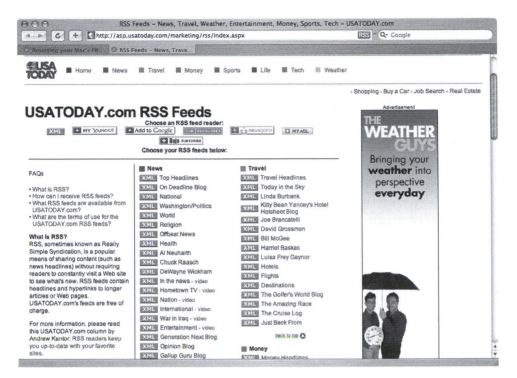

FIGURE 10.3
USA Today has more than 100 different feeds available.

podcasts. The source of a lot of news reports in the USA, Reuters, offers more than a dozen different RSS channels. These are just a few examples. There are hundreds more and range from national media to local newspapers.

The US government also uses RSS to disseminate information. For example, the Department of State offers a handful of feeds for official announcements. The US isn't the only government embracing RSS; the German government shares announcements via RSS in its three feeds.

In addition to media outlets and governments, many companies—both large and small—are using RSS as a way to share company news, product announcements, and other public relations efforts.

RSS for the Masses

Today RSS allows you to get the information you need, how you want it. RSS feeds allow content to be adopted and molded into all different types of display. One prime example and a sure vehicle for the future growth, adoption, and use of RSS, is the new operating system from Microsoft, Windows Vista. Windows Vista natively supports RSS so that it can be used within software written for the operating system and within the operating system itself. This offers a seamless user experience and a very powerful way to subscribe to RSS feeds. In Vista, when you subscribe to an RSS feed using Internet Explorer, the operating system automatically detects this new subscription and adds it for viewing. Now you have personalized content delivery right on the desktop. Once Vista reaches the majority of desktops across the world, RSS technology will reach the masses.

In addition to Microsoft's Windows Vista operating system, all of the latest major Web browsers on both the Windows and Mac OS X platforms support RSS, so that you can easily subscribe to and view RSS feeds right in the browser. This includes Internet Explorer 7, Firefox (Mac/Windows), and Apple's Safari. These browsers also support "auto-discovery," which is a feature that alerts the user to the presence of an RSS feed when visiting a Web site.

A Friendlier, More Universal RSS

Because of the integration of RSS into Web browsers and operating systems, there is an increased exposure of RSS and syndicated content to people beyond the early adopter crowd. The name "RSS" is not descriptive of what the technology does (even really simple syndication does not describe in layman's terms what RSS is and does) and could cause confusion among average computer users. In an effort to remedy this situation, a movement started to universalize how the technology is talked about and referred to. There are two main changes taking place.

The first change is an icon change. The RSS iconography (see Table 10.2 for examples) has always included either the acronym RSS or XML. For non-technical internet users, these acronyms mean nothing.

When these icons first started appearing on the Web, a user would click on them to subscribe to specific content. More often than not, the user

TABLE 10.2 History of Feed Icons

RSS Icon	Explanation
XML	The original icon for RSS. It was labeled "XML" because RSS uses the Extensible Markup Language.
RSS	An improvement on the XML icon. This icon is labeled with the technology and is still popular today.
	The feed icon of the future. It is platform and technology independent and contains only a symbol.

experience after clicking on these icons was being lead to a page that was filled with nothing more than XML code. This was a confusing and intimidating experience for the non-technical users and most didn't know what to do from there.

So, in order to embrace the technology of RSS but not its technical name, a feed icon (the image that represents a feed link) was created by Mozilla and implemented in their Firefox browser (see Figure 10.4). This new icon used a simple logo that was easily recognizable. The online community embraced the Firefox feed icon, but more importantly, it was embraced and implemented by Microsoft in their latest version of Internet Explorer. In fact, the Firefox team and the Internet Explorer team worked together to ensure they embraced a common icon.

The second change is a name change. As you can tell from the nomenclature we've been using, the term RSS is still widely used despite its unfriendly name. The idea behind changing the name of RSS to something less technology-specific (because there are indeed other syndication formats out there, like "Atom") is to make it more universal and people friendly. The "RSS Feed" name has been shortened to just "feed" or "Web feed" (or in the case of podcasting, simply "podcast feed") and has seen a huge increase in usage online. With this name change and icon change, RSS is now ready for prime time and widespread adoption among users of all technical levels.

The history of RSS and syndication formats is complicated to follow, but with one major improvement to RSS 0.93—the ability to include

FIGURE 10.4

The universal feed icon Web site. Taking a cue from Firefox, designer Matt Brett created an icon resource site for Web site designers and developers to get quality and scalable universal feed icons to use on the sites they develop.

"enclosures" that allowed each feed item to have a media file associated with it—podcasting was able to take form and see huge growth and usage in just a short time. With the new additions of a more universal icon and name, as well as an integrated experience in browsers and Microsoft's Vista operating system, podcasts and other syndicated media will no doubt become front and center of home computer user's desktop (see Figure 10.5).

RYAN'S TIP

When visiting Web sites and subscribing to new content, always be on the lookout for the new universal feed icon to subscribe to podcast or content feeds.

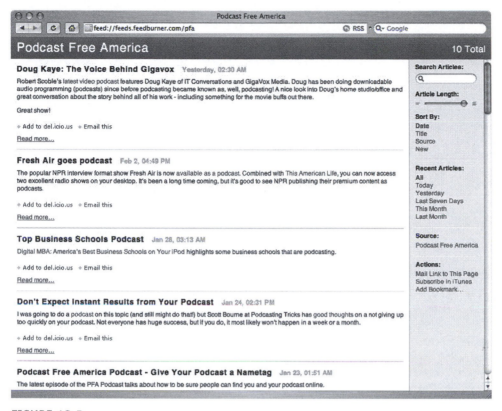

FIGURE 10.5

Modern browsers are now aware of RSS and display it in a way that is useful and usable to the user. This example is from Apple's Safari. The latest versions of Microsoft Internet Explorer, Firefox, and Apple's Safari all support displaying feeds as readable content in the browser.

How Content Syndication Through RSS Works

Now that you have a solid understanding of the history of RSS and how it evolved into a technology that enabled and gave birth to the medium of podcasting, it's now time to discuss exactly what RSS does and how it works. Similar to the last section on the history of RSS, I won't bog you down in overly complicated and technical details. The goal here is to provide a 30 000-feet view of what RSS is and does.

It is important to know why RSS and syndication technologies are such a big deal. To see why, we can just compare the old way of delivering content on the Internet and new way of delivering it with RSS. Before RSS, in order to access content on the Web, you had to go out and find it and then go back and check each Web site on a regular basis to see if new content was added or updated. This is hardly an efficient model for either the content reader or creator. What was missing was a way to alert and deliver new content directly to readers. With RSS syndication, you can now go out and find the content you like to read, see or hear, and then subscribe to it and be automatically alerted every time it is updated. Depending on the Web site, this alert may be an excerpt or the full text of the content. For podcasts, this alert of an update will include the audio file of the podcast.

I like to use the analogy of magazine subscriptions to explain how RSS syndication technology works with podcasting. People subscribe to magazines that interest them. The magazine creator completes the latest issue and then sends it off to the subscribers using the postal service. When it arrives, subscribers read it at their own convenience. The process of subscribing to the magazine requires action on your part (sending the subscription card in and paying the subscription fee), so you have to opt to receive the magazine.

Subscribing to RSS podcast feeds and receiving content updates is similar. People subscribe to your podcast by adding your feed to their feedreader software or podcasting receiving software (Apple's iTunes is a popular choice). By subscribing to the feed, the subscriber has now opted to receive any and all updates you send via that feed (see Figure 10.6). If at some point the subscriber no longer wishes to receive your podcast, they can simply unsubscribe by removing your feed from the software. This is the same way that a magazine subscription can be canceled, albeit a lot easier and quicker!

The Four Steps of RSS Syndication

RSS syndication takes place in four simple steps. The first step only happens once, while the other three take place multiple times, depending on the frequency of updates to the RSS feed and the number of subscribers.

- *Step One*: A Web site author or the Web site content management system (CMS) creates and uploads an XML file to a public Web server.

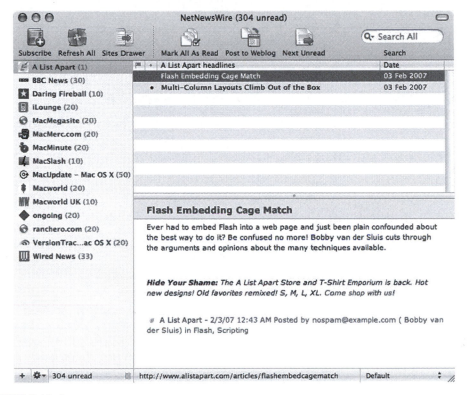

FIGURE 10.6

The NetNewsWire feedreader displaying subscribed feeds.

Contained in this file is data about the RSS feed. This generally
includes the Web site name, URL, and author.

- *Step Two*: A person subscribes to the RSS feed by adding the feed
  URL to their feedreader (Figure 10.7). Once they are subscribed, the
  feedreader will check the RSS feed at predetermined intervals for
  any new content that has been added.

- *Step Three*: New content is added to the Web site and the site author
  or Web site CMS updates the RSS feed file to reflect the new content
  (see Figure 10.8).

- *Step Four*: The subscriber's feedreader software connects to the RSS
  feed and sees the updated RSS feed file. The feedreader software
  downloads the updates and the new items are marked as new in
  the same way that your email software marks unread emails as new
  (see Table 10.3).

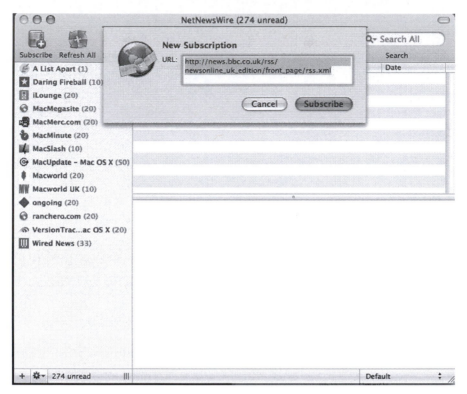

FIGURE 10.7
Subscribing to an RSS feed in NetNewsWire.

The same four steps apply to podcast feeds except for a couple of small differences. In step three when new content is added to the feed, the content creator also uploads an audio file (the podcast episode). In the feed there is a reference to the audio file called an "enclosure." The feedreader software will then download or link to the podcast audio file.

Publishing Your Podcast Feed

After you've planned, produced, and completed your podcast, it is time to publish to the world. This section will cover the basics of publishing your podcast feed, including techniques, software and processes you should consider. The goal is to give you an overview of feed publishing so you can better interface with the technical staff that will implement it.

FIGURE 10.8

A basic feed with one new update.

TABLE 10.3 A List of Some of the Most Popular Feedreader Softwares

Name	Operating System	URL
NetNewsWire	Mac OS X	www.newsgator.com/netnewswire
NewsFire	Mac OS X	www.newsfire.com
Newsgator Outlook	Microsoft Windows/Outlook	www.newsgator.com/outlook
FeedDemon	Microsoft Windows	www.feeddemon.com
Google Reader	Any platform, browser-based	www.google.com/reader
Newsgator	Any platform, browser-based	www.newsgator.com
Bloglines	Any platform, browser-based	www.bloglines.com
My Yahoo!	Any platform, browser-based	my.yahoo.com

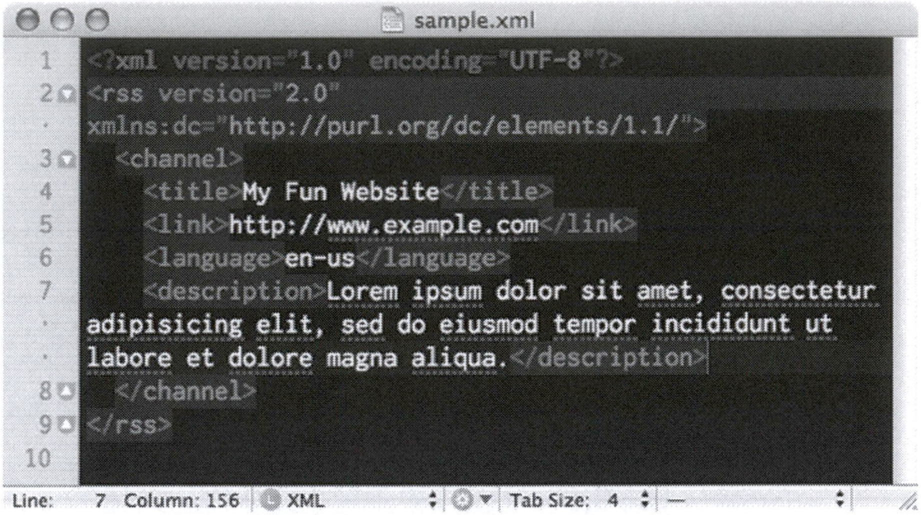

FIGURE 10.9
A basic feed with no updates.

Basic Contents of a Podcast Feed

When publishing your podcast feed, you should be prepared to include the following information:

- *Podcast title*: This is the title of your podcast (e.g., Bob's Power Tools Podcast).
- *Podcast description*: A short 1–3 sentence description of what your podcast is about. You should engage potential subscribers by clearly stating the intended goal of the podcast.
- *Podcast author*: Every podcast has an author. If it's a business podcast, that author might be the business (e.g., Bob's Power Tool Store). It can also be an individual person (e.g., Bob Smith).
- *Podcast URL*: You will want a dedicated Web page just for your podcast. This gives subscribers a way to learn more about you, your company, and your podcast. This can easily be located as a directory on your main company Web site (e.g. http://www.bobspowertools.com/podcast/).

Figure 10.9 shows what the basic feed would look like.

In addition, each episode of your podcast will have information (or metadata) about it in the podcast feed. For each podcast episode you will want to include the following information:

- *Episode title*: This title should be unique to each episode. A common usage is "Podcast Name, Episode 4."
- *Episode description*: The description briefly identifies the theme of the podcast episode.

Making Your Feed Compatible with the iTunes Store Podcast Directory

In June of 2005, Apple, Inc. CEO Steve Jobs announced that the iTunes Store would support a podcast directory and the iTunes music player software would allow you to subscribe to, download, and automatically sync podcasts to your iPod. For a young technology like podcasting, this was a phenomenal development and took podcasting from geeky basement recordings to a tool that large media companies and corporations began to embrace.

Because iTunes is on so many computers—Mac and Windows—it is important that your podcast be made compatible. Most podcast feed software will automatically make your feed iTunes compatible, but you should still be sure your technical team is aware of the iTunes podcast feed tags. More information on this can be found here: http://www.apple.com/itunes/store/podcaststechspecs.html

Using FeedBurner

One tool that has changed the way RSS feeds are made and maintained is a service called FeedBurner (www.feedburner.com). FeedBurner is a Web-based tool that allows you to manage your feed, including automatically validating it and checking for errors, so that you're always publishing a valid, readable feed. FeedBurner is a great way to control your feed without the assistance of an IT staff.

But there's more to FeedBurner than just that. It also allows you to monetize your feed using advertising and to measure your readership or listenership using reliable subscriber statistics. We'll cover more on using FeedBurner for measuring podcast statistics later on in the book. But for now, know that FeedBurner is a tool than can make managing a feed—or multiple feeds—easier.

Validating Your Feed

No matter whether your feed is created by hand or by software, it is a good idea to test it against a feed validator. A feed validator is a Web-based tool that can check your RSS feed to make it valid and working properly. This ensures that your subscribers are properly receiving your feed and content.

The Feed Validator at www.feedvalidator.org is very simple to use. Using the last example of Bob's Power Tool Podcast, to validate the feed is just a matter of inputting the feed URL into the validator (see Figure 10.10).

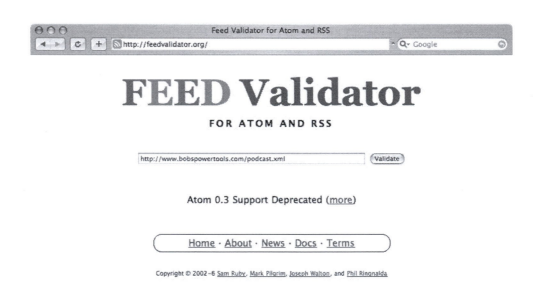

FIGURE 10.10
Validating a feed with the feed validator (www.feedvalidator.org).

If there are any errors with your feed, those will be displayed. If your feed validates, congratulations!

Lessons Learned

- RSS has a confusing history, but the innovation by Dave Winer in version 0.92 made podcasting possible.

- The name and iconography for the RSS technology is being moved away from technology descriptive words and toward generic, easily understood nomenclature that will appeal to technical and non-technical people alike.

- RSS syndication is a four-step process that allows content creators to make their Web site content distributable so that it is automatically delivered to the user's desktop.

- Caring for your podcast feed is important. Using iTunes tags and Feed Validator will help ensure that your feed is accessible and readable by everyone.

SECTION 4: PODCAST DISTRIBUTION: MARKETING, MEASURING, AND MONETIZING

Getting Your Podcast Out There

Greg Cangialosi

At this point, you should not only understand why you should be considering podcasting for your organization, but also what is involved in setting yourself up for a successful production. In the last section of the book, Ryan did a great job outlining all of the various elements that are involved in producing your podcast. From planning to producing, all the way through to the power of your really simple syndication (RSS) feed. Since we aren't writing a "technical" book, let's assume at this point you have your podcast production process down, have published your first episode, and are now ready to tell the world about all of the great content you are producing. There are many things to consider at this point to ensure that you maximize your opportunity and get the most exposure you can.

You've seen how podcasting is part of a communications revolution that is changing the way in which organizations communicate with their audiences. Furthermore, there are many steps in producing your podcast, but none are insurmountable and the return on investment (ROI) can make podcasting well worth the effort.

Of course, if no one knows about your podcast, it doesn't matter how good the content is or how well produced it is. Even outstanding podcasts can be rendered ineffective by not being properly publicized. So how do you get your podcast out there? How do you take this phenomenal content you have worked hard to produce and share it with the world and begin to build an audience?

The next few chapters of the book will be focused on how to get the word out about your podcast. I will cover the importance of where you locate your podcast, making it accessible to the rest of the world, and how to get the word out through traditional media outreach as well as various proven online marketing tactics. I will also discuss some ideas on how to build an audience and a community around your show—all key elements to a successful podcast.

Creating Awareness of Your Podcast

When determining different ways to access your podcast, you need to ask yourself "Where should my podcast live?" By this, I mean you need to consider where and how you will be able to generate the greatest amount of interest and traffic for your podcast. There are multiple ways to create access to your podcast. As mentioned in earlier chapters, your podcast should be accessible from a prominent location on your corporate Web site, a location or section that can be easily accessed by your visitors. Another popular method of posting your podcast episodes is to host them on a blog. In addition to a clear and easy-to-find "home" for your episodes, you will also want to submit your podcast to several of the popular podcast directories in order to gain maximum exposure. Adding links from blog posts, comments, and other Web properties are all effective ways of gaining exposure to your podcast.

In short, the more exposure you can give your podcast, the more likely it is that you will be able to develop an audience. Still, the sites and tools you choose to utilize for publicizing your podcast need to be appropriate for the content and the type of individuals you are trying to reach. Let's look at some of the more popular ways of gaining exposure to your podcast and why they are useful tactics.

Your Organization's Web site

As mentioned earlier, the most obvious places to promote your podcast are on your main Web site and any other relevant Web properties you may have. Since this is your organization's face online, all of your key communications should be front and center for your visitors. If you have strong search engine rankings or have a site that attracts many visitors, then you already have regular traffic visiting it for information on your products or services. Placing your podcast in a visible location throughout your Web site will capitalize on new and existing traffic and hopefully encourage downloads and listens.

Having links to your podcast from your Web site allows you to highlight new episodes and draw attention to them (see, e.g., Figure 11.1). It would be a mistake to rely solely on things like podcast directories, where there is often increased competition for downloads since your podcast will be grouped with other ones of similar or related content. Although these are also key strategies for gaining exposure, on your own Web site, there is no competition—only the information you display to your visitors.

FIGURE 11.1
Note how the whole foods Web site displays a link to its podcasts prominently at the bottom of its home page.

Ryan did a great job in covering the basics of tuning your Web site for your podcast in the "Preparing to Publish Your Podcast" chapter. Now, let's cover a few more points. Since your podcast will most likely be part of your Web site or blog, you must also decide on the format you will be offering your content. Will you simply offer a link to download your podcast with a brief description? Or will you offer your audience several options?

Offering your audience several options for each podcast episode is best practice. First and foremost, you should display your podcast's title as well as a description of the show or some basic show notes, and then offer the user several options for how they can engage with the podcast. You should offer direct downloads to files, as well as a browser-based media player that allows people to listen to your podcast while on your site. This is an important element as it is the best practice to offer your content in a way that lets your audience preview the podcast when they first see it. They may only decide to listen to 2 minutes of your podcast to test the content, but from there they will have the ability to download the actual podcast. If your content is strong, then your listener will likely return and hopefully subscribe to your podcast.

In addition to these elements, you will also want to prominently present a way for your audience to subscribe to your RSS feed. A subscriber is the best thing you can earn as a result of your efforts, so making the subscription process simple is key and should be a part of every episode's publishing. You should also include ways for listeners to subscribe via aggregators like iTunes, which we will talk about shortly. By offering various ways to obtain the information, you will be creating more opportunities for interested parties to listen and evaluate the information themselves.

GREG'S TIP

Offer your audience previews of your podcast with simple, flash-based media players, such as the Audio Player by 1 pixelout, (http://www.1pixelout.net/code/audio-player-wordpress-plugin/), and direct download options. This way, your audience can easily listen to your podcast on your Web site or blog, before they subscribe.

Hosting your podcast on your Web site or blog is a very important and effective tactic for getting your podcast out there. You already have traffic coming to your Web site, and its most likely traffic from people who would be interested in the content of your podcast. For these reasons, you are able to get a jump-start on building an audience. However, relying solely on your Web site to generate a solid audience would be somewhat short-sighted, as there are many other tools you can use that are strong auxiliaries to building your audience.

Podcast Directories

In addition to prominently posting your podcast on your Web site, you should then begin to submit your podcast to the various podcast directories that are online. Podcast directories are one of the key tools being used by listeners to find podcasts within the content they are looking for. There are many different podcast directories out there; submitting your podcast is for the most part free, and grants you exposure to a broad market of podcast listeners. Where you lose a bit of control is that you are now appealing to the podcasting market as a whole, so zeroing in on your niche market requires your consumers to be actively searching for your podcast or on keywords that relate to the content you have produced.

Regardless of your ability to reach your niche market, using a podcast directory lets you expand your reach and exposure, and your chances to increase your audience. Often times podcast directories offer a "most downloaded" list or highlight new podcasts that have been recently added to the directory. While it can be hard to compete for a spot on the "most downloaded" list, there are many ways to get noticed on a directory's Web site. Many directories offer tips on submitting your podcast and what resources to utilize in their particular directory to get the most attention.

Just as there are massive amounts of podcasts out there on just about any topic you could imagine, there are equally as many podcast directories. Take a look at Podcast411's directory page (www.podcast411.com/page2.html), and just take in the vast variety and sheer volume of the podcast directories that are out there. There are the massive powerhouses like iTunes that offer podcasts of all different categories and subjects, as well as more specific and targeted ones like Blawg, which zeros in on legal podcasts. However, just as every podcast was not created equally (variations in content quality, sound, delivery, etc.) neither are all podcast directories. Some are far more effective at appealing to an audience than others. Table 11.1 lists some of the top podcast directories in existence at present.

It shouldn't be a surprise that the current leader in podcast directories is Apple's iTunes. iTunes has been a giant in the podcasting market from the beginning, as it should be, since the term "podcast" is attributable partially to the iPod. I will discuss the virtues of iTunes and the importance of getting your podcast into their directory a little later in this section. First, I want to point out the features that these top-rated directories have in common that make them so strong and preferable to other directories out there.

An important factor to look out when deciding what directories to submit your podcast to is the number of podcasts being hosted by the directory. Currently, there is some debate over whether it is better to be listed on a directory that has a very significant number of podcasts or one that

TABLE 11.1 Leading Podcast Directories

Directory	URL
iTunes	www.apple.com/itunes
Yahoo! Podcasts	podcasts.yahoo.com
Digg Podcasts	www.digg.com/podcasts
PodcastDirectory.com	www.podcastdirectory.com
Odeo	www.odeo.com
Podcast Alley	www.podcastalley.com
Podcast.net	www.podcast.net
PodcastPickle.com	www.podcastpickle.com
Podfeed.net	www.podfeed.net
Digital Podcast	www.digitalpodcast.com

Compiled from www.jasonvanorden.com/list-of-podcast-directories.
Source: Jason Van Orden (www.jasonvanorden.com).

is perhaps more selective. The concerns with being included in a directory with a number of podcasts are that your competition may be increased and that perhaps the directory may not be well maintained (i.e., by deleting "dead" podcasts). On the other hand, a smaller directory may not have the same reach, so just because there are fewer podcasts listed it does not mean that your podcast will be downloaded or that fellow podcasts are of a higher quality. Ultimately, it is a matter of choice, the more exposure you can get the better.

If you want to determine the value of a podcast directory, you should look at how many links there are to that particular directory. The greater the number of links to the directory's URL, the greater the visibility of the directory. Resources like Alexa (www.alexa.com) can assist with these data. Clearly, since you are trying to gain as much exposure as possible for your Web site, using a directory that is linked to many other Web sites will increase the chances of directing traffic to your particular podcast.

Another characteristic of a strong podcast directory is how many blogs reference it. Sources like Technorati (www.technorati.com) are useful in finding out the popularity of a directory in the blogosphere. Technorati offers you the power to search for a variety of things being posted in blogs. Since blogs are a popular place to find podcasts (because, like podcasts, certain blogs will appeal to certain audiences, so a mention in a blog in your field would be very beneficial), a podcast directory with a lot of inbound links referencing it is definitely a place to have your podcast listed.

There are other factors that you may consider when deciding which directories would be the best for your podcast. For instance, you may find a smaller, less mainstream directory that caters to a more specific audience—an audience that may be highly interested in your podcast.

Be sure to read the fine print when submitting your podcast to any directory. You want to have all the information possible regarding the terms and conditions of having your podcast affiliated with that directory.

There is one podcast directory that you should submit your podcast to regardless of your content, and that is the iTunes podcast directory. Apple has truly been a pioneer in the podcast revolution and continues to dominate the market with iTunes and the iPod. These tools have led to the creation and distribution of millions of podcasts and currently iTunes boasts the largest number of podcasts.

iTunes is a powerful podcast directory, one that is not limited to Apple or iPod users alone. The beauty behind this tool is that it is universally recognized and accessible. Newer versions are constantly being offered, creating easier access for consumers to music, video, information, and entertainment. iTunes' ease of use makes it appealing to anyone who uses MP3 files or portable media devices and, because of its large podcast directory, iTunes has now become *the* first place to look for podcasts (see Figure 11.2).

Although difficult to prove, it is likely that iTunes has the most podcasts available compared to any other directory currently operating on the Web.

FIGURE 11.2
iTunes' podcast directory offers thousands of podcasts in dozens of different topic areas.

This often makes iTunes the first stop on any podcast searcher's quest for the ideal content. The large volume of content and the ease of accessing these podcasts make iTunes a very strong podcast directory. All that is required for a listener to enjoy a podcast is a recent iTunes program (any version from June 2005 onward) and an Internet connection. iTunes offers one-click access to its music store where the podcast directory is located. From this point, users can search for their favorite podcast, browse by category, or peruse that day's featured and top-rated podcasts (see Figure 11.3).

Overall, iTunes has served to revolutionize the podcasting medium. The podcast directory found at the music store allows a person to submit a podcast and carefully spells out the instructions for doing so with minimal effort. Christopher Penn, who I mentioned earlier in this book for his daily Financial Aid Podcast, noted that his podcasts did not begin to receive the number of downloads and listens he desired until the launch of iTunes 4.9 with podcasting. Once that version of iTunes hit the scene, fully

FIGURE 11.3

Submitting a podcast to iTunes can be done in just a few simple steps.

capable of downloading podcasts and hosting an enormous library of content, Penn was able to submit his own podcast to a directory that was being heavily trafficked, particularly from the 18–24 year-old demographic—a demographic that is highly concerned with the costs of higher education.

When a user subscribes to a particular podcast, the latest episode is loaded into his or her iTunes library each time a new episode is published. This makes transferring your podcasts to your portable media player even easier. Other services simply offer you the means of subscribing to the podcasts and accessing them through RSS feeds. iTunes delivers the entire package, ready to be listened to or watched.

iTunes has set the industry standard for media content and accessibility. Other major players, like Yahoo! Podcasts, are comparable in terms of the podcasts being offered, but as of yet no one has come close to the complete integration of the system as Apple has through iTunes, the iPod, and the iTunes music store.

One feature of iTunes that is also available on other directories is the category of "featured podcasts." A featured podcast, at least in the case of iTunes, is not there because the producer has paid for it to be there. Rather, it is selected from the many podcasts that are constantly being uploaded due to its corresponding graphics, explicit summary, and the high quality or particularly unusual content. Getting a spot as a featured podcast on a directory Web site gives your podcast a great deal of exposure, since it will be visible to every person who accesses that directory on that particular day. Often times, in order to be a featured podcast you must have at least three or four podcasts that are already available. This is ultimately beneficial for your podcast's publicity, since upon listening to the featured podcast, your listener should hopefully want to hear or see more. Having a few other episodes available demonstrates that you are publishing a regular podcast and suggests that your listener should consider subscribing so as not to miss out upcoming episodes.

GREG'S TIP

To become a featured podcast, offer new and engaging content, and be sure to include creative artwork to make your podcast stand out-the more unique and creative it is, the greater your chances of being selected as a featured podcast on a podcast directory.

Each podcast directory will offer you certain advantages and perhaps some limitations. You should carefully consider the attractiveness of each directory to your particular market, bearing in mind that some of the larger, more popular podcast directories are often the first place consumers go to search for their desired content. From there, selecting smaller, more narrowly focused podcast directories can help get your podcast to a very niche audience.

Podcast directories are not the only tools available for getting your podcast out to your audience. Rather, there are many other methods, many of which utilize traditional forms of media communications, for generating interest and awareness of your podcast initiative. These methods range from press releases to blogging, and can be managed in different ways. Regardless, the intention is the same—get people interested, and ideally downloading and talking about your podcast.

Getting the Word Out

As I have mentioned earlier in this book, new media is not replacing traditional media, but it is causing traditional media to be used in ways that it hasn't been before. Traditional media can also be an incredible tool for promoting new media, drawing attention to new ways of communicating and sharing information. Online mediums are becoming increasingly more effective for generating buzz and interest.

Consider social networking Web sites like MySpace (www.myspace.com) and Facebook (www.facebook.com). These Web sites are being used by movie production companies and bands to generate interest and hype for upcoming movies, concerts, or other events (see Figure 11.4). The power

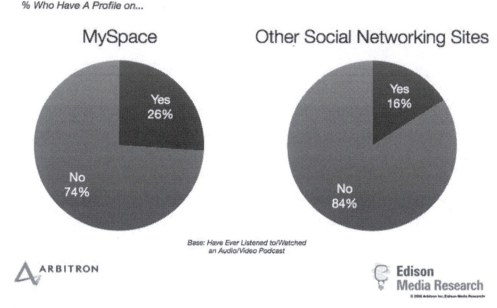

Podcast Consumers Using Social Networks

% Who Have A Profile on...

MySpace

Yes
26%

No
74%

Other Social Networking Sites

Yes
16%

No
84%

*Base: Have Ever Listened to/Watched
an Audio/Video Podcast*

ARBITRON

Edison
Media Research

FIGURE 11.4

More and more podcasters are using social networking sites like MySpace to boost their online profiles. *Source*: Edison Media Research.

of these mediums to reach their particular target group makes them prime for increasing awareness. These same tools can be just as effective for the promotion of podcasts. We will talk more about social networks in the next few chapters.

One "traditional" form of media that you should certainly consider is the medium of press releases. Press releases accomplish the task of announcing the launch of your new podcast initiative. While you would not want to release an announcement to the press every time you publish a new podcast, it certainly doesn't hurt to make sure that the media (and thereby your consumers) know that your organization is, in fact, podcasting. Using traditional media to create the buzz and awareness at the beginning is a useful component during the formative stages of your podcast.

What is additionally useful about issuing a press release is that the same information that is being released to standard media like newspapers will

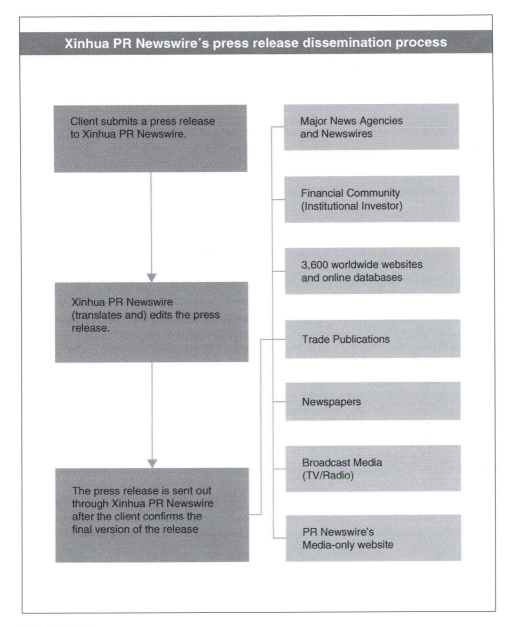

Xinhua PR Newswire's press release dissemination process

Client submits a press release to Xinhua PR Newswire.

Xinhua PR Newswire (translates and) edits the press release.

The press release is sent out through Xinhua PR Newswire after the client confirms the final version of the release

Major News Agencies and Newswires

Financial Community (Institutional Investor)

3,600 worldwide websites and online databases

Trade Publications

Newspapers

Broadcast Media (TV/Radio)

PR Newswire's Media-only website

FIGURE 11.5

Chart showing how PR Newswire disseminates press releases. *Source*: PR Newswire.

also most likely be posted on the Web. The key syndication services like PR Newswire (www.prnewswire.com) and PR Web (www.prWeb.com) are excellent ways to get your information out to a very wide audience, from major media outlets to the top search engines (see Figure 11.5).

Also, submitting your press release to sites like podcastingnews.com is an excellent way to get your podcast in front of an already savvyaudience. You want to maximize the power of your press release by extending its reach beyond that of the traditional media. The Internet clearly offers many opportunities and channels for exposure in this regard.

Participating in the Blogosphere

Using various online mediums to promote new media is clearly one of the most effective means of creating awareness of your podcast. Blog outreach, especially, is an excellent tool to consider when thinking of how you will get your podcast out into the hands of your audience (Figure 11.6). The blogosphere is constantly growing and feeds off of new information and dialog within it. Because of the social, viral way in which the ecosystem

Most Podcast Consumers Read Blogs...

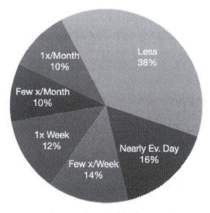

Base: Have Ever Listened to/Watched an Audio/
Video Podcast AND familiar with Blogs

FIGURE 11.6

More than 40 percent of podcast listeners say they read blogs at least once a week. *Source*: Edison Media Research.

that we call the blogosphere works, your podcast can gain a lot of exposure if posted and talked about in the right places.

Using the blogosphere to gain exposure can be done in a variety of ways. Of course, having your own blog is useful, and promoting your own podcasts on it is a very efficient way of converting your existing blog subscribers into podcast subscribers. If someone has already subscribed to your blog, they are clearly indicating an interest in what you have to say. When you publish your podcast and write about it on your blog, you're playing off the fact that you already have an audience that is keyed in to you. Most likely, your podcast reflects some component of your blog's content, so at the very minimum you have a group of people who would be willing to explore your new podcast. If your company has or maintains several blogs, they should all have a cohesive process for linking to your most recent podcasts.

As your blog audience begins to visit and download your podcast (assuming it is good content), there is a good chance they may write about it and link to it themselves on their own blog. Thus, by initiating the conversation by using your own blog as a platform, you have spawned an online conversation in the blogosphere. Of course, in order for this to work you need two key elements: a blog with an audience and a podcast with content strong enough to generate interest (Figure 11.7).

Still, at this point in time, more and more organizations are blogging and are using blogs outside the confines of the corporate structure to reach an audience beyond their own employees. Hopefully, you already have your organization's blog up and running, so mentioning your stellar podcast in an entry or two should not only be an easy step, but should generate a great deal of interest from your audience. This is a great exposure for your podcast, and most importantly it doesn't cost you anything.

Other bloggers or podcasters who listen to your podcast and like what they hear will begin to include mentions in their own posts, as well as start linking to your podcast. In some cases they may even want to

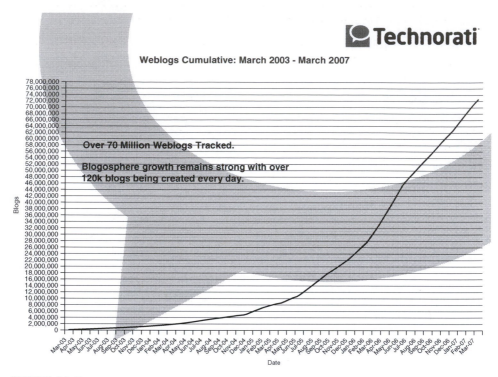

FIGURE 11.7

Between March 2003 and March 2007, the number of blogs tracked by Technorati rose from 0 to more than 70 million. *Source*: Technorati.

include your podcast in their own communications, getting you even more exposure. As a quick example, take my podcast, ROI Radio (www.roiradio. com). I publish the show on a regular basis, and my content is very much tailored to professionals in technology, marketing, and online media. The show also happens to attract other podcasters and bloggers in related industries. I was recently asked if I wanted to be included on a popular and fast-growing podcast network called MediaSwamp (www.mediaswamp. com). Giovanni Gallucci from Dexterity Media (www.dexteritymedia.com), the company that runs the network, is a colleague of mine in the online and social media space, and was not only a guest on my show but is also an active subscriber to both my podcast and my blog The Trend Junkie (www.thetrendjunkie.com). This type of exposure gets my show in front of thousands of people, who are most likely to be my target audience and who may otherwise have never found my show.

Once other people start talking about and linking to your content, your audience will grow because you are now extending beyond your core audience (which may be only a small group or a conglomerate of hundreds), and incorporating the audience and reach of other blogs. You want to create a dialog—put information out there that is relevant and pertinent and will stimulate conversations. The more people talk, the more people will become aware of what started it all—your podcast.

Waiting for others to pick up on your podcast is a very passive and extremely slow way of attracting an audience. However, by taking action you will begin to build momentum. You have to engage and participate in the blogosphere on an ongoing and consistent basis if you want to be seen as a "voice."

What I mean by this is you should go out and find blogs of similar topics and interests to that of your podcast and start commenting, and participating in the conversation that is taking place. Blogs are fascinating Internet organisms that thrive off of dialog. By commenting on others' blogs, you are provoking conversation. Conversation leads to information dissemination and thus the opportunity to put you and your podcast front and center for another audience to check out.

GREG'S TIP

> **By actively participating in the dialog that is taking place in the blogosphere, you are also creating the opportunity for other individuals to learn more about you and your organization.**

Dialoguing is one of the features of social media that set it apart from the traditional "one-way" media outlets. It is an element that you should truly understand and engage in order to effectively promote your podcast. You cannot simply put your podcast out into the blogosphere; you must create conversation about it. This requires that you actively engage other bloggers by commenting on their posts, linking your name back to your podcast, and getting people interested in what you have to share. Your comments and posts should not be blatant plugs for your podcast, but rather relevant and constructive information or opinion that builds off of the blogger's post or another comment that came before yours. As a participant in this type of dialog, other readers may take interest in who you are and what you or your organization is all about. From there you may have your next subscriber.

This is where we see once again the importance of the content in your podcast. The content of your podcast will determine which blogs are most useful for you to participate in. You should ideally keep things parallel between your contributions, your podcast, and the blogger's content. Remember, you are seeking out blogs because you are trying to reach out to a larger audience. The audience you are trying to reach is not going to limit themselves to one or two sources for the information they desire. Instead many people are hungry for the newest, most useful and intriguing content. Social media is designed for user interaction, dialoguing, and information sharing. Thus, participating in the blogosphere can work in perfect unison with promoting a podcast.

WARNING Remember to keep things in perspective when blogging and commenting on blogs. If you are commenting on someone else's blog, remember, it's not about you. Your comments and podcast need to contribute to the topic. Engaging in blatant self-promotion, especially with information or opinion that's not directly relevant to that blog, is counter-productive and can actually hurt your reputation in the blogosphere.

Establishing relationships and a network with others who actively participate in the blogosphere will help in getting the word out on your podcast. As more and more bloggers come to know of your podcast, the better chance there is that they will link to your podcast, dialog about it, and refer other information seekers to your Web site. The blogosphere survives on this sort of symbiotic relationship between content producers and consumers.

Optimizing Your Podcast for Search Engines

The use of search engines is one of the most popular online activities for everyone, just behind email. Search engines like Google and Yahoo! are often the first places people go when looking for information, whether it be found on blogs, podcasts, or specific Web sites. There are thousands of books, blogs, and Web sites containing tips, insights, and strategies for search engine optimization (SEO) to increase your Web site's rank when a user conducts a search using certain keywords.

SEO is a crucial part of any Web-driven component of your business. You want to develop your Web site and blog so that it is rich in keywords that consumers are likely to search for when using a search engine. Because SEO is powered by keyword searches, it is a key element to tailor your blog or Web site for SEO than a podcast, since podcasts contain audio or video content, not text. Often, to improve SEO, be careful in wording headlines or URLs to include specific words that are most frequently used for Internet searches. As you can imagine, there are literally millions of keywords that are searched depending on what category you are in. In order to find out what are the most popular keywords that are being searched in your category, there are several resources out there to choose from (e.g., Wordtracker (www.wordtracker.com) and Yahoo!'s Search Term Estimator (http://inventory.overture.com/d/searchinventory/suggestion/)).

What is even more important about search is that up until very recently, search engines could not search audio or video content. Now, this is all changing. With new search technologies coming out that can actually search within an audio or video file, search is more important than ever. A search engine called Everyzing (www.everyzing.com), which employs voice-recognition technology originally developed for military use, is one of the best-known tools out there for searching audio and now video content.

As cutting-edge as these technologies are, it's still important to focus on organic SEO. So how, then, do you get your podcast to be a top-ranked search engine result?

There are many ways you can use the power of search to highlight your podcast, from optimizing your main Web site, or the site or blog where your podcast is hosted, to transcribing the content of your podcast, to including a text file that can be posted with your podcast containing your show notes. Let us first look at the simplest ways you can draw attention to your podcast using keywords.

As you know, search engines work by looking for the keywords entered by the user. One way to increase the chances of your podcast getting picked up during a user's search is to create a keyword-rich title for your podcast. For example, if your podcast is about team-building exercises for small businesses, you may want to include the words "team," "building," and "business" in your podcast's title. To further increase your chances of getting a higher search engine rank, you should write a description of your podcast to accompany it on the same page it is hosted.

Again, keywords are the focus here. Your podcast description needs to be just as rich in keywords as your title, repeating the same point. The more keywords you can include, the more attractive your podcast will become to search engines. It is very important to use the power of the keyword search in your favor. Additionally, including a brief description of your podcast will aid your audience in evaluating the content of the podcast and increase the chances of them listening to it. Overall, including a description of your podcast increases its appeal for search engines and creates a greater ease of use for the listener in deciding whether or not to download the podcast.

Another way to take advantage of the keyword-driven nature of search engines is to include a transcript of your podcast on the Web. While transcribing your podcast can be a minor hassle, it can serve a similar purpose to including a brief summary. Your transcription will be infused with certain keywords throughout simply due to the nature of your content. Posting the content as text will give your audience a chance to skim through and glean an idea of the content, and then download the podcast to listen to it at their leisure. Furthermore, it gives you the chance to infuse the script with more keywords to gain a higher search engine rank. The key thing to remember with SEO is that the more you have out there textually, the more likely your podcast or pages that link to your podcast will appear in search results (see sidebar, "Transcribing Your Podcast").

TRANSCRIBING YOUR PODCAST

Similarly, when creating text content for your podcast, you should consider transcribing your shows and posting those transcriptions where your podcast lives. The key thing to remember with SEO is that the more you have out there textually, the more likely your podcast or pages that link to your podcast will appear in search results.

Transcriptions of your podcast differ from show notes in that they offer a blow-by-blow account of the content of your episode (see Figure 11.8). If a user so desired, he could read your entire podcast transcription rather than listen to the actual show. Most users who are searching for podcasts do desire to listen to the episode itself, so instead may find the transcription useful in determining their interest in the podcast. While show notes may mention a particular topic that is covered by your podcast, your transcription will tell your listeners how much detail you go into regarding that topic.

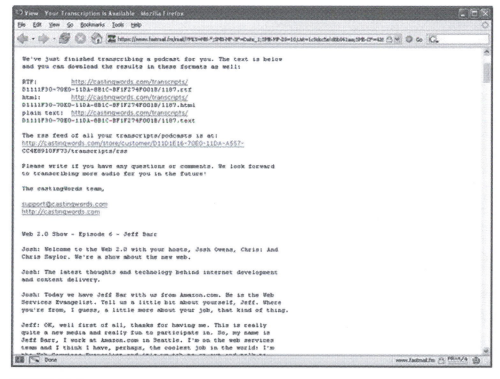

SIDE NOTE

FIGURE 11.8
Casting words is one of many services that will transcribe your podcast.
Source: www.castingwords.com.

SIDE NOTE

Getting a transcription of your podcast doesn't have to be a time-consuming chore. The availability of speech-to-text software makes it easy to select a good program and have the software do the bulk of the work. However, be sure that you are willing to review your software results since these programs, while yielding a relatively high degree of accuracy (usually between 80 and 95 percent) are not 100 percent accurate in converting speech-to-text. These software programs often have difficulty with accents, or can misjudge words because of background noise or other audio issues.

Still, transcribing your podcast is a great asset for SEO and can help your podcast climb the ranks of any search engine. SEO is an important component of online marketing, and when done well can drive large amounts of traffic to your Web site.

Another key element to SEO, as it relates to being ranked in Google, is what is called your site's PageRank. This weighs the amount of incoming links that are pointed to your site. In short, a link to your site is good, but a link to your site that includes a high-value keyword as part of its text is great. Links to your site build your PageRank (Google's importance rating determined by how other sites link to your site), what the link says builds weight for a particular keyword.

So clearly, the more solid content you put out, the more people will link to you, and the more they link to your podcast, the higher your search engine ranking will be. Take IT Conversations for example, if you search for "Steve Wozniak" on Google, the IT Conversations podcast will be the 4th result out of millions.

Finally, consider adding keywords in the domain name URL that you create for your podcast. The same keywords you use in your title, your summary, and your transcript can appear in your Web address. This step alone can help increase your search engine rankings, as well as make it easy for your audience to identify your podcast. For my podcast, ROI Radio, the Web address is http://www.roiradio.com. By creating a URL that is easy to remember and includes the topic, I make it easier for my listeners to access the podcast and to see what topics are covered. My podcast is hosted on a WordPress (www.wordpress.com) blog where I offer a synopsis of each episode. Not only does this give my audience an introduction to the pod-cast, but it also helps my podcast achieve higher search engine rankings.

> **GREG'S TIP**
>
> Keep in mind the top keywords that are searched for your particular subject matter and include them in your audio and on the Web site where your podcast lives. This will increase the appeal of your podcast for search engines, as does having high-quality inbound links from other blogs and Web sites.

All of these steps are useful in gaining a higher search engine rank. Naturally, the higher the ranking you receive, the more prominent your podcast will become. It is important to create your podcast with SEO in mind. Think like your audience: What words would they use if they were looking to find the type of content that's in your podcast? Try several com-binations and try to work in a few possibilities for searches. Consider our "team building for small businesses" example. While the obvious keywords are right there, you would want to think of other ways that your audi-ence would search for this topic. Perhaps someone would use the keywords "collaborative exercises." The key is to choose your keywords carefully, and your podcast will have a better chance of achieving a higher ranking.

Another important thing to point out as it relates to SEO is that this should by no means be thought of as a process that occurs overnight. It takes time, sometimes up to many months to get ranked and included in the major search engines. There are several variables that are not in your control, for example the algorithms on which Google or Yahoo conduct searches, the way they spider and index the Web, etc. That said, it is good to put the elements into play that will give you the best chance of being ranked in the shortest amount of time.

Optimizing Your Natural Search Ranking

Now that you understand the power of search engines, you need to begin preparing your podcast and its home for SEO. We have already looked at the power of keywords, so how should you include them in your podcasting strategy?

As mentioned before, there are many places on the Web in which you can find out the most popular keywords. Popularity of a word alone, however, will not help you in selecting the best keywords. You must consider the entire combination that someone may use to look for information. Various companies offer their services in determining the best phrases and words for you to use make SEO consultation a top priority.

Your content will help you decide what types of keywords are most relevant to your audience. What drives your content? What is the main point? What are you trying to inform your customers of? The answers to these questions will help guide you to the proper optimization of keywords.

Once you have determined which keywords you feel you should be optimizing for, you can think through your format and/or interview questions for your podcast, and make sure you're considering some of these keywords. These keywords will most likely be brought up naturally throughout the course of your podcast production. When you are complete, if you post a transcription of the podcast, your likelihood of being ranked using those words will be higher. It goes without saying that you do not want your podcast to be completely scripted, but make sure to have talking points or key areas within your show that include core keywords.

As with every other step of podcasting—research, research, research. You must know your content, your audience, what's been done before, and what is working. Because your content will be changing with each podcast you produce, you may want to consider optimizing keywords that strike at the core of your podcasting initiative rather than ones that might only appear in a few of your episodes.

Another key element is the metadata and show notes that you should include with every episode that you publish. As Ryan described in an earlier chapter the metadata included in your podcast can also help with making your content easier to find. These elements include the author, title, subject, and description, among other assets that allow your podcast to get more visibility.

Incorporating Show Notes

Another excellent tactic to enhance your search rankings is to include show notes that go along with each episode. Show notes can be included on the main page of where each episode is located, or can be linked on a separate page.

Including show notes on your podcast is an excellent way to increase your podcast's appeal to search engines (see Figure 11.9). In general, the more keyword-rich text you can include with your podcast, the more likely that key search engines will notice it. Show notes offer your listener a

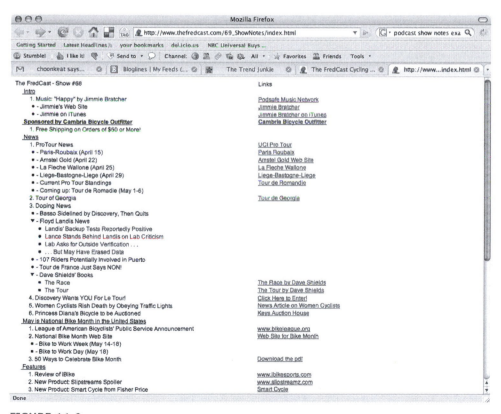

FIGURE 11.9

Examples of show notes from the FredCast Cycling Podcast.

chance to review the content of your podcast without actually download-ing the episode. These highlights from the podcast allow you to showcase the main points of your episode and entice your audience to listen. And just as important, show notes provide you with the chance to infuse your podcast's home with keywords to lure search engines to the site and list it among users' results.

Show notes are not a transcription of your podcast, but rather a snapshot of the highlights of your show. Let's say that you produce a weekly pod-cast that is usually around 30 minutes long and covers topics pertaining to deep-sea fishing. Each episode you put out will cover different aspects of this theme, but even the greatest deep-sea fishing enthusiast may not be interested in every single show you put out. Show notes of your podcast will cover the main points of each podcast episode, so that listeners who have not subscribed can decide which show they want to download. Perhaps one show you post covers new equipment being used to catch sailfish, and another discusses the hottest locations to go on a fishing excursion. A lis-tener who is planning a vacation may be enthralled with the information in the latter podcast, whereas someone who is new to deep-sea fishing may be inclined to listen to the episode on equipment. Without show notes, you could potentially lose both of these listeners, since they may not download the podcast that most pertains to their interests.

Aside from the benefit of appealing to your listeners, show notes give you the chance to attract the attention of the ever-powerful search engines. Before you decide to depend solely on the emerging search engines that search for content, you need to consider the opportunity you have for SEO by including show notes for your podcast.

GREG'S TIP   When including your show notes, post them just beneath the title of your podcast. Bulleted formats work very well for drawing attention to the key points, making it easier for your listeners to get a quick feel for the content in that particular episode.

If you begin taking these steps from the initial launch of your podcast, you will be positioning yourself for greater results sooner rather than later. Because podcasts deal with content and specific audiences, it takes time to get them noticed and into the right hands (or ears). Additionally, prior to launching your podcast beginning to blog about it in advance, lends itself to creating relevancy and "buzz" around the arrival of your podcast.

One of the most important steps in optimizing for the search engines is to prepare and do your research. Know your content. Know your audience. These factors will guide you to the appropriate keywords and lead you to the best blogs where your audience is already trying to gather information on the subject matter. Creating the buzz early will help launch your podcast, and creating the buzz where your audience is will help get your podcast off to a running start.

Searching by Content: The Next Generation of Media Searching

I mentioned earlier that there is, at present, no defined means of searching for podcasts by content other than that what might get picked up in a title, file name, summary, or transcription. Keyword-powered search engines dominate the search sector—that is, for now.

New ways to search are emerging as a consequence of the recent emergence of audio and video content as a popular means of communicating online. Ask yourself, what is easier—searching for something general by title or by content? Clearly, in the case of podcasts and video podcasts, since so many new ones are being created, searching for something that is content specific will yield more results than just hoping you've selected the right keywords for a search. This is merely one reason why we will begin to see more and more content-driven search engines in the near future.

Audio and video search engines are in existence right now, even if they are not as popular as their purely keyword-based siblings. Podscope (www.podscope.com) and Everyzing (www.everyzing.com) are both examples of this new type of search engine, highlighting the content of audio and video on the Web. More and more of these kinds of search engines are appearing.

The basic functioning of these search engines is similar to that of traditional ones in that keywords are used to narrow in on the desired information. The difference is, however, that unlike traditional searches that search text, these new engines are searching spoken words. How exactly does this work, you may be wondering? The most popular method being used at the moment is that these engines go out and create a text index of audio and video files, which is then searched for keywords.

There are some kinks that need to be worked out when using speech-to-text to transcribe audio and video. Right now most speech-to-text programs are only about 80 percent accurate, meaning that it is harder to get the correct context of all the audio and video, so some strange results can appear when searching. Optimum conditions for transcribing a podcast (meaning no background noise, clear vocal broadcasting) will yield higher degrees of accuracy. However, many podcasts and video podcasts do include some sort of background music, or are not always completely clear. Furthermore, speech-to-text software often has difficulties understanding accents, again reducing accuracy.

GREG'S TIP

There are many transcription services available that are affordable, either through an outside source like CastingWords.com or through software you can purchase yourself. Regardless, one of the best ways to get search rankings is to publish transcriptions of your podcast.

Just as consumers at home have shifted the media playing field and changed the way in which we communicate, we are now changing the way in which we search by pushing for multimedia-driven search engines. Primary search engines are relatively blind to media on the Web, be it podcasts or streaming video. The producers of this content are just as concerned as consumers that their content get noticed and shared.

Wizzard Software (www.wizzardsoftware.com) is a software company that focuses on text-to-speech technologies. They work on having computers, telephones, and other electronic devices deliver information to users in a human-like voice, in response to human queries. With the focus on text-to-speech technologies, as well as their recent acquisition of Switchpod (www.switchpod.com) and Liberated Syndication (www.libsyn.com), Wizzard Software has positioned itself for a huge move into the podcasting arena.

At present, Wizzard Software is working in conjunction with IBM and AT&T to offer Voice Tools, which include an assortment of text-to-speech tools. While these tools are marketed for several different uses, they are becoming more important in the realm of podcasting to increase the efficiency of searching for content.

Audio and video on the Web is still somewhat difficult to index at this point in time. The technology that is currently available, while effective, does not transcribe text accurately enough to make it used globally yet. New developments in technology will help move transcription forward, allowing for more accurate and detailed accounts of audio and video content, and thusly increasing the searchability of the content of podcasts and video podcasts alike. As more and more content goes up on the Web in audio and video format, the need for search engines driven by content will be huge and force the technology to evolve at an accelerated rate.

Chris Macdonald, who was part of the recent merger between Liberated Syndication, and Wizzard Software, described some new ways in which searching for podcasts and video podcasts will most likely develop. First of all, in conjunction with the portable nature of podcasts, it is likely that in the near future we will begin to see portable ways to search for podcasts. The present method requires that users return to their computers to obtain new feeds and information. As podcasting becomes more mainstream, users will demand a way to search for content without being connected to their computer.

What we are also likely to see emerge is the embedding of information that can be searched within the podcast itself. Just like RSS was further developed with the ability to carry along the media files themselves, and not just a link, the next generation of those files will carry text or pictures within them, searchable to users. What this means with regards to searching is that engines can be designed to search the file for this additional data, be it text or a sort of algorithm that pulls out keywords and phrases from the audio content.

GREG'S TIP

Search engine technology is evolving at a rapid pace. The next generation of content-driven search engines will have a very large impact on the way podcasts, both audio and video, are found by consumers. Make sure to keep abreast of these new technologies.

Until the use of embedded information becomes more mainstream, most search engines for content will rely on transcriptions of podcasts and video podcasts. Users will need to continue returning to their computer and run a standard Boolean search to find the podcasts they want to listen to. But just as podcasting itself evolves, so will the tools that support it.

Lessons Learned

- Post and link to your podcast in several locations such as your own Web site or company blog(s).

- Take advantage of the reach of podcast directories. Submit your podcast to a few large directories, like iTunes and Yahoo! Podcasts, but also look into smaller, more targeted directories.

- Distributing a press release on the Web can be an effective way to get the word out.

- Blog about your podcast. The more the conversation, the greater the awareness.

- Search is still a key way to discover podcasts, be it through a major search engine like Google or through a content-driven search engine like Everyzing or Podscope.

- Transcribing your podcast is one of the most effective ways of getting noticed by search engines at present.

- Technology is emerging to make podcast searches more geared toward content and more portable.

Online Marketing Tactics that Generate Results

Greg Cangialosi

In the last chapter I covered some of the ways to get the initial word out about your podcast. As discussed, you can create this initial exposure through prominent placement of your podcast on your Web site or blog, launching press releases, submitting to podcast directories, engaging in the blogosphere, and starting early to optimize your podcast and its home in order to get naturally high search rankings. Getting the word out on your podcast is how you generate interest and build your audience, because you can't share your content if no one is listening!

In this chapter we will look at different online marketing tactics that have a proven track record of generating results, and how you can incorporate these tools in your podcast marketing efforts. These tools, like the ones mentioned above, are intended to get your podcast in front of your audience, and can sometimes provide immediate results. We are now going to be talking about some of the core elements of any successful online marketing program. The key areas of focus will be search engine marketing (SEM), email marketing, and online display advertising, as well as some other useful tactics to help generate awareness about your podcast. All of these mediums are useful, proven online marketing channels that will help put your podcast in the spotlight.

Proven Online Marketing Mediums

As the Internet has evolved into a huge sea of information and communication, many tools have evolved as powerful marketing mediums. At the core of any effective online marketing effort should be three key elements, no matter what medium you are using. Your efforts should be targeted, relevant, and measurable.

Throughout this chapter, think about how you can use a variety of online marketing channels for both audience acquisition and audience retention. By using the power of search marketing and online advertising, you are getting your message in front of your prospective podcast audience. Once you have them, you should do everything you can to retain them. That includes getting them to subscribe to your RSS (really simple syndication) feed, but you can also ask them to sign up for frequent email communications or a monthly newsletter as well. Audience retention is key to your ongoing success. Let's jump into some proven online marketing tactics.

Search Engine Marketing: Pay Per Click

We already examined in detail the importance of search engine optimization (SEO), and optimizing the various elements of your podcast so that you have the greatest chance of getting high natural rankings in the search engines. As discussed, this process can sometimes take months to accomplish and it is an ongoing effort to optimize your position. So what can you do in the meantime to gain interest and drive traffic to your podcast? The immediate solution is to develop an SEM or pay per click campaign and start bidding on the keywords that are most likely to be searched by your target audience.

SEM is a very useful, highly effective means of driving traffic to your podcast. Unlike SEO, SEM offers immediate gratification and placement within the major search engines. Of course, it goes without saying that this type of immediate gratification comes with a price.

Much as a podcast appeals to a specific, content-driven audience, SEM capitalizes on the keywords a person uses to provide them with targeted, relevant advertisements. Think about any time you have conducted a search on Google. Invariably, your search will produce two or three links at the top of the page in a blue box, as well as several other links in a column on the right-hand side of the screen. These are all "sponsored links" or advertisements and are often incredibly pertinent to your search. These are placed by organizations participating in SEM.

How does this work? How do you participate in SEM? SEM functions on the principle of pay per click. In short, pay per click means that you pay only when someone clicks on your sponsored link, which can be a very effective way of spending marketing dollars. You pay for what drives traffic to your site, and only that traffic. Your ad may show up a thousand times in Google, but you only pay if someone clicks on it (see Figure 12.1). This also presents a great branding opportunity as well.

Here is how it works. Much as we discussed in the last chapter, you should first do research on the various keywords that are being searched on in your particular category. You can select 10, 20, 50, even hundreds or, if appropriate, thousands of keywords that relate to your topic and interest category. The keywords you choose to sponsor can also be broken

FIGURE 12.1
How Google AdWords works. *Source*: Google AdWords (adwords.google.com).

down into different keyword groups, so you can measure their performance against each other and see which is giving you the highest yield.

With SEM you are dedicating a specific budget amount—in this case, let's say it's a monthly budget of $1000—and you bid on the particular keywords that you want your ads to show up under. You simply dictate how much money you're willing to spend per click on each keyword. With services like Google's AdWords and Yahoo! Search Marketing, their suite of technologies will assist you in optimizing your overall ad spend so you get the furthest reach for your dollar.

As mentioned, with SEM you choose the words you desire your ad to be associated with. If your podcast caters to the slightly more obscure and less often searched terms, then you will have greater chances of being able to bid on a large quantity of several different words for most likely a few cents per word. If, however, your podcast deals with subject matter like mortgages or perhaps tax services, then the selection of words you would most likely bid on becomes increasingly more expensive due to the amount of other organizations who are focusing on those keywords. This can vary from a few cents to several dollars per word per click. It does not take a math genius to see that paying 2 cents for a click yields more "bang for the buck" than paying 15 dollars per click. But it all depends on your particular category. If you are in a highly competitive category, there will be a lot of competition for your top keywords, and you will need to pay careful attention to your SEM campaign so that you can stretch your marketing dollars as far as they can go.

As mentioned earlier, both Google and Yahoo! will assist marketers with optimizing your ad budget. For example, once your quota for the day or the month has been met, your ads will cease to appear in search results until the following day or month when you have your next purchased allotment. Regardless of whether you are in an obscure category that isn't expensive or a highly competitive one, it is a good idea to keep a close eye on your SEM campaign to make sure you are getting the most for your dollars.

Larger search engines like Google and Yahoo! will offer support tools to help you decide which words you should bid on and how to optimize your campaign. Check out Google AdWords (http://adwords.google.com) and Yahoo! Search Marketing (http://searchmarketing.yahoo.com) to learn more.

The power of search engines like Google and Yahoo!, and their ability to get your ad in front of Web users, is a great asset when trying to build an audience for your podcast. SEM is a great tool since it supplements some of the responsibility of seeking out your audience. Search engines have an enormous reach into mass culture and an immeasurable amount of data to determine when your ad should show up at the right time.

Pay per click marketing offers you an opportunity to buy your way to immediate search engine results. Before you launch into a full-blown SEM campaign, buying up different words and spending lots of dollars, you should test the waters with a few different words in smaller quantities. You may find that the keywords you thought would be the most successful actually yield poor results, and that consumers are searching for your content in a completely different way. Be prepared to test several combinations and then, after you have tracked your results, you can move forward with an SEM campaign that will land your podcast at the top of the list (or near it).

WARNING

Be careful not to set your budget and bids and walk away. You should pay careful attention to your SEM campaign to ensure that your keyword bids are optimized. You don't want to spend your monthly budget in the first week of a month. You may also consider getting help from an outside firm to help maximize your marketing dollars.

There are many SEM tactics you can apply to podcasting. As one simple example, if your show features interviews with guests from other organizations, you should bid on their names and their company names in addition to your regular set of keywords. People's names are always being "Googled." Why not take advantage of these searches and get your podcast ad in front of those individuals? After all, you do have content that is relevant to the search term. You should continuously be adding and deleting search terms from your campaign.

The need to optimize the copy in the ads for an SEM campaign is also of utmost importance. For instance, when displayed with search results for the names of people or companies, the title of the ad should be relevant to the search. For instance, if we do a search for "Craig Syverson" we are much more likely to click on an ad with a title of "Podcasts by Craig Syverson" or "Listen to Craig Syverson" than we are for "VentureCast" or "Listen to VentureCast". The first two titles appear to be more relevant to my search than the second set. The same advice goes for the description. Most ad platforms give the user the ability to use wildcards, which allow certain search terms to be auto-populated with the keyword or keyword phrase the user has typed into the search engine, thus adding more relevancy to the ad headline. Used correctly, they can dramatically increase the click-through rates on your ads.

When you are involved in SEM, it is very important that you also monitor your natural rankings as well. Tracking your SEO efforts at the same time will allow you to gauge the success of your efforts and will suggest what keywords you should bid up or down, or drop from your campaign altogether. Why spend money on a keyword on which you already rank high in the search engines? You can use a tool like Web Position Gold (www.webpositiongold.com) to monitor your natural search rankings. Tools like this will tell you where you naturally rank on the major search engines under particular keywords.

The major search engines will offer you plenty of data and reporting around your SEM campaign so you can see exactly what's happening at any given time. Most reporting is done in real time or batched daily. You can tell which keywords are performing the best, which ones are non-performers, and where every penny of your SEM budget it going.

It's clear that Google and Yahoo! are the largest search engines out there, and they carry the largest amount of inventory. Therefore, they also carry the highest click costs. Table 12.1 shows several other options in addition to these search engines that you should explore.

For more ideas on where to find SEM bargains, users can check out the "Lists of Search Engines" page on wikipedia (http://en.wikipedia.org/wiki/list_of_search_engines).

If you are a larger company it's highly likely that you already have an SEM program in place, either in house or via an outside SEM vendor. If this is the case, all you need to do is ask them to create some new keyword groups that are focused around your podcast and its content.

Remember once again that when you bid on keywords, you are not the only organization looking to capitalize on those words. You will most likely have competitors and they will drive up the costs of the campaign. You do not need to achieve the number-one rank when involved in SEM, but the closer to the top of the page you can keep your advertisement, the more likely it is you will have traffic driven to your Web site.

Email Marketing

Email marketing has become an essential component of nearly every organization, no matter what industry they are in. Businesses, non-profits, educational institutions, and other organizations of all sizes engage in email marketing. Over the last few years email marketing has become the primary online channel for organizations to communicate with their customers, prospects, employees, and the media. Email builds loyalty and retention and creates dialog between organizations and their audiences.

TABLE 12.1 Alternative Search Marketing Options to Google and Yahoo!

Microsoft AdCenter (www.adcenter.microsoft.com)
Ask.com (www.sponsoredlistings.ask.com)
Looksmart (www.adcenter.looksmart.com)
Stumbleupon (www.stumbleupon.com/ads/)

According to eMarketer (www.eMarketer.com), over 147 million people across the US use email either through a personal account or work account nearly every single day—and this statistic only includes those over the age of 18. Considering that, in 2006, the estimated total US population was at nearly 300 million, almost half of the US is online and using email (see Figure 12.2). Email marketing allows for access into this market in a way that television, radio, and other forms of traditional media cannot.

Email marketing is useful in that your audience can subscribe to receive updates, information, and promotions via email. A database of permission-based email addresses provides you with an audience that has confirmed their interest in your organization's activities and correspondence. This creates opportunities to open dialog between you and your audience, from something as simple as asking your audience to redeem a code they've

US E-Mail Users as a Percent of Internet Users and Total US Population*, 2003–2010

	E-Mail users % of Internet users	E-Mail users % of total population
2003	88.1	52.0
2004	88.5	53.6
2005	89.1	55.1
2006	89.7	56.4
2007	90.4	57.8
2008	91.1	59.0
2009	91.8	60.1
2010	92.2	61.0

Note: eMarketer defines an e-mail user as a person aged 3+ who sends an e-mail at least once per month.
*Internet users and total population aged 3+.

075274   www.e**Marketer**.com

FIGURE 12.2

Number of email users in the US from 2003 to 2010. *Source*: eMarketer.com.

received in an email to requesting direct feedback on a certain issue. Email marketing is versatile and can be developed in a variety of ways to suit the different needs of many organizations.

One major factor that lends itself to the power of email marketing is that it builds loyalty and retention with your recipients. Email campaigns, newsletters, and special promotions can also create an exclusivity factor that appeals to your audience. Building off of these factors, you are able to increase subscriber retention by remaining in the view of your audience and gaining mindshare of each recipient. Emails that arrive in their inboxes continuously remind your subscribers of your brand and offerings, and that will keep them returning to you.

Understanding that email is an extremely valuable marketing tool, be ready to collect email addresses wherever possible. If you have a blog, offer your content via email as an option or offer your readers a supplemental email newsletter they can subscribe to. You should make the opt-in process easy and accessible from every appropriate place within your Web presence. It is also important to understand that some individuals may choose to subscribe to your RSS content via email as well. The mainstream use of RSS feed readers is still emerging and many prefer to use their email inbox as their primary application for all subscription-based content. At any point that you can collect an email address, make sure that it is clear to your audience so that they can subscribe to your content.

Once you have a database of consumers that have subscribed to your email communications, depending on what kind of campaign you are sending to them, be sure to emphasize a clear call to action in each email. Even the most beautifully crafted emails that are attractive, easy to read, and so on can fail in the long run by not including a strong call to action. Your call to action is the part of the message that asks your reader to do something. The requested action can be as simple as visiting a link to read the full article, or clicking on a promotional rate for a product offering, etc. Regardless, the part of your email where you ask your audience to engage needs to be clear and prominent within the message.

In the case of podcasting, email can be used in a variety of ways. First and foremost, you should include a mention in your company's existing monthly or quarterly email newsletter that is consistent and has a place in every edition. At my company, Blue Sky Factory, Inc. (www.blueskyfactory. com), we always highlight the latest and most relevant ROI Radio episode in our monthly newsletter, Factory Direct. Even though our newsletter is about email marketing tips, best practices, and industry trends, including a mention about ROI Radio in every edition keeps people coming back to the podcast as well. Since our brand is tied into the podcast, it generates more mindshare to our clients, prospects, and listeners. In addition to the branding and messaging it provides, we are also actively converting some of our email newsletter subscribers into podcast subscribers. It's a win–win, the subscriber gets more value-added content, and we pick up more subscribers to the podcast.

You can also develop email marketing strategies based solely around your podcast. For example, you may want to let your subscribers know what you will be covering in the upcoming episode to build some anticipation. Or you simply may want to alert your subscribers to when a new podcast has been published. Even though they may already be subscribed via your RSS feed and be alerted to your new content via their RSS aggregator or through a directory like iTunes, it still can't hurt to let them know. It is more likely the case that your audience will be checking their email before their RSS reader and as mentioned above in some cases they are the same.

Not everyone will subscribe to your podcast immediately, and therefore they will not necessarily go to your podcast's home to see if new content has been added. Email offers a means of notifying new listeners or infrequent downloaders of new information that is available to them and, even better, offers them a direct link to it.

Other tactics include creating supplemental content around your podcasts and offering it to your audience via email. This can be a newsletter, tips, highlights, etc. You may also find that some people subscribe to your email content first before engaging with your podcast. The key is to develop a dialog and get people engaged with your subject matter.

Email can also be used as a survey tool. As mentioned several times throughout the book, the more you know about your audience the better. Create a simple online survey and poll your subscribers, learn more about them, what their interests are, what they think of your podcast, take suggestions, etc. Drive them to these surveys via email, or better yet, in some cases you can include quick polls right in the body of the email. Gathering this type of information will allow you understand your audience better, produce more engaging content, retain your listeners, and gain more subscribers.

Keep in mind that the people who are receiving your emails have made it very clear that they are interested in hearing from you, so long as you have a proper opt-in method in place and have collected emails on a permission basis. An email subscription form is generally a very easy element to set up. Any email service provider that you use will be able to offer you a simple form that you can generate and begin to collect email addresses, almost in minutes.

Because you have a database of interested subscribers, you should take advantage of the access you have to this group and send out emails that are targeted and relevant. Tell them about your latest show, what you cover and what they can expect to get out of it, and why it is different. Since RSS is still foreign to some people, allowing your visitors to subscribe to your email communications can be key in staying in front of these individuals.

Another key element in email marketing is the viral nature of the medium. Think about it: How many times have you passed on an email to a friend that you think they would be interested in? We all do. Email is viral by its very nature—it's easy to hit the forward button and share something interesting with a friend. In fact, most email technology services offer what's known in the industry as a "forward to a friend" feature, where recipients can click a button within the email creative and it will pop open a Web browser with a form to type in a friend or colleague's email address and often provide a space for a brief note.

WARNING While email marketing is a very powerful and often incredibly successful tool, be careful not to inundate your recipients with too many emails. There is a careful balance that needs to be maintained when using email marketing, and too much of a good thing can lead to opt-outs and being flagged as spam.

Email marketing is not a new concept in online marketing (see Figure 12.3). So what's the big deal? As we will explore in another chapter, metrics for measuring podcasts are still evolving and thus tracking and measuring the success of your podcast can be challenging. Email marketing, however, is extremely well established with baseline metrics that are easy to track and understand. For example, with most email service providers, you can view the open rates and click-through rates of any campaign you send out. In

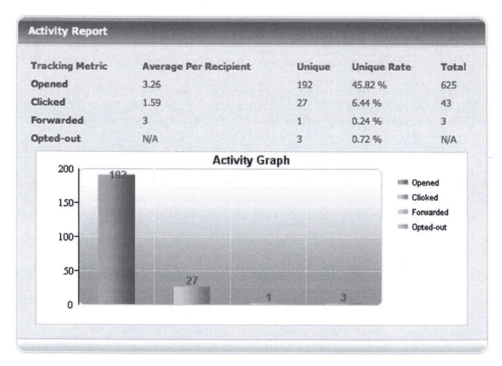

FIGURE 12.3

A sample email marketing tracking report. *Source*: Blue Sky Factory's Publicaster Email Marketing Platform (www.publicaster.com).

most cases, you can see which individuals or segments of your list clicked through to your podcast and directly downloaded it. These types of metrics are important to be able to measure the success of your efforts.

Most email providers will also offer a comprehensive toolset for list management, bounce backs, and subscriber preferences, as well as manage the deliverability aspects of your campaigns. These are all the features that allow you to focus on the message and not worry about the technical details.

Another reason to consider email marketing for your podcast is that it is fairly cost effective. Due to the targeted and relevant nature of email marketing, your response is likely to be higher than if you follow broader, more general marketing strategies. With email marketing (like podcasting) you have already been able to narrow down the audience to those who have confirmed an interest in your organization, products, or services.

Overall, email marketing is an exceptionally useful tool in promoting your podcast and should be included in all of your marketing efforts.

Online Display Advertising

One area that should not be overlooked is online display advertising. Banner ads and button ads can be extremely effective in driving traffic to your podcast if you target them appropriately. There are several ways to take advantage of this medium and many resources to consider depending on your budget and how much reach you are looking to get.

First and foremost is the sponsorship or ad buy on a particular Web site, blog, or network of sites. Most popular Web properties, including blogs, are generally represented by a third-party company that will assist in developing an ad campaign that will target your sponsorship to the most appropriate audience. Companies like John Battelle's Federated Media (www.federatedmedia.net) can assist in getting display ads on a large network of publisher sites, mostly blogs that are geared toward your target audience (see Figure 12.4). There are several other organizations that can help guide you in the right direction in this regard.

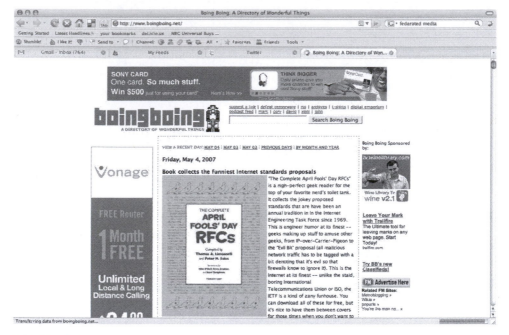

FIGURE 12.4

Sample display advertisements on the popular BoingBoing.net blog.

There are also many opportunities for you to do your own outreach and sponsor specific Web sites and/or blogs that you think have the audience that would most appeal to your podcast content. Don't be shy; reach out to ask what a particular publisher's protocol is for sponsorship. Ask them about how they charge for banner ads or button sidebar ads, and get some exposure working direct.

After ensuring your ads have the best chance of being presented in front of your target audience, the next step is to develop some compelling creative. Your display ads should invoke interest and curiosity in order to get a decent click-through rate on your efforts. Much like email, online display ads should be to the point and offer a clear call to action for the user (see Figure 12.5). For example, I sponsor the Web site www.citybizlist.com, a Baltimore-based publication that updates its content on a daily basis, including a daily email blast that goes out to over 7000 business folks in Baltimore alone. Citybizlist also includes my podcast display ads in their

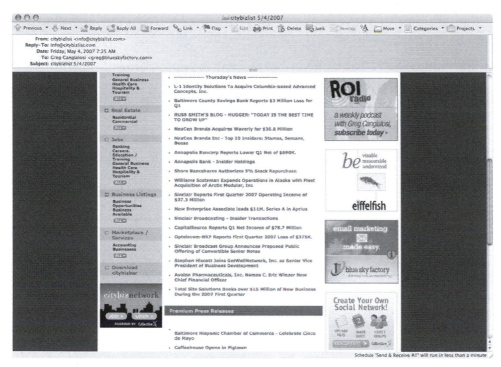

FIGURE 12.5
Examples of email sponsorship display advertisements.

Washington DC, Boston, and Philadelphia editions as well. Although citybizlist's overall audience is much wider than my exact target audience, that is, marketers, the ads still generate a ton of hits to ROI Radio and have converted many loyal listeners and subscribers.

Outside of direct sponsorships or network sponsorships that generally run on a cost per thousand (CPM) basis, meaning you pay a certain dollar amount for every 1000 impressions of your ad, there are also what are known as ad networks that allow you to buy online media on a performance basis as well. By performance basis, I mean models like cost per click (CPC) or cost per acquisition (CPA). Much like an SEM campaign, these types of buys only charge you when someone takes an action. Although they can be wider in reach, many of the top networks offer both demographic and behavioral targeting for your ad buy.

The leaders in this space are Advertising.com (www.advertising.com), ValueClick (www.valueclick.com), and Commission Junction (www.commissionjunction.com). All three of these leaders offer a variety of solutions to get your ad in front of the right audience.

Additional Tools and Tactics to Keep People Coming Back

In addition to these proven online marketing tactics, there are several other ways to develop an audience and keep listeners returning to your podcasts.

Creating Evergreen Content

One way to support your podcast does not involve a marketing tactic or search engines, yet it is still a tactic of sorts. When you are creating content for your podcast, most often people are interested in current information, things that are new and relevant. But your audience may be most likely interested in another kind of content—"evergreen" content.

What do I mean by "evergreen?" Evergreen content is content that is virtually timeless, or at least something that will remain pertinent for a long period of time. Not every single podcast you produce will be or needs to be classified as evergreen content, but having a few gems in the pack can definitely help in attracting a wider audience. Generally, over time, evergreen content is linked to by many people and in some cases widely referenced.

It is important to remember that a big motivating factor behind downloading a podcast is not only convenience and a desire to learn more about a topic, but also the desire to learn about what is going on in particular subject matter *now*. That said, offering some content that will be relevant for months (or even years) to come is useful for a variety of reasons.

This speaks to the importance of having an organized way of archiving your podcast content. Archiving all of your podcasts, along with their corresponding show notes and transcripts, will allow future visitors to download and enjoy this timeless content, assisting you in potentially converting one-time listeners into subscribers. Because evergreen content is relevant and ageless, your audience can continue to grow and expand by accessing these successful podcasts. By keeping evergreen episodes archived on your Web site, along with their corresponding textual supplements, you are once again increasing your search rankings and attractiveness to the larger search engines.

There is no real rule of thumb in determining which of your podcasts should be evergreen and which should have a shorter "shelf life" with timely rather than timeless content. But if you find that your podcast relies most heavily on current event-type content, consider producing one or two with longer-lasting content, perhaps as special editions that are more timeless than the norm so that you may capitalize on the benefits of evergreen content.

Make Your Own Headlines

When developing your podcast, you should be thinking about making headlines and not just in the traditional sense. While gaining media exposure by producing a podcast would be phenomenal, the type of headlines you should be focusing on are the ones for your podcast episodes.

One great form of spreading the word about your podcast is the Headline Animator from Feedburner (www.feedburner.com). This is an excellent tool you can use to display and rotate the most recent podcasts that you have posted. Completely customizable, the Headline Animator can be tailored to display in many formats. The one that I have seen the most success with is the email signature version. I use it to promote my podcasts and blogs. In fact, I have deployed this feature across my entire organization so that at the bottom of every email that goes out from a staff member of Blue Sky Factory, the five most recent blog postings or podcasts that have been published rotate in the signature file (see Figures 12.6a–c).

The service is free with a Feedburner account and affords you another way to publicize your podcast on the Web.

FIGURE 12.6

Feedburner's Headline Animator is used to merely offer users a "brushed metal" appearance; but it is now far more customizable. Also here is an example of the signature file that rotates headlines. *Source*: Feedburner Blog, blogs.feedburner.com.

With a Headline Animator from Feedburner, you can post information about your podcast just about anywhere that will allow you to. Some good starting points would be to post the headlines on your Web site and blog, so that you are not only drawing attention to your new podcast but also displaying a quick summary of your most recent podcast content. Using some of the tools provided by Feedburner, interested parties can generally click through directly to the downloadable file.

GREG'S TIP

A side note about Headline Animator: If you use Feedburner to power your headlines, you also have access to an entire suite of other tools to promote your content. Feedburner is constantly working to improve upon their existing tools and metrics, making it easier to get your content into the hands of your audience.

The folks at Feedburner believe in continually improving upon their existing tools. New improvements to Headline Animator are frequent and are geared toward enhancing the customization features of your content. Recently, Feedburner enabled a "grab-it" feature for headlines, meaning that interested parties in your content can "grab" your Headline Animator and post it somewhere as well. This is a great example of social media working to promote itself, and will hopefully spur a viral takeoff for your podcast as Web users continue to view your headlines and pass them on.

Another popular public space to display your headlines is on social networking sites like MySpace and YouTube. With social networks becoming ever prominent on the Web, more people and businesses are joining in on them. For instance, it is now a commonplace for almost any band to have its own MySpace page. Posting your Headline Animator on your own unique social networking page creates one more space for your audience to access your podcast.

Podcast Album Art

Another tactic you should consider utilizing is album art for your podcast. Creating an image for your podcast is not dissimilar from developing your organization's logo—you need something unique to distinguish your podcast from the crowd and make it immediately recognizable as your content.

Think of the power of cover art in the music industry. Logos and imagery can build loyalty and recognition in a way that words alone cannot. The same principles can be applied to podcasting. Developing artwork to accompany your podcast will be useful in a variety of ways in promoting your podcast online.

One reason to design a logo for your podcast is it assists in getting your podcast noticed on a directory like iTunes. Most of the podcasts that are popular in iTunes—the ones that achieve featured podcast status, or new releases, etc.—have some sort of accompanying artwork to draw attention to them. iTunes does not typically feature podcasts that don't offer some sort of logo or artwork since it detracts from the attractiveness of the page.

As you will recall from Chapter 11 when we discussed promoting your podcast through iTunes, the benefits of being featured on such a directory were also discussed. Being featured is essentially free publicity for your podcast, putting it front and center for every visitor to see. Many people download podcasts or explore their content simply because they saw it as a featured podcast. Eye-grabbing cover art will help divert traffic to your podcast through directories that publish the art alongside the podcast (see, e.g., Figure 12.7). Not all directories provide the space to submit cover art, but having artwork ready for those that do will help brand your podcast and draw attention to it.

Another reason you should create artwork for your podcast is brand identification. Anyone who has been involved in business can tell you the importance of brand recognition. For example, Nike would not be Nike if not for the trademarked "swoosh" that is proudly displayed on all their gear. Often when you see an advertisement for this company, their name is not even included—the image alone is powerful enough. While that kind of notoriety is an extreme example of successful branding, a solid image that is associated with your content will help establish your podcast's identity.

Finally, developing artwork for your podcast gives you one more tool that you can use to promote your podcast online. Just as we discussed the use of the Headline Animator, you can use your podcast cover art as your personal

FIGURE 12.7
Unique album art, like the image for VentureCast shown here, will make your podcast stand out on iTunes.

image when blogging, posting bulletins, or creating links to your podcast. The more you are able to associate an image with your podcast, the greater the chances of your audience recognizing it for its high-quality content.

Now that you have produced your podcast, designed some eye-popping cover art, and are actively promoting it online, the next chapter will take a look at growing your audience, and how to build interactivity and community around your podcast. Then it's time to measure the success of your efforts and drill into the importance of metrics; how to measure your podcast, and what the future holds for measuring podcasts.

Lessons Learned

- SEM is a quick way to get exposure and build immediate traffic to your podcast. This can help in building up an audience quickly.

- Email marketing is a great tool for building loyalty and retention with your audience. Sending timely and relevant content to your subscriber base will keep them engaged with your brand and your podcast.

- Online display advertisements can yield great results. Consider banner ads and button ads on targeted and relevant Web sites and blogs to attract new subscribers.

- Creating evergreen content allows you to build your archive of content with some timeless shows. These are great anchor shows for your podcast.

- Make use of tools like Feedburner's Headline Animator to increase the reach of your podcast awareness.

- Include album art with your podcast.

Building Community and Interactivity

Greg Cangialosi

Up to this point we have looked at how to bring your podcast from its nascent stages and successfully produce and promote it. You have followed the steps, produced a great podcast, and are beginning to build an audience of listeners. So that's it, right? You can put your feet up and watch your podcast blossom before your eyes?

Not quite. Once you have begun building an audience who is engaged with your content, you then have an opportunity to take things to the next level. One way to continue to develop and enhance your podcast and your audience is by creating community and interactivity around your show. Creating a community around your podcast is a great way to enhance the experience of your audience and foster loyalty in listeners. In the following sections, we will take a look at some of the different mediums you can use to build a sense of community among your listeners, and take your podcast to the next level.

Beyond Written Comments

In the previous chapters, I've extolled the virtues of blogging and participating in the blogosphere to garner awareness and exposure for you, your organization, and your podcast. Sometimes the most intriguing conversations begin in the comment sections on blogs. Comments are useful in that they are one of the simplest ways to engage your audience. Most people understand how to post comments and are willing to do so, if they have something to say in reaction to your content.

Creating the space for comments on your podcast's Web site or home (however you have set it up) is a great way to begin dialog with your audience. By prompting your listeners to engage, or by asking them to post their thoughts on your site, you can begin to develop some basic rapport with them.

Participating in an online conversation is a much more dynamic and interactive experience now than ever before. Dialoguing in the comments is a good place to start interacting and communicating with your audience. In most cases, when people engage in dialog online, they expect a response just as if they were involved in a face-to-face conversation. Therefore, it's important to pay attention to the activity on your blog and Web site, and to respond in a timely manner when people begin to engage. I make this a key practice for both my personal and business blogs.

The emergence of social media has made several tools available to create community around your podcast. Community can be fostered beyond just words, actually encouraging participation and collaboration and even real conversation between audience members and you.

Audio Comments

Podcasting is different from other forms of social media in that it does not easily allow for listeners to engage in dialog. Unlike blogs, where thoughts are posted and responded to through the written word, podcasts provide information audibly and, in the case of video, visually, with no real way for a listener to respond the instant they hear it. Audio comments are emerging as a way for your audience to respond to your podcast in kind—audio for audio.

Allowing and encouraging your audience to send in audio comments makes it possible for listeners to not only leave their thoughts and comments about your content, but to do it verbally. Several programs exist that allow your audience to record messages, which can either be set to be private and listened to only by you or left public for all to hear.

Audio comments are exactly what they sound like—actual vocal comments that are recorded by your audience and then submitted to you, the publisher. Depending on how you set up your options, audio comments also can be shared with others who are visiting and listening. As the producer of the content, you can determine who can listen to the audio comments and also set limits on the recording time.

What are the benefits of allowing your listeners to communicate verbally with you? One is that it gives your audience a new way to reach out to you and communicate their thoughts, suggestions, and opinions. You can start an actual dialog by asking your listeners to leave questions that probe deeper into the topics you are covering. Verbal comments and questions can provide excellent feedback that will help direct you in the development of future podcast content.

Many podcasters that use audio comments take the remarks of the listeners and work them into their next or future episode. This is useful for two major reasons. First, it helps produce content for your next podcast and adds variety to the show so that it is not just the host talking or interviewing. Second, including audio comments helps build loyalty and community around your show.

Audio comments foster community by showing your listeners that you are actually listening to and incorporating their thoughts and opinions into your content. If you include the pertinent comments or answer some of the more poignant questions in your next podcast, your listeners will take note and appreciate the inclusion and the response.

People engage in online dialog because of the chance to share ideas and become a part of a community. If you begin to include audio comments in your podcast, people will listen and respond not only to your content, but use your space to comment on each other's remarks and build from there.

As more listeners become familiar with your podcast and one and other, the conversation can become deeper and more extensive.

Audio comments are yet another way to find out more about your audience and your target market. The information you can acquire through this kind of interaction is not something you can achieve with a focus group or a survey. This is a direct consumer input, telling you specifically what your listeners are interested in, what they think, and what they are looking for in terms of content.

Responding to audio comments shows a commitment on your part. If you begin accepting audio comments from your audience, then responding to them regularly is essential if your podcast is to become a success.

GREG'S TIP

You should respond to a listener's comment on an individual basis to address a specific question or opinion. This deepens the bond between your audience and your podcast by demonstrating your interest in the individual as well as the audience as a whole.

Everyone likes to be heard. Including audio comments from your audience in your podcast gives your listeners a chance to share their opinion globally, to make an acute observation or profound statement. Allowing this space to be shared by your audience creates a sense of participation and ownership of the podcast. These sentiments lend themselves to greater loyalty among your listener base.

There are many different services you can use to begin harnessing audio comments for your podcast. MobaTalk (which replaced MyChingo in early 2007), Odeo, Skype, and k7.net are different services that will allow your audience to record audio comments (see Table 13.1). Each works slightly differently, but the basic principles are the same: you are given a means to record audio and the ability to have it posted publicly or privately. Some services request a fee for use of their system, while others are free of charge and each has certain advantages and drawbacks.

TABLE 13.1 List of Audio Commenting Services

Service	Cost	Features
MobaTalk	Free	Integrates multimedia for audio comments, video comments, voicemail, and more.
Odeo	Free	Can also be used on MySpace for audio comments. Includes an online player.
Skype voicemail	Under $10 per month	Skype users can leave voicemail when you are not online. Service is free with SkypeIn, which also provides you with a phone number that others can call.
k7.net	Free	Free phone number is provided that allows you to receive voicemail. Can be accessed online or emailed to you.

The features of these systems vary, since some are true tools for audio commenting whereas others are voicemail that is sent as VoIP (Voice over IP). MyChingo and audio comments from Odeo provide simple Web-based widgets to record audio from listeners. For the free services, there are often time limits to how long a person can record, which can prove beneficial in the end because it keeps comments concise and therefore easier to respond to or incorporate in your podcast.

Of course, for audio commenting to be accessible on the Web you need to have a designated area on your site for commenting on your podcast. Using a simple JavaScript-based widget on your podcast's site can work great if you have the space. Generally the setup is rather simple, requiring you to cut and paste some code within your site or blog template. If, however, using a service like this is not ideal for receiving audio comments, you may want to consider voicemail.

Voicemail

Using a voicemail service instead of a commenting service does not reduce the quality or effect of incorporating your listener comments. The principles behind leaving comments on voicemail parallel those of a Web-based audio commenting system, and work in a very similar fashion.

Most of the top voicemail services for receiving comments utilize VoIP technologies to record the calls of your listeners. These services offer listeners a phone number to call and leave their comments. Upon calling this service, they are able to leave their comments and thoughts, which you can then incorporate into your podcast in the same manner as with standard audio comments.

The benefit of using voicemail through a service like Skype or k7.net is that the messages are recorded digitally, so the sound files are ready for use without further encoding. This is in contrast to the one in which the recording went to an external machine as with standard voicemail.

WARNING

One drawback to voicemail is that if you are using a designated telephone number, you may be excluding overseas listeners. Remember that your podcast can travel around the globe, so some of your most frequent listeners can be on another continent entirely. For them, calling to leave a voicemail can be a rather pricey endeavor.

Services like Skype and Google Talk offer high-quality sound and recording for a fraction of the cost of traditional phone services, if any cost is incurred at all (computer to computer calls are often free, and a minimal fee is charged for calling a land line). Voicemail through Skype is available for a minimal fee, but Google Talk offers voicemail free of charge.

Using a voicemail service can often allow your listeners a greater amount of recording time, so the quality of the comments may be better since your contributors will have more time to expand upon their thoughts. Google Talk, for example, allows up to 10 minutes of recording time, whereas the free component of MyChingo only allows for two.

Offering a combination of audio comments and voicemail technologies will allow you to maximize your audience's ability to engage your podcast's community. Not everyone who listens to your podcast will have the tools to record using an audio comment recording program, nor will everyone want to dial a phone number to leave a message. Regardless, most people like to express their opinions, and the more options you can provide them to do so, the better your chances of getting high-quality audio comments.

GREG'S TIP

Providing a variety of options with which your listeners can submit their audio comments is best practice. They should be able to use a Web-based system for leaving comments or be able to pick up the phone and leave a voicemail comment. Allowing your listeners to email their audio comments as attachments is another option.

Thoughts on Comments

Not every comment or contribution you receive from your audience will be a gem that needs to be shared with the world. Some comments may just be praise or criticism of the show, other remarks may be completely off-topic, and others may be so fantastic that you can't wait to broadcast them. But there are certain things that you can do to solicit the next talking point or get the kind of feedback you can use in your podcast. You can begin the next episode with thoughts and comments from listeners on the last one, and highlight the points that were brought up.

Audio comments can provide a variety of uses for your podcast. Some of the comments that are more praise than contribution can be included on your podcast's site as testimonials to your program. Testimonials are powerful marketing tools, since new listeners may be interested to hear what other listeners think of your podcast before downloading it themselves. Word of mouth can be very powerful, and putting together a string of positive comments from actual listeners helps add credibility and can attract new listeners.

The uses for audio comments in building community can be tailored to your individual podcasting needs. Your goals and objectives will vary depending on the kind of organization you are. For instance, posting listener testimonials in either text or audio format on your podcast's home page might be more appropriate if you are promoting your company's products, whereas including listener comments in your next podcast would be better if your podcast is more in the education and outreach realm. Regardless, you do not need to incorporate audio comments to build community, but they are becoming a very powerful tool to do so.

Collaboration, Knowledge Sharing, and Community Development

Audio comments are not the only tools available for building community around your podcast. Web 2.0 encompasses the creation and development of several different methods of collaboration and knowledge sharing that can build communities. You should be thinking along the lines of wiki's and social networks at this point. These tools not only ask for participants to share information, but to actually help build it. In the next section, we will look at how you can use these mediums to build stronger community around your podcast.

Launch a Wiki

At this point of the information age, almost everyone has not only heard of Wikipedia (www.wikipedia.org), but has also used it at some point. Wikipedia is perhaps the most prominent example of the use of a wiki to develop and share information, and even form community. People from all over the world contribute to Wikipedia, working to keep information current, in depth, and accurate. It is a truly global endeavor.

Creating a wiki for your podcast may not result in a community of the same breadth or depth as Wikipedia, but it certainly can be used to for fostering community and developing an information resource for your podcast's content. There are multitudes of ways that wikis can be used by your organization, but here we are going to focus on how you can use the collaborative nature of the wiki to support your podcast.

Like podcasts, for a wiki to be successful it needs to have a focus and targeted goal in order for people to want to engage. If left open-ended, people may comment, but these contributions will probably not be very pertinent to the topic. Few people want to read a wiki that is just a mix of unrelated topics. Thus, creating a wiki in conjunction with your podcast content creates the common link for successful community building.

When starting your wiki, you need to consider what your main purpose will be. Obviously, you are looking to build community, but that is a natural side effect of this particular tool. Instead, you need to consider if your wiki will be for documentation, event planning, and information building ...— the possibilities are almost endless.

Before launching your own wiki, check out several different examples of them in addition to Wikipedia. Look for examples of different formats, methods, and means—seeing them used in different ways will help you decide how you want to shape your wiki. Check out www.wikia.com for a directory of wikis on a variety of subjects.

GREG'S TIP

Your wiki can be either open for anyone to edit, or secure and limited to contributions by registered users. Limiting access to your wiki can some-times generate better content, and encourage other visitors to check out your podcast, but open access allows others to engage in your community and then possibly be converted to a new subscriber. Ultimately, you need to choose what best works for you and your audience and determine the level of participation that is available based on that decision.

If you choose to limit wiki participation to subscribers, it may be a good idea to require that a contributor's name be attached to a post, article, or revision. This will clearly identify the contributor and force them to consider their words just as much as if they were speaking with colleagues.

GREG'S TIP

The first step in getting people engaged in your wiki after you launch it is to let your audience familiarize themselves with the space and to register

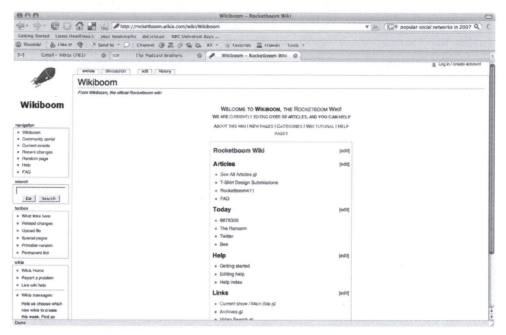

FIGURE 13.1

Wikiboom, the official community wiki of the popular videoblog. *Source*: www. rocketboom.com.

on the wiki if they are going to participate. As described before with audio comments, you want to endow your participants with a sense of ownership so as to foster greater loyalty. If your participants feel that they have a stake in the wiki, they will take pains to ensure the accuracy of the information that is shared and the maintenance and provision of information (see Figure 13.1).

After you start promoting the fact that you have launched a wiki, it becomes time to then start building the content that will foster participation and help your community grow. At first, your wiki will be a clean slate—barren, untouched, with no content. It will most likely fall on you to take the initial plunge and post the initial content. Fortunately for you, deciding on your content should not be too challenging, since it should be relevant to the content found in your podcast. For instance, if your podcast is about marketing strategies for antique dealers, you can start developing content on how to start generating new inventory or even posting the tips you describe in your podcast into text. Regardless, it takes the wiki and the podcast publisher to start the ball rolling.

Once the initial content is posted, you can start building momentum and participation by hosting collaborative events. These "barn-raising" events are a great way to familiarize your audience with your wiki and create the mass content that will appeal to future listeners and community members. An additional benefit to organizing a collaborative event for your wiki is that it gets the community off and running as individuals work to support and assist one another in the creation of content. Bear in mind although most people today are familiar with what a wiki is, many are not familiar with how to edit and participate with them. Introducing a group of neophytes at the beginning and helping them learn and grow will foster not only community, but also the confidence to continue building.

Not everyone will want to or be able to participate in a collaborative session for your wiki. Still, inviting your audience to explore and contribute is a fantastic way to begin audience engagement. I want to emphasize the invitation component of your participation request. In your podcast, you can either direct people to "go to" or "check out" your wiki—but inviting them to explore and contribute holds an entirely different connotation than the aforementioned phrases. The phrases as mentioned essentially direct traffic to your wiki, whereas an actual invitation to explore and participate creates more of a notion of exclusivity and community—exactly the notion you want to convey.

Wikis are a great way to start a community around your podcast. Not only will your podcast be seen as a valuable source of information, but your wiki will serve to support it and be just as highly valued. But as with audio comments, a wiki is only as effective as you make it, and perhaps the best way to increase participation is to acknowledge your participants.

One way to acknowledge those who contribute to your wiki is by welcoming first-time users, and also acknowledging when someone has made a useful contribution. Taking the time to recognize a person's contribution shows that you are actively maintaining the space and are interested in seeing the community's interests being met.

Another way to recognize contributions is to use information posted in the wiki as a reference in your podcast, or even as material for future content. These applications of incorporating your wiki into your podcast are not dissimilar from the uses of audio comments, just that instead of utilizing audio, you are utilizing textual content.

Finally, just posting your own contribution or amendments to existing information are ways of building community. You audience does not want you to leave them hanging, fending for themselves. Make yourself a wiki master of sorts—go in, edit content as necessary (perhaps there are typos that are just unseemly), and organize the information so that it is easy to use and is visually appealing. If your podcast is professional, your wiki space should be too.

Social Networks

It should be no surprise to anyone that one of the fastest-growing mediums of Web 2.0 is that of social networks. News and headlines today are constantly talking about YouTube, MySpace, Facebook, LinkedIn, and the power these types of sites bring to the table. Social networks are a stellar example of community building at work, since their main objective is, in essence, to build community. However, breaking into these networks takes finesse and can be tricky, so it must be done correctly if you are to successfully build a community for your podcast using these sites.

Social networks like MySpace, Facebook, and Xanga are growing at an enormous rate. Nielson//Netratings conducted a study that was released in May 2006 that revealed a growth rate of 47 percent for social networking sites (see Figure 13.2). Perhaps even more astonishing than the growth rate is the retention rate of these Web sites, with the top five retaining roughly a 50 percent average.

Market Share of US Internet Visits to Top 20 Social Networking Sites February 2007

Rank	Name	Domain	Market Share
1	MySpace	www.myspace.com	80.74%
2	Facebook	www.facebook.com	10.32%
3	Bebo	www.bebo.com	1.18%
4	BlackPlanet.com	www.blackplanet.com	0.88%
5	Xanga	www.xanga.com	0.87%
6	iMeem	www.imeem.com	0.73%
7	Yahoo! 360	360.yahoo.com	0.72%
8	Classmates	www.classmates.com	0.72%
9	hi5	www.hi5.com	0.69%
10	Tagged	www.tagged.com	0.67%
11	LiveJournal	www.livejournal.com	0.49%
12	Gaiaonline.com	www.gaiaonline.com	0.48%
13	Friendster	www.friendster.com	0.34%
14	Orkut	www.orkut.com	0.26%
15	Windows Live Spaces	spaces.live.com	0.18%
16	HoverSpot	www.hoverspot.com	0.18%
17	Buzznet	www.buzznet.com	0.18%
18	Sconex	www.sconex.com	0.14%
19	MiGente.com	www.migente.com	0.11%
20	myYearbook	www.myyearbook.com	0.11%

Note - data is based on custom category of 20 of the leading social networking websites ranked by market share of visits, which is the percentage of traffic to the site, based on Hitwise sample of 10 million US Internet users. The percentages represent the market share of visits among the websites within the custom category.
Source: Hitwise

FIGURE 13.2

According to Hitwise, MySpace was still by far the most popular social networking site in early 2007. *Source*: Hitwise.

The power behind these sites is the user-driven and user-generated content. What can make social networks appealing for you and your podcast is the highly developed community that is already built and at your disposal. Many of these sites form groups for common interests, announcing events, and meeting others based on information provided in user profiles. Social networks offer huge access to audience, but this audience can also be fickle and extremely particular.

It is also clear that not all social networks are appropriate for every podcast. Depending on who your audience is, you may want to stay clear of certain networks. For example, if your podcast targets individuals who would be interested in a particular business topic, you have no need to consider getting involved in a blogging social network like Xanga (www.xanga.com) that focuses on Generation Y. In this case, creating a profile and highlighting your podcast on targeted groups within Facebook (www.facebook.com) may be more appropriate. On the other hand, if you're a clothing company like American Apparel, your podcast would be very appropriate to have a presence on Xanga.

As described earlier in this book, you can utilize social networks to promote your podcast by creating your own profile on one of these sites. Such a profile will allow your podcast to be searched for within the network by users, and likewise allow you to search for them (e.g., you can search groups of users who would be interested in your podcast's content).

These same principles apply to using social networks to build community around your podcast. First and foremost, you must register and have a profile on the network. Your access to information and communities is key, and typically you cannot obtain this access without first registering. When building your profile, consider the audience you are striving to reach and gear your content toward them. Include pictures (such as your podcast logo), links (to your Web site and related Web pages), and even join a few groups and communities.

Once your podcast is a member of a social network, with "friends" that you have reached out to or who have reached out to you, you can begin using the social network to create community and awareness around your podcast. One way to do this is to create a group and start a discussion. Many of these social networking sites also have a blog-like function where people can post comments and start conversations. Other members can then comment on these posts and continue the conversation from there.

Another useful aspect of social networks is the ability to announce and host events. This function can be used to sponsor events and put out a notice to interested members, creating a movement around your content. Events on social networks can be invitations to an actual physical event, or simply be used to raise awareness about your podcast or alert members of new content.

GREG'S TIP   Create a profile for your podcast on the social networks that are the most appropriate for your content. Don't overlook the diversity of participants in some of the larger social networks; it's not just a bunch of kids who are networking with each other.

Social networks are useful for podcasting because they offer so many cross sections of markets that are breaking themselves down by interest. Search through any listing of groups and you will find a great many common interests, many of which will relate to your podcast and its content. This clearly complements the narrow and specific nature of a podcast. Social networks take what can be a challenging part of podcasting—finding your niche market—and simplify it by allowing the market to segment itself.

Building a community around your podcast using social networks takes a bit more effort on your part than some other Web 2.0 tools, but the payoffs can be huge. The power of social networks is in their retention rate and widespread use. Of the aforementioned tools at your disposal, most of the general population is familiar with how to use social networks. Thus, you may be able to build a community more quickly using this tool than some of the others.

There is concern that, due to the rapid success of these social networks with mainstream audiences, the same audiences who flocked to this medium may be just as quick to abandon it. However, current data shows positive growth for nearly every social network, so this fear, while not entirely unfounded, is not likely to occur in the near future if at all.

Another option in regards to building a community around your podcast using social networks is to simply create your very own. The simplest way to do this is to use a site called CollectiveX (www.collectivex.com). CollectiveX (Figure 13.3) enables you to create what they call "groupsites" around any topic of your choice. These groupsites are part Web site, part blog, and part social network. The service started out of founder Clarence Wooten's frustration with being involved in so many different organizations and the difficulty of staying in the loop and keeping track of meetings, events, documents, etc. Out of this frustration, CollectiveX was born. The site allows anyone to set up a groupsite for his/her own purposes for free. You can quickly and easily create a network for your podcast and ask your listeners to sign up and interact with one another. There are several features that foster community and knowledge sharing amongst the members of each group.

FIGURE 13.3

CollectiveX allows users to create their own social networks, like the one shown here, which it calls groupsites. *Source*: CollectiveX.

Social networks are a force for change in community building. Segmentation of the audience by groups is a huge aid in finding your foundations for community and the massive ability to share information through these networks. If you can construct your profile well, social networks are a fantastic platform for building community around your podcast.

Online Forums

Another tool you can use to build community is an online forum. Forums allow for individuals to post topics and for others to respond to and discuss them. These generate what are known as discussion threads. Users can read the dialog taking place, much like they can in the comments of a blog post. There are a ton of free online forum services online for you to take advantage of. As the moderator of your forum, you can suggest topics to discuss that relate to your podcast, or allow your community to engage on their own. This is yet another way to get your audience engaged with each other, and build community.

If You Build It ... You Need a Strategy

When you are beginning your efforts at building community, there are several things that you should consider and decide upon before venturing into new territory.

First, you will want to have a champion within your organization for the medium (or mediums) you choose. Just as when you began your podcast, you should find someone who is already familiar with the workings of the medium so that you are not struggling to work a tool that your users are more familiar with than you. Your champion will be your moderator and supervisor of the community building efforts as a result. In many cases, the podcast producer can do all of these, but in larger organizations, some delegation can be particularly helpful.

Second, you can certainly use multiple tools to build community, but remember that there can be such a thing as too many choices. Don't saturate your audience with so many options that they become fragmented amongst themselves. A couple of carefully implemented options can be more than sufficient, such as perhaps a combination of audio comments, a blog, and a social network around your podcast.

Third, in order to engage your audience, make sure that you give them something to respond to. You want to allow them the space to ask questions, and thusly allowing you the opportunity to respond to those questions in a timely and interested manner. Interaction on your part is essential not only for getting the conversation started, but also in addressing the needs of your audience.

Fourth, never antagonize or intimidate your audience or allow them to treat each other with disrespect. Part of building a community involves meshing different opinions and personalities into one forum, but this process does not need to be unpleasant or in any way threatening to any-one who wishes to participate. Your role as the host is to help foster a wel-coming and open community for communication and the sharing of ideas and common interests. This includes establishing and enforcing rules of conduct for participation.

Finally, be sure that your audience knows that you are putting toge-ther a community for them. A call to action in your podcast invit-ing your audience to explore your new forum will help generate interest and direct traffic to that medium. For example, including an easy to remember phone number at the beginning and end of your podcast will encourage those who have just listened to your episode to call in with comments.

As you conclude each podcast episode, try and find some way to show that your podcast's reach is beyond the spoken word. Your podcast is also a community—a community of individuals joined together by a common interest or pursuit. This is a powerful message to get across, especially as new listeners come across your program and enjoy the content.

Lessons Learned

- Building a community around your podcast increases listener loyalty and helps generate new content.

- Audio comments and voicemail are useful in collecting listener's thoughts and verbal remarks, and can be incorporated in upcoming episodes.

- Wikis can be used for compiling additional resources about your content, articles, and discussions built by you and your listeners.

- Social networks are one of the fastest-growing and prominent community tools of Web 2.0. Harnessing their power can help you build a solid community around your podcast.

- Make use of forums as another option for your audience to discuss relevant topics.

- Make your community known through your podcast. No one will contribute if they don't know that they can.

Show Me the Metrics

Greg Cangialosi

Anyone with any experience in marketing or communications understands the importance of tracking and measuring the success of those efforts. The same applies to your podcasting initiative, whether you are using it to generate leads and drive sales, to educate and inform, or to increase brand awareness. Measuring the success of your podcast will help you refine your strategy, increase your market penetration, and provide a picture of the overall success of your efforts.

Tracking and measuring your marketing and communication efforts can lead to optimized performance over time if the data is reviewed often and acted upon. Your findings highlight your strengths and weaknesses and can shed light on areas where your campaign may need to devote more attention. There are many key performance indicators (KPIs) that can be used depending on what form of communications you are using.

Traditional KPIs include metrics that track customer-related numbers, such as new customer acquisition, returning customers, or demographic data. These indicators can be broken down into different categories: quantitative, practical, directional, and actionable. These same categories can also apply to the practice of measuring your podcast, and tracking the core metrics around your efforts will provide a wealth of valuable information as you continue to move forward.

The Current State of Podcasting Metrics

Measuring the success of your podcast, however, may not be as easy as measuring the effectiveness of an email campaign or an online advertisement. This is because, during the time this book was written, the field of podcasting metrics was still developing; at present there are no agreed-upon industry standards or uniform practices for measuring the effectiveness of a podcast.

This is not to imply that podcasts are not being measured, monitored, and tracked. In fact, that is not the case at all; almost everyone who is publishing a podcast is tracking it on some level, using a handful of metrics available today. The question becomes, then, how effective are those metrics? In earlier chapters, we discussed several things to consider when developing your metrics strategy. Your metrics should somehow represent the success or achievement of your podcast's objective and provide a means to measure how close you are to that goal.

Podcasters have established a variety of ways to measure their goals, but since no podcast is exactly alike, and since not everyone has the same objective, what works for one podcaster may not work for another. Additionally, since there is a lack of uniformity, comparing metrics can be extremely difficult. For example, most podcasters agree that tracking the number of downloads their podcast has is a reasonable metric that applies industry-wide. However, how downloads are actually being defined can vary. For example, some define a "download" as the download of the file by a listener, regardless of whether the download completes or not. Others may argue that a true download is not only a complete transfer of the file from the host to the user, but also the opening and listening or viewing of a particular file (i.e., consumption).

You can see where this can get confusing. Similar arguments surround the other metrics used by podcasters. The contentious nature of podcasting metrics is not necessarily a disadvantage, however. Instead, it reflects the growing pains that are inherent to any burgeoning industry, and as podcasters continue to try new metrics and question the accuracy of existing definitions, eventually a standard will emerge that is both stable and precise.

Governing Firms

By now you are probably thinking that surely this cannot be as big of a challenge as it sounds. After all, other social media tools have established various performance indicators, and the Internet itself has built a strong, solid arsenal of metrics that can be tailored and applied to the various functions and uses of the Web. So what, then, is prohibiting podcasting from developing streamlined metrics like traditional media and online marketing and the Internet as a whole?

Two major hurdles are resources and research data. Podcasting is a relatively new addition to the new media landscape, and as such, it does not have the same luxury of experience as many related mediums have. Other mediums that have been around much longer have had time to build a track record and experiment with different metrics until the best ones were standardized. Consequently, by the time the business world realized the value of these tools, they were already reaping data and had statistics to back up their efforts.

As these other mediums continued to grow, Internet research and marketing firms began collecting data with standardized metrics throughout the entire industry. Now, with regards to the majority of the Internet industry there are these "governing bodies" that hold the reins to metric standards and analysis. ComScore and Neilsen//NetRatings are examples of firms that conducts in-depth research and analysis of Web traffic, audience demographics, online advertising, and various other services.

COMPANY PROFILE: NIELSEN//NETRATINGS

Nielsen//NetRatings is a global company that reports on nearly 70 percent of the world's Internet usage. Research is conducted using the same methodology and standards worldwide. The advantage of using the same methods globally is that it establishes the foundation for comparing trends and usage regardless of which country is being evaluated.

The company uses a variety of methodologies depending on the information being obtained, using the best methods for the most accurate data. This data is used to track demographics, Internet usage, advertising research, streaming media, consumer habits, and much more.

Nielsen//NetRatings is a highly reputable source for Internet statistics and data, largely because of its proven and consistent methodology. Its acquisition of this data allows them to effectively track and research those trends that matter most to advertisers and businesses.

These organizations offer a host of resources and collective market research data that is currently unavailable to podcasters. This is primarily due to the fact that these organizations have been addressing metrics from a mass audience model, whereas in contrast podcasting requires assessment within and between thousands of distinct niche demographics. Second, because some podcasts are designed to monetize these niches, the economic support for providing these services on a widespread level simply may not exist. That said, the industry as a whole is working diligently to provide a way to measure the niche aspect that podcasting metrics bring to the table. We will discuss this further later in this chapter.

Many of the firms that offer market research on Web mediums can offer comparisons between your company's efforts and campaigns and those of your competitors. Such reporting can indicate your market share compared to your competition, or offer a breakdown of revenue being driven by online marketing. The data these firms have is crucial in determining consumers' computer usage habits—everything from online purchasing to instant message usage—and provide valuable insight into the kind of consumers that comprise your audience.

Information on the audience you are trying to reach is very important when trying to formulate any communication, but the catch with podcasting is that you need to get information about *your* specific audience because of the niche content-driven nature of podcasts. The information provided by these Internet market research firms tells more about general audience Internet usage than what sort of content they are seeking. Sure, you can target the audience that has purchased a particular product, but that does not give you appropriate information regarding the driving force of your audience.

The podcast industry demands a different kind of measurement, and without a central body to develop an industry standard, it is harder to gauge and compare the success of podcasts. If one podcast is measuring success based on the number of downloads, while a competing podcast is focused on the number of listens, and yet another is tracking the number of listeners that are converted into sales, there is clearly no common ground on which these podcasts can be compared.

Because many advertisers are looking at podcasting as a new potential advertising medium, a great deal of additional pressure is being applied to podcasters to develop some sort of standard similar to cost per thousand (CPM)/impression models for determining advertising rates. This additional pressure, plus podcasters' own needs for developing a standard, is giving rise to efforts like the Podcasting Open Metrics Initiative, a group of individuals within the podcasting industry who have helped start the conversation around the importance of defining standardized metrics. We will discuss this in more depth a bit later in the chapter.

Between formal organizations and industry-based initiatives, it won't be long before a standard means of measuring podcasts emerges. The establishment of standards will help create a uniform system for communicating with advertisers, podcasters, and audiences. The resulting metrics will allow podcasters to compare the success of their efforts with that of your competitors, as well as compare revenue and market share.

At present, however, no such standard exists, and so we must work with what we have available. As you will see as we delve deeper into this chapter, the metrics that are currently in place are, though imperfect, far from meaningless. Furthermore, you will see that a little creativity and ingenuity on your part can result in powerful measurement that is unique and specific to your podcast and your objectives.

Podcasting Metrics Today

There are several metrics used by most podcasters today, even if the definitions of these metrics vary from person to person and from podcast to podcast. These current metrics are likely to help shape the industry standard in measuring and tracking podcasts, and currently offer a very basic means of following certain aspects of your podcast. While newer, more narrowly defined metrics are likely to emerge in the future, there will almost assuredly be a place for the existing metrics in the industry.

Fortunately, many services exist to track the metrics for your podcast, so after you have put all your energy into creating your content you simply need to use the right tools and services that are available to help you with measurement. Throughout this book, we have talked about the value of services like Feedburner, Libsyn and Podtrac in keeping you current with the metrics around your podcast. It is important to recognize that any service you enlist to track your statistics may use different methodologies and so you should be familiar with what they define as a download, how they track really simple syndication (RSS) subscriptions, file requests, and so on.

GREG'S TIP

Each data provider attempts to deliver the most sound and accurate data possible regarding your podcast. Since there is no set industry standard, you should select your provider based on which manner of reporting best suits your needs.

The weight a given metric has for you and your podcast depends very heavily on the goals and objectives you have laid out for your initiative. Below, in no particular order, we will examine some of the most common metrics that are applicable to nearly every podcast. At present, each lacks an accepted industry-wide definition, but as more people and organizations engage in podcasting, the closer we are to arriving at a working solution for each of these metrics.

RSS feed subscribers

We have already discussed in detail what an RSS feed is, how to create one, and how and what can be measured. Still, to gloss over the value of using your RSS feed as a source of metrics that are used today would be a mistake. RSS feed metrics serve as useful metrics in determining the reach of your podcast and the loyalty of your audience. What is even more appealing is that they are quantifiable and measurable.

Not every metric that you will use will be quantitative. Some metrics may be more subjective and have far less substantial roots in regards to measurement. For this reason, having a few quantitative metrics will help add concrete numbers to track and offer direction. RSS feeds are entirely quantifiable, and there are already several services out there that track how many people are subscribing to your podcast.

Knowing the number of people who are subscribing does not indicate how many people are actually listening to your podcast, but it does offer you insight into the number of people who are interested in your content. For someone to take the effort to subscribe your podcast's RSS feed indicates an ongoing interest in the content, and thereby helps you determine the size of the audience your podcast is building. Although the number of RSS subscribers doesn't provide an exact representation of your podcast's market share, it does offer an overview of the core group of individuals you are reaching.

You should also consider evaluating your RSS subscribers over particular windows of time. Your 30-day average of RSS subscribers should increase or decrease proportional to your downloads.

Your RSS subscribers offer only a representation of people who are committed to your content in the sense that they wish to know when updated information is available. RSS hosting service Feedburner currently offers the most detailed snapshot of RSS subscribers as well as how your subscribers are interacting with your content, both text-based content and audio/video (Figure 14.1).

Downloads

Tracking the number of downloads of a podcast is another popular metric. Downloads differ from RSS feeds in that they track the number of times a particular media file is downloaded to an individual's computer. This metric provides a more realistic view of how many people a podcast is actually reaching.

The problem with tracking downloads is that there is no uniform definition of what counts as a download. Some podcasters feel that any attempt made by a user to download the file should count, whether the download is completed or not. The mere intention to access the information makes the download viable in their minds, since there may be things beyond the user's control that interfere with their download (such as a server error).

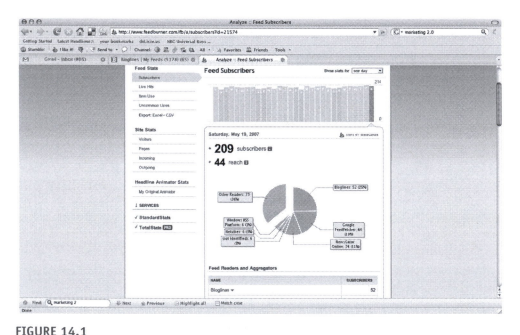

FIGURE 14.1
RSS subscriber metrics as displayed by Feedburner. *Source:* Feedburner.

Some may argue that a partial download clearly cannot be considered a true download. However, such a perception ignores that a listener may have only desired to listen to the beginning portion of the podcast, or perhaps listened to 90 percent of the podcast. Does the fact that the listener did not listen to the podcast from start to finish disqualify their action as a download? As you can see, the issue is not as cut and dried as it initially seems.

Other podcasters, however, believe that a download is truly a download only if the file has been completely and entirely transferred from the host site to the user's system. While this does offer a more focused and firm definition, it may also limit the true scope of a podcast's audience. At present, a commonly accepted means of tracking downloads ties to tracking "unique" downloads. That is to say downloads to specific, unique IP addresses. Providers of tracking information like Libsyn, Feedburner, and Podbridge use this method for measuring downloads (Figure 14.2).

While monitoring downloads to specific IP addresses offers a more specific metric than simply tracking hits or downloads, it has its own set of hurdles to overcome. For instance, a member of your podcast's audience could download your podcast both at home or at work, and each of these computers has a separate IP address. Therefore, your one audience member has now been counted as two, and in turn inflates your numbers. Additionally, in tracking downloads to IP addresses you are not able to determine if the file was completely downloaded—partial downloads are still counted.

As mentioned above, you should also analyze your downloads over specific periods of time. This will give you a good idea of how popular a particular episode is. For example, Chris Penn from the Financial Aid Podcast measures each episode in periods of 1, 7, 30, 90, and 365 days. Penn finds that some of his podcasts become popular long after they have been published.

Measuring downloads offers you great information from podcast to podcast. This metric provides you with data to compare the growth of your

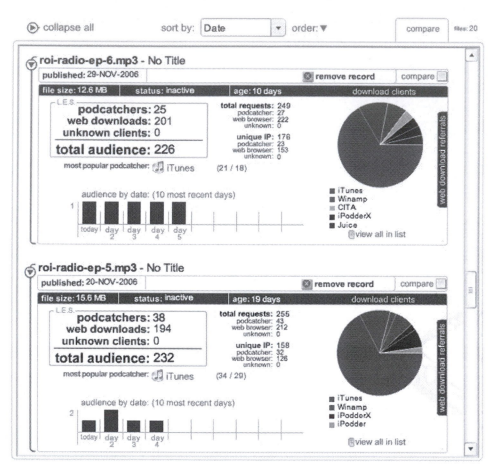

FIGURE 14.2
Sample reporting on unique downloads from Libsyn. *Source*: Libsyn.

audience from each episode. So while it may not be the most perfect metric, measuring downloads is still useful in gaining a general overview of audience size, growth, and trends.

Audience reach

Audience reach is a metric that defines the number of people who have viewed or listened to the content of a podcast within a given time period. The time-dependent component of defining audience reach is what makes it more challenging to develop an industry-wide standard. Furthermore, the complications regarding the definitions of complete vs. partial downloads, and the weight of listens vs. file requests, adds to the difficulty of defining this metric.

Still, determining your podcast's audience reach is crucial for measuring the success of your initiative. Knowing your podcast's reach will help you in determining if you are reaching your desired number of listeners in a given time period—be it a measurement per episode, per week, or per month. Tracking this data will allow you to monitor the growth of your podcast as well as its sustainability.

Knowing these statistics is akin to knowing the circulation of a newspaper or magazine in which you are running an advertisement. Obviously, you want to reach as large an audience as possible within a given time period, since that means your information is reaching more potential consumers or clients. If you are considering having advertisements on your podcast, determining your audience reach is crucial to selling the sponsorship on your podcast. Even if you are not looking to run ads and your podcast is committed solely to your organization's goals and objectives, you should be tracking how many people you are reaching.

GREG'S TIP

Just as with other podcasting metrics, definitions of audience reach vary. Some define it by actual listens, others by downloads. Be certain to be consistent with the way you measure your reach.

Audience reach is also a metric designed to assist in the calculation of return on investment (ROI). Think back to the beginning of your podcasting initiative, when you were initially trying to gain support from the management of your organization. You should be able to provide evidence that your podcast is not only reaching your intended audience, but also yielding a positive ROI. Depending on what your podcasting objective is, how you calculate your ROI will vary, but almost assuredly your audience reach will come into play since it is a measurable unit of people against time.

The challenge with using audience reach as a metric is that it may never reflect the same reach numbers as some traditional forms of media. Because many podcasts appeal to niche markets, the number of people the content will reach is far smaller than for a more general and broadly targeted magazine on fashion, for example. These smaller markets make the figures less impressive size-wise, but no less valuable. A top-rated podcast may be able to reach over one hundred thousand people in a week, but these are podcasts like National Public Radio (NPR) and other well-branded, long established programs. At the same time, podcasts such as Queso Compuesto (www.quesocompuesto.com) and Marketing Over Coffee (www.marketingovercoffee.com) may only reach one or two thousand people a week, but those listeners comprise classic niche audiences whose members share many of the same characteristics and so are potentially quite valuable to the right advertisers.

As standard metrics emerge for downloads and subscriptions, the metrics defining audience reach will also become more solidified. A standardized metric will enable you to calculate more accurate ROI as well as measure your podcast against the successes and failures of your competitors.

Engagement

When measuring the success of a podcast, many podcasters now turn to engagement metrics to determine the value and strength of their content. Engagement means different things to different podcasters, but in general, it is a means of tracking and measuring the level of interest, participation, and actions of your audience.

Some podcasters simply depend on metrics such as RSS feeds and downloads to evaluate the overall measurement of their podcast. Others track more unconventional means of participation, such as new leads, sales, or blog posts and online conversations that have started as a result of their own content and efforts. Regardless of how a podcaster tracks engagement, their objective is the same—to measure how actively their audience is engaging with, absorbing, and spreading their content.

The Word of Mouth Marketing Association (WOMMA), an association dedicated to setting standards in order to encourage the use of word of mouth marketing as a medium, has actually defined a framework for measurement, and has defined a popular metric dubbed a WOMunit or a "Word of Mouth unit." This metric is defined as a unit of marketing-relevant information, describing the process of how a message is passed from one consumer to another. This can be through a conversation, a comment on a message board, an email, a blog post, etc. WOMunits are very relevant when thinking about the various ways to measure your podcasts effect in the marketplace.

GREG'S TIP

Tracking the number of times individuals post comments on your blog or in a forum, or write blog posts about you or your organization, are key metrics around engagement. Use tools like Technorati (www.technorati.com) and Google Blog Search (blogsearch.google.com) to search the blogosphere and see when and where you or your organization is mentioned.

There are several organizations that are actively involved in measuring engagement and influence around the Web. WOMMA and Nielsen BuzzMetrics are helping to move measurement forward in this space, and companies like Buzzlogic and Visible Technologies are offering dashboards that can show companies what is being said about them in blogs, social networks, and other consumer-generated media outlets. A popular tool to search the blogosphere is Technorati (www.technorati.com), which allows you to search by term or tag. This is a great way to see where, when, and how you or your organization is being discussed or referenced.

Podcasters using engagement metrics also often encourage communication between their listeners and the host. We talked about these in detail in the last chapter. They may be using wikis, blogs, audio comments, or any variety of ways to get listeners to not only listen to their podcast but also actively contribute to the generation of new content and share ideas amongst themselves and the producer. Engagement in this case can be measured by how often listeners contribute, what they are contributing, and the size of the community that not only listens to your content but does actually engage beyond that. Tracking metrics such as these gives you insight into the popularity and consumption of your podcast's content. Knowing the frequency and means of your audience's contributions defines the success of your podcast in terms of participation.

Engagement as a metric adds supplemental data to the tracking of growth and involvement of your audience. From this data can come useful information regarding the demographics of your group, as well as crucial input regarding listener habits. All of this data has a use in measuring the success of your podcast and even developing a means of calculating ROI.

Web analytics

Another source of metrics for your podcast is looking at your Web analytics—the base information you would want to know for any Web property that you create. What Web analytics refers to is the number of times your podcast's Web site is visited, how many hits and page views it receives, what resources are being accessed, and how people are finding your site. This type of information is essential to any online medium since it provides basic but necessary data regarding traffic and user habits.

Obtaining these metrics is fairly easy and very affordable. There are many service providers that track this data, such as Google Analytics and WebTrends. Some services, like Google Analytics, are free to use, and others produce software for purchase or licensing. Most companies have at least one of these programs in place to track this data, be it a free service or an enterprise software program. The reason for obtaining this data is that it will allow you to assess different components of your podcasting initiative on a macro level from broader data covering basic actions of your audience.

By tracking the number of visits, hits, and downloads, you are able to determine several different things. For one, you can determine your conversion rate from visits into actual downloads of your podcast. This sort of data will help you determine your strengths and weaknesses, showing where you are capturing visitors and where you may be losing them.

Web analytics also allows you to track where your audience is. This is a key metric for two major reasons. One is that you want to make sure that you are reaching your target audience in the right geographic region. The Internet is a global tool, so even if you are targeting a US market there is nothing prohibiting people in Asia or Europe from accessing the same information. Tracking who is accessing your content and in what part of your country or the world helps you ensure that you are reaching your target as well as help you expand your reach into new areas.

The other important reason for knowing your audience's geographical location is that you can continually optimize your content. If you are specifically interested in reaching an audience that is located in the Mid-Western US, then tracking the number of people in that region who are downloading your content is extremely important. From the data that is returned, you can then fine-tune your content to reach even more individuals in that particular region.

Web analytics are useful no matter what your podcasting objective is. Numbers indicating positive Web traffic, numerous hits on supplemental information, and various resources being accessed all serve toward building the platform to engage your audience and disseminate your podcast in the most effective manner. Without this basic data offered by Web analytics software and programs, you will find yourself lacking key information for improving your understanding of other performance indicators. Web analytics not only offers valuable information, but also enhances the quality of the data you obtain through other metrics.

Listener habits

Listener habits include such things as the time of day that a podcast is downloaded, when it is consumed, where a listener is downloading the content, and even how they respond to what they have listened to. This sort of data is obtained through various tools like the ones we have just discussed, or through specific programs that are embedded in the podcast file itself and are designed to track specific user habits.

Knowing the most popular time of day that your podcast is downloaded can give you an idea as to the age group of your audience, since the younger generation would be more apt to download right after school or very late at night, whereas the older working crowd may download more frequently during the work day or late evening.

New advances in software and algorithms enable podcasters to track not only when a podcast is downloaded, but also when it is listened to. This is a crucial piece of data because it not only offers you real numbers regarding how often your content is actually consumed, but also when and how people are consuming. You are able to distinguish if the file has been transferred to a portable player, or whether it was simply played while the listener was seated at their computer. The value behind this sort of data is that it allows you to see how your listeners actually listen. If you find that your audience typically transfers your podcast to portable device, you can conclude that they are a mobile, on-demand audience, and can then build your content in a way that is more conducive to listening on the go. The more you can tailor your content to suit your audience, the more engaged and committed they will be to your podcast.

Measuring Success and Effectiveness

Obviously, the standardization of these metrics will be critical to the future of podcasting. The goal is to accurately measure the success and effectiveness of podcasting as an industry. Even after a standard means of measuring podcasting emerges, you will need to consider what will be the most effective way of measuring success for *your* podcast.

There are many different ways to use the metrics listed above to measure your own success. If you take some time and explore the organizations that provide tracking and monitoring services, you will see that in the reporting they offer there are several different charts, stats, and graphs that explain what is happening with your podcast and, in some cases, your brand. Sticking with some of the more popular metrics, you will find that almost all of these reports keep close tabs on the number of downloads and subscribers that are following your podcast.

These particular statistics allow you to measure your efforts based largely on growth. Following the growth of your audience gives you an indication as to the popularity of your content as well as the reach that you have into your market. The statistics offered up by downloads allows you to gauge the size of your audience beyond your subscriber base. Metrics such as these are often very useful when trying to assess the success of a podcast geared toward educating or increasing brand image. In these situations, you are most often just trying to raise awareness about your organization, be it through free information or tips that appeal to the consumer market that you are targeting. Thus, the continued growth of that audience illustrates success on the part of your podcast initiative.

There are various ways you can tell if these sales have come from your podcast or if they are related to other factors. Linking sales to your podcast requires some sort of call to action on the part of your consumer, and when there is a call to action there should be a clear way of tracking it. For instance, you can direct those who listen to your podcast to a Web site that is only mentioned and publicized through your podcast. Any transactions that occur on that site can then be linked back to your podcast. Another option would be to include a promotion or easy-to-remember code in your podcast. Again, since this information will only be available to those who are listening to your podcast, the sales that include this particular code or promotion can be directly linked to your podcast.

Success can also be defined in terms of listener loyalty, active subscriptions, and audience participation. Developing a loyal audience is just as much a measure of success as continually reaching new listeners. Listener loyalty indicates that listeners engage with and prefer your content. Tracking not only how many listeners you have, but how many continue to download your content from episode to episode, shows that you have produced a quality production that is connecting with an audience.

Overall, the success of your podcast can only be measured against the goals and objectives you had laid out initially. The metrics that exist can all be used in some way to express a measurement of your acquisition of these goals, and certainly some metrics will be better suited to that task than others. What is essential for measuring your podcast is defining which metrics will reflect your results most accurately, and the best way to achieve this is to define what your ROI should be.

Defining ROI for Your Organization

In defining your podcast objectives, you should also be thinking of how to measure the ROI for your podcast. Depending on your objective, establishing your ROI could be as simple as tracking the number of downloads or the size of your subscriber base. Or, tracking your ROI may need to be more complex, combining the use of several metrics and creativity on your part.

Earlier in this book, we looked at ways that some organizations are employing a little ingenuity in creating metrics for measuring the success of their podcast. Think back to Chris Penn, who can directly track the number of loans generated by his Financial Aid Podcast due to the leads he captures by sending listeners to his own specific affiliated Web sites. This is a prime example of how an organization can develop a metric that measures exactly what the podcast was intended to do—in this case, generate leads that lead to closed loans.

Obviously this is a metric that cannot be applied industry-wide, but not every measurement needs to apply to every podcast. Instead, when you are determining your ROI you need to consider what will offer you the most comprehensive and accurate reflection of how your podcast is doing against your goals. So what does ROI mean for you, your organization, and your podcast?

Your ROI for your podcast will depend on how you answer several questions. What was your goal in launching a podcast? Were you looking to promote a new product? Was your goal to reach a new demographic within your market? Did you simply want to build customer loyalty? Additionally, once you have reflected on your objective, you need to answer one more question: *Is producing your podcast worth it?*

Not every podcasting initiative will be a success. Some attempts may be overly ambitious, and others may not be given the attention and care that they needed to be a success. Thus, in calculating your ROI you need to consider the costs, the time, and the effort that went into building your podcast and then compare that to the results. Initially, your results may lead you to believe that podcasting is not worth the effort, since the first few months your numbers will likely be rather low. Keep in mind that it takes time to build a podcast audience, particularly since the medium is still so new to consumers and businesses alike.

ROI will vary from business to business. Fortunately, the costs of podcast production are usually rather low, particularly compared to traditional marketing, sales, and public relations campaigns. Still, you want to be sure that the efforts and funds you are putting forth are yielding results. To return to the example of the Financial Aid Podcast, the number of loans generated by the podcasts is very small when compared to the number of loans produced by its parent, The Student Loan Network. However, the costs of producing the podcast are so small that it is worth the time and effort to continue putting out episodes.

Ultimately when you are determining the ROI for your podcast, it comes down to the same principles that an organization needs to ask itself when dealing with any expenditure. The benefits of producing the information should outweigh the physical costs, whether these benefits are financial in nature or express themselves in stronger consumer relations. Only your organization can decide if the ROI is strong enough to continue on a given course—just be sure that the way you calculate your ROI is an accurate reflection of your efforts and your results.

Industry Initiatives for Defining Standardized Measurement

To help you determine the best metrics to use and various ways to calculate ROI, the podcasting industry is working arduously to put forth standards that provide that data in a clear and measurable way. As we discussed earlier in this chapter, podcasting as an industry does not have a host of firms that track and develop metrics for it. Rather, definitions are still organic and podcasters are constantly testing new ways to measure and define their metrics. So who better to turn to when looking to create an industry standard than the podcasters themselves?

Podcasting Open Metrics Initiative

The Podcasting Open Metrics Initiative (www.openmetrics.org) is an effort that was spawned by a group of individuals in 2006 that recognized the importance of establishing standard metrics for podcasting. They saw that individual podcasters lacked the data necessary to persuade advertisers that podcasting offers a viable niche market that can be successfully used to promote goods and services. Additionally, these same individuals noted that standardized metrics would enable collaboration, comparison, and discussion of podcasting efforts in a way that is currently escaping the industry. The Podcasting Open Metrics Initiative is not unique in these observations, but they were one of the first to note and suggest that the conversation around industry-wide standardization get started.

Open Metrics has emerged as a movement to help make podcasting a more marketable and measurable industry—and thereby more lucrative for everyone involved. Because podcasting lacks a common means of comparing shows and defining audience reach, it is difficult to convince advertisers to look at not only the quantitative value of a show, but also the qualitative value. The qualitative impact of a podcast can be worth far more than the numbers, since a podcast with a small audience may actually be the authority for that group—and thus advertisers would be wise to capitalize on that particular show. But many still remain skeptical, unwilling to look beyond the numbers.

The proposed path Open Metrics has chosen to follow is a three-phase program involving different levels of demographic data that will be obtained at different times. Phase One is the most basic step and will help lay the foundation for the other two phases to blossom. What is involved in Phase One is the collection of standard data to accurately represent both the number of downloads per week and month and also create a truly universal means of measuring the number of subscribers each podcast has.

The most important goal of Phase One is for a standard metric to emerge. While naturally the most accurate measurement is being sought, it is more important that this metric be uniform across the industry. If the metric that emerges does not measure every single download for a podcast, but is accurate enough to the point that all podcasters adopt it, then this metric would be far more useful and successful than more accurate one that is not accepted industry-wide. Developing this comparable, standard metric will open the door for organizations and advertisers to look at two podcasts side by side and compare different aspects of them in a truly measurable way. For organizations, this means a better idea of where your podcast stands when compared to your competitors as well as essential information for tracking the growth of your audience.

The second proposed phase will focus on more specific demographic data (Figure 14.3). The data to be collected and standardized in Phase Two will include such categories as gender, age, household income, and marital status. Naturally, there are other components—such as the number of children in a household and education level—to be factored in, and this is the sort of data that will be added as the initiative moves forward. With this information, podcasters will be better able to define their markets, thereby helping them target the audience they desire as well as potentially attract advertisers.

Phase Three will move a step beyond the second stage and seek out psychographic data. This data will be even more valuable to podcasters and advertisers alike, since psychographic data encompasses aspects of consumer habits such as what they buy, when they buy, and their preferred buying method. The data will also incorporate components of audience demographics such as their personal interests and hobbies. Again, this makes podcasting more marketable as a medium for advertisers, businesses, and organizations alike.

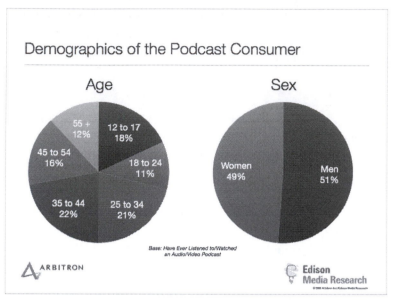

FIGURE 14.3
Demographic data of podcast listeners in March 2007, as obtained by Edison Media Research by survey. *Source*: Edison Media Research—"2007 Podcast Presentation" March 2007.

The Open Metrics Initiative is still very young and has a long road ahead of it. As I mentioned, the Open Metric's group has served primarily as a conversation starter around the importance of this standardization. Further progress may be made through another organization's efforts, one that can dedicate more time and resources to this initiative. That group, the Association for Downloadable Media, (www.downloadablemedia.org), was coming together as this book went to press and was scheduled to be announced in the summer of 2007. Its goal will be to support independent podcasters, publishers, tools, vendors, agencies, and marketers in order to increase the effectiveness and efficiency of advertising and sponsoring downloadable media across multiple platforms by creating standardized ad units, reporting, and audience measurement for the industry.

Because of this eagerness and willingness to work collectively to arrive at a solution, these initiatives promise to work by delivering an industry standard that allows for the measurement of podcasting. Quantifying the efforts of podcasters and their shows is critical for the medium to reach its full potential as a mainstream form of communication between organizations and their audiences.

> **GREG'S TIP**
>
> To learn more about the proposed initiative from the Podcasting Open Metrics Initiative, visit the Web site at www.openmetrics.org. Also, look out for more information from the newly formed Association for Downloadable Media.

Lessons Learned

- Podcasting does not have universally defined metrics nor independent firms controlling existing metrics and research. However, the metrics that are in place are functional and are actively being crystallized by the industry.

- The metrics that indicate the success of your podcast don't necessarily relate to the size of your podcast or the number of subscribers, but rather the attainment of your goals and objectives.

- Calculating your ROI will require that you draw upon several metrics and perhaps develop your own custom metric for determining the cost–benefit analysis necessary.

- Podcasters are working with advertisers, public relations firms, and other industries in a joint effort to define metrics from within the industry in a manner that meets the demands of all parties involved.

Making Money with Your Podcast

Tim Bourquin

In the course of creating and producing your podcast, you've probably spent time considering how much it's going to cost in time, money, and personnel resources. Depending on what your overall podcasting objectives are you may want to monetize your content. This chapter will show you how to make your podcast pay for itself and even generate a profit.

A podcast doesn't have to be considered an expense line-item on the budget. With a little planning and extra focus on generating revenue, a podcast can also be an income line item. Obviously, adding additional income to the bottom line is always an easier sell to upper management than adding additional expenses. Making your podcast pay for itself will make the job of convincing your colleagues and bosses to back a podcasting initiative a much easier task. Even if you are only using your podcast as a marketing tool for your company, I would urge you to consider it an asset—an asset that can be leveraged to generate income.

This chapter will help you think about your podcast in ways you may not have considered in the past. You may initially think the money spent to create your podcast would fall under the marketing and advertising budget. It's true, of course, that your podcast will generate awareness for your products and services and even generate direct sales—the very definition of marketing and advertising. It would be a mistake, however, to lump in your podcast with other traditional advertising such as magazine ads or Web banners. Podcasts differ from those ads in a very important way: it is content that can be leveraged in many different ways.

Thinking Differently About Your Podcast

When a magazine ad is designed and submitted to the publisher, the ad runs and gives you exposure to the publisher's audience. The publisher controls access to that audience and you can only reach them again by writing another check to the publisher to run the ad in the following month's issue. The same is true for Web site banners, radio and television ads, and billboards. All of these media are middlemen between you and the audience you want to reach.

Podcasting effectively allows you to cut out the middleman and build an audience for your own content. You can then reach out and "talk" to this audience as frequently as you desire without having to pay a middleman additional dollars to reach that audience on a regular basis.

I don't mean to infer that the end of traditional advertising is near. On the contrary, it takes a great deal of effort to build any audience, so sometimes it's just easier and more cost effective to advertise with someone that has already spent the time, money, and resources to build an audience you want to target rather than building your own. I am, however, saying that your organization should be doing both—building your own audience with your podcast and reaching out through existing content creators who also have the attention of your customers and prospects.

This chapter will not only show you how to build your own audience, but also have the efforts pay for themselves and even generate profit. Imagine that!

> When you are proposing a podcast, don't forget to mention the fact that cutting out the middlemen between you and your customer will result in savings that can offset any expenses needed to produce the content!

Advertising efforts that go from the expense side of the budget to the income side of the budget are not a totally new idea. For many years, AM radio has sold airtime to "hosts" who deliver content that is educational but in essence is an infomercial for the "hosts" services.

Consider the example of a mortgage company that buys time on a local AM radio station on a Sunday afternoon. The mortgage company pays a flat fee for the airtime and then does a call-in show where homeowners and homeowner hopefuls ask questions about how to apply for a mortgage, how to improve their credit score, and things to look for when shopping for a loan. Each week during the show, the host mentions his company name numerous times and even takes a few of the station break ads for themselves to run 30-second spots. The remaining spots, the company sells to related but non-competitive services like title and escrow companies, real estate agents, and home inspection services. If they do it right, the mortgage company not only breaks even on the cost of the airtime, but actually makes a profit.

This same thought process and revenue model can and should be applied to your podcasting efforts. You are creating valuable content and building an audience that others will want to reach as well. This is not to say that you should design your podcast to mimic the format of traditional radio and immediately go out and try to sell 30-second ad spots. After all, podcasting has grown so quickly, in part, because listeners are tired of hearing so many commercials on traditional radio. Instead, I want you to start thinking about your podcast as an asset and not a liability—an asset that you can leverage to bring in direct and indirect dollars.

Every Company is Now A Media Company

Now that you have begun to think about your podcast as a revenue source rather than an expense, you should also begin thinking of your company as a media enterprise, regardless of what you sell or service. This is not as far a leap as you may first think. Everyone from plumbers to airlines have been creating interactive media since the beginning of the Internet. Your company Web site is media, and few people would consider starting any business these days without a Web site. A podcast is simply another weapon in your media arsenal to capture the attention of your prospects and customers and increase sales.

Companies that have had success monetizing their podcasts and attracting a listening audience quickly have done five things right. I call them the five "E's" of podcasting:

Entertain

Your podcast must be more than just a scripted rundown of the features and benefits of your product or service. No matter the subject, you've got to find a way to entertain your audience or they'll stop listening. Interviews are an easy way to do this quickly because a conversation between two people is always more interesting than listening to one person blather on for the entire show. The more you can make your podcast sound like a conversation between people in a coffee shop, where you allow everyone else to "eavesdrop" on your chat, the more entertaining it will be.

Engage

I'd like to be able to say that you have several chances to get it right, that if you start off slow, people will stick around to see if your podcast gets interesting. That's just not reality. You've got to capture your listener's attention within the first 20–30 seconds or they will simply stop playing the podcast and move on. Don't wait to get into the "meat" of your show— do it immediately and tell your listeners they are about to learn something they can use right away to improve their business.

Educate

Let's face it—no matter how fascinating or relevant we think our company's products or services are, no one is going to subscribe to a 20- or 30-minute commercial each week. You may fool a few people into listening for a while, but in the end you will lose them because your content is nothing more than a sales pitch. You've got to educate and inform the audience from start to finish while ensuring that you get your message out.

Easy to Consume

Don't make the listener hunt around on your site for the link to the MP3 file. Give the link front and center attention and if possible, make your podcast play in a variety of formats such as Windows Media and RealAudio. You can find a free white paper on this to read (or hand to your IT department) here: http://www.newmediaexpo.com/whitepapers/Making_the_Most_of_Your_MP3_File.pdf.

TIM'S TIP

In many surveys, podcasters find that more than 60 percent of their listeners play the content straight from the creator's Web site rather than on a portable device. This is why it is critical to make it easy to listen to on your Web site in addition to on an iPod or MP3 player.

Encourage Action

This is where most podcasts fail. Companies can do an amazing job of fulfilling the goals of the first four "E's" and then forget this last one. Every podcast you produce should ask the listener to take some sort of action after (or while) listening. Whether that is visiting a certain page on your Web site, submitting an email address, completing a survey, or simply leaving a comment, you need to make sure the listener begins to communicate back with you on a regular basis. Even if the action is simply clicking a radio button that responds to the "poll of the week," it keeps your audience engaged and the two-way street of communication alive.

Start by having your listeners complete small tasks and get them used to being asked for action on their part. Without the final "E," your podcast will fail to provide the results you and your bosses are looking for no matter what your goals are.

Direct Revenue Streams from Your Podcast

Now that you are creating compelling content that can be monetized by meeting the goals of each of the five "E's," it's time to start generating revenue.

DANGER ZONE

You may be hesitant to begin taking sponsors or selling a product via the podcast for fear of it getting in the way of the original message you are trying to convey with the show. It's a valid point. Part of the challenge of making money with podcasts is that people are drawn to this type of niche content precisely because they have grown tired of the constant screaming advertisements in traditional media.

An Arbitron "Spot Study" conducted for the radio industry in 2005 found the following:

- **Eighty-four percent of radio listeners think that listening to commercials is a fair price for free programming.**

However...

- **Thirty-four percent of radio listeners find that radio ads become so "annoying" and "intrusive" they sometimes turn it off (it's 38 percent if the survey respondent owned an MP3 player!).**

And not surprisingly...

- **The younger the audience the more they find ads intolerable.**

Traditional radio stations have a tremendous amount of overhead and therefore have to run a great deal more commercials in order to turn a profit. Furthermore, because the audience demographic is so varied, only very general advertisements for things that nearly every listener is a potential customer for (think mortgages, cars, or diet and nutritional supplements).

We get annoyed by the advertisements not only because of their frequency in interrupting the content we're really interested in hearing such as music or talk, but

I would argue it is mostly because 90 percent of the advertisements are for things we are not in the market for at that moment. You might be looking for a new car or a mortgage once every few years. For the 1 percent of the listeners who *are* ready to buy at that moment, it's a welcome notification. For 99 percent of the rest of us, it is simply an annoyance to endure until the real content comes back on.

What this means is that podcasters need to be careful about how they place advertisements in their shows so that they don't alienate the very audience that has come to them out of frustration with other media.

However podcasters have several unique advantages over traditional media:

1 Overhead is lower and therefore podcasters can run fewer commercials and still break even or even profitable.

2 The audience is much more focused, and therefore the podcaster can attract advertisers that are relevant to the entire audience, greatly reducing the "annoyance factor."

Using our previous example, if you're not in the market for a new car, you tend to ge annoyed with those ads because you have no reason to be interested. However, if your podcast was for those listeners who are looking for new car information, that same annoying ad now becomes a needed information your audience is open to receiving.

Another example can be found with a podcast I started and later sold, EndurancePlanet.com. This podcast for triathletes, marathon runners, and adventure race teams has a very narrow audience. Only people who are truly interested in endurance sports are subscribing and regularly tuning in. Normally, an advertisement for a new sports drink that, in tests, showed that triathletes could swim, run, and bike 12 percent faster during races would be a waste of time and get lost on traditional radio—an annoyance for 99 percent of the listeners. For the EndurancePlanet.com podcast, however, the 1 percent of the target audience from a traditional radio model is 100 percent of the listener base. The advertisement is seen as a valuable information that is of interest to every single listener.

It's great for the listener because the advertisement isn't an unrelated and annoying interruption. It's great for the advertiser, because they know every penny spent will reach the target audience and not be wasted in a shotgun approach to marketing. It's great for the podcaster, because they now act as a gateway to a valuable audience that can be monetized in literally hundreds of ways.

All this is to say that you can be confident that if you reach out to the right advertise or sponsor, your audience will not abandon your show because of the annoyance factor.

SIDE NOTE

Listeners will respond better to your sponsor messages when you ask them personally to do so! Letting them know sponsors will help keep the content free, will remind them to click on sponsor ads, and buy their products whenever possible.

Once you've made the decision to sell sponsorships in your podcast, the question then becomes, "Do I use one of the several advertising services to get sponsorship or do I sell my own?"

Ad Networks

Much like the popular Google AdSense service, where anyone can sign up for an account and begin showing ads on a Web site that are relevant (theoretically) to the words it finds on the site, you can leave the work of actually getting advertisers to someone else.

If you have a Web site or a blog, you may have already tried one of these ad services. Google acts as your salesperson, attracting advertisers to the search engine and network of millions of Web sites and blogs that agree to show the ads and receive a small portion of what the advertiser has paid. You don't have to pick up the phone and "dial for dollars" or ask anyone for money.

The trouble is that, although there's no work on your part other than pasting some html code into your Web site, you may also find out that the service generates just a few dollars each month. In fact, it may generate so little revenue for the Web site owner that it's just not worth giving the ads the space they take up on the site at all. Sure, there are some folks out there that make thousands of dollars each month. But for the vast majority of content owners, it's chump change at best.

Typically, if you are willing to "pound the pavement" a bit, knock on some doors, and make phone calls to advertisers you think are the right fit, you'll be able to make more money selling the advertising on your own. Most podcasters, however, aren't willing or don't have the time to dedicate to sales efforts, so the new podcasting ad networks are probably their best bet.

Podcast ad networks operate a bit differently than Google AdSense, in that most I've spoken with are out pitching in front of potential advertisers, either directly or through their ad agencies, in an effort to get advertisers on board for their network. They are starting to get traction in convincing advertisers of the value of advertising in new media but getting consistent renewals month after month has been a challenge.

Podcast Ad Networks

These are some of the services that have already booked advertising dollars for independent podcasters.

Blubrry: www.Blubrry.com

Blubrry negotiates advertising deals for podcasters that are members of the blubrry podcast directory. Blubrry is owned by Raw Voice.

Kiptronic: www.Kiptronic.com

Kiptronic's Podcast Marketplace is an open-access podcast sponsorship network designed to put the podcaster in the driver's seat. Includes free Promo Exchange service whereby podcasters can exchange promotional ads for each other's shows. Can be used with any hosting services where Kiptronic's Apache module can be installed such as Libsyn.com.

Podango: www.Podango.com

Podango monetizes niche-focused networks of podcasts called Podango Stations. Each station is put together by a station owner/director (the podcaster). Revenue comes from both station- and podcast-level sponsorships. The company offers potential sponsors ad creation services, and campaign tracking tools. Seventy percent of the revenue is split according to agreements between station directors and the podcasters on their stations.

Podtrac: www.Podtrac.com

Connects podcasters with advertisers. Specializes in highly targeted podcast advertising, by precisely matching audience demographics and interests with the appropriate advertising for those listeners and viewers. Company actively solicits major

SIDE NOTE

advertising agencies to entice their clients to advertise within the podcasts the company represents. Also includes audience survey tools for podcasters.

SIDE NOTE **RadioTail: www.RadioTail.com**

RadioTail works with podcasts that have highly focused content and engaged audiences. Their technology takes care of rotating ad spots and tracking campaigns, so podcasters and advertisers can get the statistics they need to understand their return on investment (ROI).

Each service has its own pros and cons so be sure to contact each to determine which is the best fit for your podcast. The choice boils down to this: if you are willing to make sales calls in addition to creating your content you should sell your own sponsorships. If the thought of sales makes you cringe, then the networks are the best place to go to generate revenue. Let them make the calls on your behalf and just concentrate on creating great podcasts.

Note: At the time of this writing, Google is rumored to be developing audio ad insertion for podcasts that is similar to their Google AdSense program. Google recently purchased dMarc, which allows radio stations and advertisers to connect for advertising spots. Adapting the technology for podcasts would seem to be an inevitable step and will probably be launched by the end of 2007.

Selling Your Own Sponsorships and Advertising

One reason to sell your own sponsorships is that you already have relationships and connections within the industry subject you are covering in your podcast. Chances are you already know the players in the industry and can make a pitch to people who already know you. If this is the case, start with those current relationships and work your way out from there.

WARNING

Important Note: Keep in mind that you are not just selling mentions in the podcast itself. You also have value in the accompanying Web site, in an email newsletter (which I always suggest podcasters should have), and the really simple syndication (RSS) feed that carries your podcast to the audience!

You'll need two tools in order to sell sponsorships:

1. A media kit
2. An advertising agreement

The media kit

A media kit tells the advertiser what your show is about, who listens, and why they should advertise with you. It also outlines the various choices the advertiser has when it comes to advertising on your Web site and podcast.

Media buyers and marketing managers are used to asking for information packaged this way, so having a media kit will show you are serious about your content and that you are conducting your podcast as a true media business. Magazines, radio, and Web sites have been using media kits for many years to attract business and showcase their properties to prospects in a positive way.

> **Your first sales efforts for sponsorship should start with companies you already have a relationship with. If you are not sure where to start, make the "sponsor" your own company products or services so that sponsors who may happen to be listening will understand how they will be promoted if they sponsor your show themselves.**

 **TIM'S TIP**

The media kit doesn't have to be long. In fact, I recommend it be 2–3 pages maximum. Marketing managers are inundated with sales pitches on a daily basis from media properties who want them to advertise. Keep your information short and to the point and the person you are pitching will appreciate that you have not wasted their time. Get to the point but give them all the information they need to make a decision (Figure 15.1).

The media kit should include four sections:

1. *Introduction to the podcast*: This section gives the advertiser general information about your show including its frequency, topics covered, and the format (interviews, stories, etc.)

••• General Information •••

TraderInterviews.com is a unique online audio media company. We interview active traders, technical analysts, hedge fund managers, tax accountants and risk management experts about all aspects of short-term securities and forex trading. The interviews are then streamed online, available as podcasts and archived on the site for one year. The mission of TraderInterviews.com is to educate, inform and entertain active traders and investors in order to help them make more consistently profitable trading decisions.

Over 5,000 traders (unique visitors) listen to interviews and visit TraderInterviews.com each month. The interviews are available in both streaming and downloadable mp3 format as – giving listeners the ability to either listen while visiting the website, checking email, trading or doing research online. Listeners can also subscribe to the site's RSS feed podcast and interviews are automatically downloaded to their iPod or other mp3 player to listen later while commuting, exercising, or at the office. The interviews are kept between 12 and 15 minutes in duration, as our findings show this to be the "attention span" for most online listeners. At this duration, we find that 86% of all interviews are listened to *in their entirety*.

We offer an interactive way for traders to listen and learn from fellow market enthusiasts who share stories about what has worked and what hasn't in their own trading strategies.

In addition to daily interviews, TraderInterviews.com also produces special multi-part audio presentations on specific topics such as more complex options hedging strategies.

••• Competitive Edge •••

No other website allows advertisers to reach such a highly targeted listening audience of small business

FIGURE 15.1

The TraderInterviews.com podcast media kit.

2 *Your competitive edge*: This section should discuss how you reach out to your listeners and grow, why your show is different from other media and from other podcasts in the same market, and why the advertiser should spend money with you as opposed to or in addition to their existing marketing efforts.

3 *Listener/viewer demographics*: This section should tell the advertiser who your audience is and why they listen. If you have not already surveyed your audience, this is the reason to do it now. There are several good Web-based survey tools available including SurveyMonkey.com and Zoomerang.com. Advertisers will want to know more about your listener than just how much money they make and where they live. You should include no less than five but no more than ten survey question responses that will help the advertiser learn about your audience and determine if it is a proper fit for their products and services.

Advertising rates: This section tells the advertiser how much a sponsorship costs and what is included with each ad buy. List out very clearly what the advertiser gets for their investment.

We'll talk about how much you should consider charging for sponsorship in a moment. First, let's discuss what you should offer to advertisers.

What to sell

Web sites with text content typically offer a buffet of choices when it comes to advertising and sponsorship. A variety of different banner sizes and placement on the page are offered, each with a different price. This is certainly a legitimate way to offer advertising on your podcast. An advertiser could choose to have just a banner on the sidebar of your site, while another advertiser could choose to purchase a host read 20-second pitch for the advertiser's product or service.

My experience has been, however, that this wasn't of interest to companies I pitched. When I first began pitching companies on advertising on the EnduranceRadio.com podcast for triathletes and marathon runners, I offered a variety of choices ranging from banner ads to audio ads to text links in our weekly email newsletter. I initially thought that the more choices I offered, the better chance I would have of getting the buyer to say "yes" to sponsoring the podcast. My "cafeteria line" of choices was overwhelming and probably confusing to the reader. It lead to "paralysis by analysis" on the advertisers' part because they could never decide which banner, text ad, or audio mention was the right choice.

By offering potential advertisers too many choices, you might actually discourage them from buying ads. A single, focused opportunity like a sponsorship will likely yield more sales. **WARNING**

After 2 weeks of telephone sales calls to at least 60 companies, I finally sold a single lousy banner on the site for 1 month for $250. It just wasn't working.

I decided that there had to be a better way of capturing the attention of the advertiser. I decided offering a single sponsorship for a single episode and packaged everything I had been offering "a la carte" into one large sponsorship package for $500 per show with a four show minimum buy. It was a single choice and the advertiser got an exclusive sponsorship of a single show once per week for 4 weeks. Bingo! It worked—the advertiser now had just one choice—buy or not.

I found out later that the real value that advertisers are looking for these days is exclusivity—not having to share the attention of the listener with any competitors. We've all been to Web sites that look like Las Vegas slot machines with flashing banners and buttons for 12–15 different companies. This not only de-values the advertisement for everyone but overwhelms the content.

Here is what a show sponsorship includes for the podcasts I produce:

- A 20-second host-delivered audio mention of the advertiser's special offer to be run within first 120 seconds of podcast.
- A product mention and thank you by interview host at end of podcast interview.
- A 200 × 33 logo and hotlink on TraderInterviews.com home page.
- A 200 × 33 logo/hotlink in podcast RSS feed.
- A 200 × 33 logo/hotlink in weekly email newsletter.
- A 468 × 60 banner/hotlink on TraderInterviews.com home page in interview block.
- A 468 × 60 banner/hotlink in TraderInterviews.com weekly email newsletter.
- A 468 × 60 banner/hotlink in TraderInterviews.com RSS feed.
- A text hotlink and phone number in "presented by" area of interview display block.
- A text hotlink and phone number in podcast RSS feed.
- A text hotlink and phone number in weekly email newsletter.

- An advertiser-provided 200 × 33 logo/hotlink in podcast RSS feed.

- A text hotlink in email newsletter featuring interviews from previous wee.

- An advertiser-provided 300 × 300 graphic displayed in iTunes while the program plays in iTunes.

- An advertiser-provided 200 × 33 logo and hotlink in Windows Media Player window.

- Advertiser Web site in RealPlayer window.

- Archive of the sponsored interview for at least 1 year with text and advertiser-provided graphic and hotlink.

- Hotlink title and 75-word description of special offer on "Marketplace" page of TraderInterviews.com.

> **TIM'S TIP**
>
> **The more ways you can give sponsors exposure, the better chance they will see results and continue to renew each month.**

As you can see, the audio mention is just one very small part of exposure a sponsor receives. Don't discount the fact that most people still listen to podcasts right on the Web site and that those eyeballs have value! Also, you'll notice that we offer our content in both Windows Media format and RealPlayer format. Each of these players allows you to do some slick things like showing the sponsor's Web site within the player window while the content is playing.

Because of the popularity of iTunes, I found that prospective sponsors ears perked up when I mentioned that their graphic would be visible in iTunes while their sponsored podcast was playing.(see Figure 15.2). Below is a screenshot where GFT is the sponsor of this particular interview:

Figure 15.3 shows the sponsorship in action.

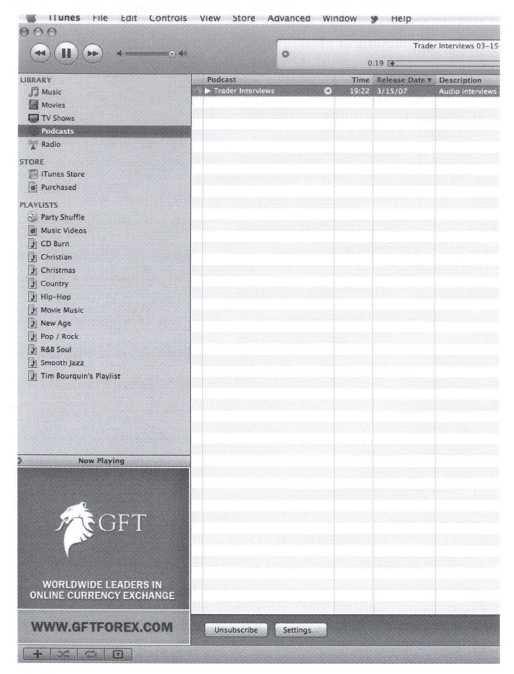

FIGURE 15.2
Sponsors can have their logo shown in iTunes while their sponsored podcast is playing, as shown in the lower left.

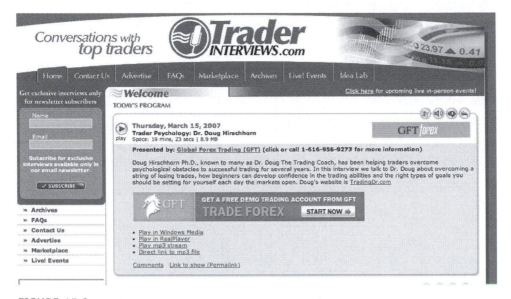

FIGURE 15.3

The TraderInterviews.com home page displaying podcast sponsorship.

By offering a single sponsor per show for a higher price, I was able to greatly increase the value to the advertiser and respect our listeners by not overwhelming them with advertisements. It also resulted in having to make fewer phone calls, because by increasing the minimum buy from $250 to $2000 I was able to sell quality instead of quantity.

The results for the advertisers have been outstanding. Because there is just a sponsor per show, the resulting click-through percentages and sales for the sponsor products and services have been tremendous and we're actually running into the good problem of not having enough inventory of shows to sell. But the beauty of this method is that you can simply do more shows to fulfill the sponsor requests you have. Start by doing one show per week and when that's sponsored, move to two a week and so on.

How to price podcast sponsorship

I get phone calls at my office almost on a daily basis from podcasters who want to know how much they should charge for advertising on their podcast. As with most things in life, the answer is, "it depends." Most podcasters greatly undervalue their shows and the audience they have attracted.

Deciding what to charge is more art than science, but I'm going to guide you in the right direction by first showing you what not to do.

The first thing you need to do is throw the old cost per thousand (CPM) model of determining banner advertising out the window. CPM was used early on with Web sites to standardize for advertisers what they were paying for banner ads. For every one thousand times a banner was viewed on a Web site, the advertiser would pay, for example, $15. The CPM was $15 and the advertiser could then budget how much they wanted to spend. For example if XYZ company had a budget of $30 on the Web site that offered a CPM of $15, the advertiser's banner would be loaded two thousand times. Clicks on the banner were tracked, although the cost was the same no matter how many (or how few) times a Web site user clicked on the banner.

CPM worked well for sites like Yahoo.com and MSN.com because the demographic range of age, income, etc. were so wide that it was impossible to target a specific group. Advertisers paid the requested CPM and hoped that the audience they were hoping to target would click.

For Web sites and podcasts with highly targeted and niche content, the audience is also much targeted and niche. Think of it this way: if your Web site attracted only three visitors a month, you'd never be able to collect enough money on a CPM model to make it worthwhile. There's just not enough traffic coming through to make the numbers work.

But now imagine that those three monthly visitors are Bill Gates, Steve Jobs, and Larry Ellison. How much would advertisers pay you now to get in front of those three CEOs each month? It's an extreme example, of course. But the point is that everyone needs to stop thinking in terms of audience quantity and start thinking about audience quality.

Using the example podcast site of EnduranceRadio.com, we charged $500 per episode with about 5000 downloads per show. This works out to a CPM of $100! When advertisers were trying to compare "apples to apples" they'd say, "we only have to pay $15 per thousand on Yahoo.com—why are you so much more expensive?" The answer, of course, is that our audience is

100 percent the target audience, while only 1 percent of Yahoo's visitors were the target audience (triathletes).

For this reason, I recommend charging on a per-episode basis instead of CPM. There's just no fair and easy way to compete with general population sites on a CPM basis so don't bother trying to convince the advertiser otherwise.

The true answer to "what should I charge" question lies in the value of the audience you have attracted. *The more difficult to reach that audience by other means, the more you can charge advertisers to reach them through your show.*

> **WARNING**
>
> Most new podcasters make the mistake of giving a new advertiser huge discounts to "prove" the value of their show. Don't do it! You are much better off waiting until an advertiser is willing to pay you a fair price. Add additional value but be very reluctant to give more than a 10 percent discount even to new advertisers who, in our experience, will be unwilling to pay the full price from that point forward even if they get results.

If your advertiser is selling laundry detergent or some other item for which nearly everyone on the planet is a potential customer, there are millions of ways to reach the general population so you'll likely not be able to charge a premium. However, if your audience happens to be purchasing managers who are looking to outfit large offices with furniture, that audience is worth more not only because a single customer could result in a multi-million dollar account, but because that highly targeted audience would be difficult to reach by other means. The fewer choices your advertiser has to reach an audience like yours, the more leverage you have to charge a premium.

Finally, like everything else in business, start with a figure you believe the market will bear and then negotiate from there (if necessary) for multi-show buys.

The advertising agreement and insertion order

Once you have an advertiser on board, they're probably going to ask you for an insertion order (IO). The IO contains a few legal items to protect

|TraderInterviews.com
ADVERTISING AGREEMENT and INSERTION ORDER

THIS PODCAST ADVERTISING AGREEMENT (the "Agreement") is made between TNC New Media, Inc., a California corporation ("TNC") and Global Forex Trading ("Advertiser"), a --- corporation the undersigned advertiser ("Advertiser").

In consideration of the mutual promises and covenants contained in this Agreement, the parties hereto agree as follows:

1.   Advertising. TNC shall use its diligent efforts to provide the Internet-related advertising specified in Insertion Order. Any advertising submitted by Advertiser must be in form and substance acceptable to TNC.

2.   Payment. Advertiser shall pay the fee set forth in Insertion Order to TNC, due and payable as indicated therein.

3.   Cancellations. Except as otherwise provided in the Podcast Advertising Agreement, the Podcast Advertising Agreement is non-cancelable by Advertiser. If Advertiser cancels the Advertising Order, in whole or in part, Advertiser agrees to pay the full amount detailed in the Podcast Advertising Agreement.

4.   Indemnity. Advertiser represents and warrants to TNC, and Third Parties (if any), that Advertiser holds all necessary rights to permit the use of the advertisement by TNC for the purpose of this Agreement; and that the use, reproduction, distribution, transmission or display of advertisement, any data regarding users, and any material to which users can link, or any products or services made available to users, through the advertisement will not (a) violate any criminal laws or any rights of any

FIGURE 15.4

A sample advertising agreement for the TraderInterviews.com podcast.

you and also outlines payment terms and what type of "creative" like banner ads and logos you'll need to fulfill the sponsorship.

Although I recommend you have an attorney review your advertising agreement (see, e.g., Figure 15.4) and IO, you can download a template at http://www.PodcastExpo.com/PodcastAdvertisingAgreement.doc

Having an agreement and IO for the advertiser to sign will again show you are a professional media property using the right tools to protect both you and the advertiser. It also puts in writing exactly what is expected of you so that you can fulfill all of the obligations you have promised to do.

WARNING Contract law varies from state to state, so be sure to have your attorney review the advertising agreement template and make any adjustments necessary to comply with your state and local laws.

Helping Your Advertiser Track ROI

I've known many podcasters who have had success landing an advertiser, only to have them do a one-time buy and not renew again for more show sponsorships. Part of the problem is that the podcaster has not helped the advertiser clearly determine whether or not their investment actually worked.

Consider it as *your* job to make sure the advertiser knows that their sponsorship actually resulted in leads or sales for their company. Part of the way you can do this is to insist that every banner, graphic, and URL mentioned in the podcast is unique to your podcast and Web site so that it can be tracked back to you.

Most advertisers are sophisticated enough these days to use unique tracking links for banners and graphics they purchase on a Web site. However, these same tracking links aren't practical to be read in the audio of your podcast. But don't make the mistake of just mentioning the advertiser's home page in the podcast itself. You'd be missing out on learning how many people actually heard the sponsor mention in the podcast and typed in the Web site address the host mentioned.

Imagine trying to read the following tracking URL in your podcast: http://www.XYZCompany.com/558728.asp?2d8c9c.

It would be impossible to expect anyone to remember that. Instead, have your sponsor's Web team, create an easy to remember URL with your show name that can be tracked, such as http://www.XYZCompany/yourpodcast

It's a bit more work on the part of advertiser, but this will ensure that you get credit for every single visit that is a result of you r podcast.

If you have the capability, I'd also recommend tracking the links on your side, so that you have backup confirmation of the visitors you are sending to the sponsor. The technology involved in doing so is beyond the scope of this chapter on monetization, but it's something you should look into with a Web site expert. If you do take this route, be sure to provide the advertiser with a report of the results within 30 days of the end of the campaign.

What Ads Return the Best Results?

When first selling sponsorships of several of our podcasts, I conducted tests to see what type of ad returned the best results for the advertiser. I wondered, for instance, what the results would be if the only place I mentioned the sponsor Web site URL was in the audio? What would be the response if I added a text link to the RSS feed in addition to the audio?

In this case it was a sponsorship that I gave away on EnduranceRadio. com to a company selling a $34 product for endurance athletes. We also tested different methods to announce the offer.

The results were surprising.

Advertiser Web site mentioned in podcast

For approximately 22,440 downloads where the offer Web site address was mentioned *only* in the podcast:

- *10-, 15-, or 30-second ad*: *340 clicks, which resulted in 24 sales (1.5 percent click through)*. Here we ran a pre-recorded advertisement (more like traditional radio) at the beginning of the podcast.

- *Host endorsement*: *462 clicks/32 sales (2.0 percent click through)*. Here the host of the podcast read the ad himself and added a few words about how he liked the product.

- *"Celebrity" endorsement*: *613 clicks/22 sales (2.7 percent click through)*. Here we had a "celebrity" in the industry—a well-known triathlete—read the sponsor's offer.

- *"Average joe" endorsement*: *643 clicks/28 sales (2.8 percent click through)*. This one was the most surprising. Here we had just a regular "weekend warrior" athlete who used the product endorse it on the show. I believe this one worked best because listeners like to hear people like them recommend a product rather than a "celebrity" they feel is simply paid to pitch.

We then tested the offer using the same types of campaigns as above but also included the offer Web site address in the show notes, RSS feed and in our weekly email newsletter.

As you would expect, the click-through percentages went up dramatically when the listener simply had to click on a link rather than type it into the address bar of their browser.

Advertiser Web site mentioned in podcast and displayed on Web site

For approximately 22 500 downloads where the link was mentioned in the audio and placed on the Web site, in the podcast RSS feed, and in our weekly email newsletter.

- *10-, 15-, or 30-second ad: 580 clicks resulting in 32 sales (2.6 percent click through).*
- *Host endorsement: 1112 clicks/68 sales (4.9 percent click through).*
- *"Celebrity" endorsement: 1402 clicks/63 sales (6.2 percent click through).*
- *"Average joe" endorsement: 1225 clicks/62 sales (5.4 percent click through).*

Offer as Much Exposure as Possible

The point of showing you this data is to prove that while there is definite value in the audio mention only, your sponsor will get a much better response by utilizing all of the resources at your exposure. Pile on as much exposure as you can manage and you'll have an easier time getting sponsors to renew each month.

Keep in mind that if you archive your podcasts on your Web site, the advertiser is getting a tremendous amount of value for as long as their sponsored podcast is in those archives and downloadable by listeners. At some point you may want to investigate ways to update those archives on-the-fly to be able to monetize the archives again and again with whomever is the newest sponsor.

A relatively new service that assembles your show on the fly in real time is now available. GigaVox Media (www.GigaVox.com) allows you to produce your show in pieces so that you can include updated information in your archives and current shows simply by inserting a new ad one time. This enables you to sell your archives again and again rather than just one time to that particular sponsor.

Proactively Share Information with the Advertiser

Finally, be sure to keep in touch with the sponsor during the campaign to ensure they are satisfied. Send them screenshots of their graphics on your Web site and wherever else they can be seen. Don't assume they will see their sponsorship in action. If the campaign is not performing for any reason, you'll be able to make adjustments to how the ad is read by the host, for example, while the campaign is still running. The time to make sure they are happy is not after the campaign is over! Keep in touch along the way and asking for a renewal will be much easier.

Direct Sales

While the first thought most people have to generate revenue with their podcast is advertising and sponsorship, podcasts are a particularly good medium for direct sales of everything from white papers and eBooks and other information-based products to washing machines and video games.

When using your podcast in this way, think of it as content used like a fund-raising show for public television. Several times a year, Public Broadcasting Service (PBS) stations run programming that is intended to get viewers engaged and calling to pledge funds. The shows are usually special in that they tend to draw the viewers emotionally with music, guest interviews, and great stories. Your podcast should do the same!

Let's face it—listeners are not going to tune in for a weekly commercial for your company's products and services. You've got to find a way to provide information that draws them in and then entertains and educates them on the things that are important to them.

Whirlpool is a corporate podcast that is often cited as a great example of a podcast done right by a Fortune 1000 company. It would have been very easy for them to do a podcast on ways to get the most of their appliances. They could have conducted weekly shows that educated their customers on the nuances of getting their whites extra white and how to keep their colors from fading.

> **The more subtle your pitch, the more likely your listener will respond and continue to listen to your content because you are not giving them a "hard sell."**

TIM'S TIP

Instead, they decided to do a podcast on the issues important to the family called "The American Family" (see Figure 15.5). Each week the host, Audrey Reed-Granger, interviews people from all walks of family life about the issues families go through at various stages. Balancing child care with careers, potty training, and teaching young children to swim have all been covered on the show.

By focusing on what is important to a large segment of their customer base instead of what is important to the company, Whirlpool is developing a close relationship with current and future customers. While they may not be selling washing machines and dishwashers directly, when listeners of their podcast go into an appliance store to purchase an appliance, I guarantee Whirlpool is top of mind.

The lesson here for direct sales via a podcast is this: don't sell washing machines—"sell" information that is going to help your customers who will one day be in the market for washing machines.

My brother Emile and I do a weekly podcast about the business of podcasting to promote the podcast and New Media Expo, a convention we produce annually for audio and video creators who want to distribute compelling digital media. If we simply did a 20-minute weekly show that "sold" people on

FIGURE 15.5
Whirlpool's American Family podcast, which promotes the sponsor indirectly, by building a relationship with the listener.

buying conference tickets and booth space, we'd never grow the audience. However, each week we cover the latest news and information that independent media creators need to produce better content and monetize it in creative ways. Of course we start off each show telling our listeners about the newest keynote speaker added and a few reasons to attend, but we quickly move on to what the listener is really there for—information they can use immediately in their own small media business.

Determine what information your customers need to make their business or personal lives better and create that content via interviews, stories, and lists of tips. Of course you'll sprinkle in references to your products and services, but the show itself doesn't even have to be about your industry directly. In this sense, think of your company as the sponsor of your own podcast that reaches the exact target market you want to reach. Remember, the Whirlpool podcast isn't about selling washing machines, although the end purpose of the show is to do just that.

Even as you indirectly sell your product or service, don't forget the final "E"—encourage action. End every podcast with a request for your listeners to do something—subscribe to an email newsletter, send your email feedback you can read on the next show, or respond to a survey. Every podcast should solicit some sort of real response from your audience.

Affiliate Programs

Now that you have the right frame of reference from which to design a podcast to sell your products and services, what if you're producing original content and don't know what to sell?

Affiliate programs are an easy way to get started monetizing your podcast. An affiliate program is one where you earn a commission or bounty for every product you sell. Companies from Amazon.com to Best Buy offer online affiliate programs you can sign up for and immediately begin earning revenue.

The beauty of affiliate programs is that they now exist for nearly every product sold. It's very easy to find products that are a good fit for your audience. Technology podcasts probably have the easiest time, but even sports, religion, and arts and crafts podcasts can find products that would be of interest to their listeners and earn a commission on every item sold.

A search engine will yield thousands of results for the term "affiliate programs." Paul Colligan of PodcastSecrets.com, who has had great success lusing affiliate programs to generate revenue for his Web sites and podcasts, recommends three directories to get you started:

1. Commission Junction: www.CJ.com
2. Associates Programs: www.AssociatePrograms.com
3. Click Bank: www.ClickBank.com

One way to implement an affiliate program easily is to simply make it "the sponsor" of your show. Give the affiliate banner and mention the same exposure listed earlier in this chapter. It's an unobtrusive way to make money and pick up "sponsorship dollars" for your show.

Most affiliate programs provide banners of varying sizes that you can use on your Web site, in the RSS feed, and in your email newsletter.

I would also recommend purchasing your own domain names and having them forward to your unique affiliate link. Much like using an easy to remember URL in the audio podcast for sponsor links, it will make it much easier for your listeners to remember and type into an address bar on their browser. For example, if you are doing a sports podcast and your "sponsor" is an affiliate program for sports memorabilia, your affiliate link might look like this: http://www.sportsmemorabiliaaffiliates.com/refer="127487"

This would be fine as a link to your banners, but much too difficult to read in the beginning of your podcast. Instead, register a domain name such as www.SportsHistoryNow.com through one of the major registrars and then "forward" it to your unique link. We use GoDaddy.com to register all our domain names, although there are several reputable firms. Registering and then reading www.SportsHistoryNow.com is going to be easier for you to do on your show and easier for your listener to remember in the future.

Using affiliate programs is a good way to insert sponsorship and advertising into your show until you are able to get direct sponsorship dollars.

It is also a good option for those who are unable or don't want to take the time to make sales calls to perspective sponsors.

> **TIM'S TIP**
>
> If you are selling your own product or service in your podcast, you should also consider setting up an affiliate program so that other Web sites, podcasts, and blogs can sell your product on your behalf and generate additional revenue you might not earn otherwise. You can find out more about setting up your own affiliate program by going to www.AssociatesProgram.com or at www.AffiliateShop.com.

Free vs. Premium vs. Subscription Podcasts

Most podcasts start out as free content available for anyone to download. Making your podcast free will allow you to build an audience quickly and get people talking about it. Making it easy for your listeners to consume and sharing your show will build buzz and a following. Of course, submit your show's RSS feed and Web site address to as many podcast directories available including iTunes (e.g., an excellent listing of podcast directories can be found here: http://www.podcast411.com/page2.html).

Once you have built an audience and have several months of weekly shows in your archives it's time to consider generating revenue with either a paid subscription version of your show or stand-alone premium editions of your show that can be downloaded for a one-time payment.

I recommend you have at least 6 months of weekly shows in your archives before attempting to sell content. Six months will be a sufficient time to gain the confidence and trust of your listeners. Your current listeners, who know the quality of what you produce for free, are the most likely to then purchase any premium content you produce.

Premium downloads

An excellent way to gauge your audience's interest in paid content is to produce a special edition show that you sell via download. For example, we produced EndurancePlanet.com (Figure 15.6) for over a year for free before we decided to produce a series of special episodes. Each week we

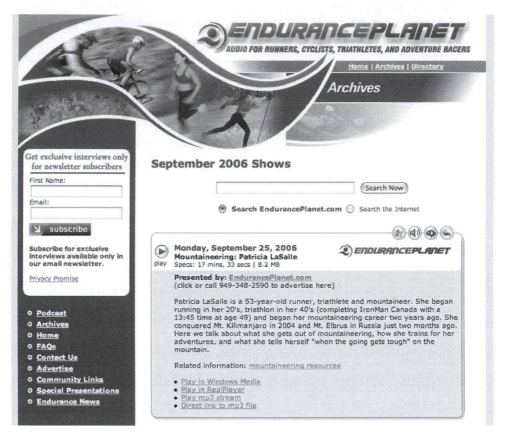

FIGURE 15.6

The EndurancePlanet.com podcast began as free content, and later started including content only available for a fee.

interviewed endurance athletes about how they trained, raced, and ate for peak performance. After we had proven to our audience that we could produce quality, useful content on a regular basis, we decided to produce a series of three podcasts that contained specific details for training for an Ironman Triathlon.

Based on feedback and questions we had received over the past year from our listeners, we learned that this was information that was difficult to find elsewhere and they were hungry for details.

We produced three 1-hour podcasts and sold the series for $19.95. It was a tremendous success (by our measures) and over 400 of our listeners purchased the content in the first month. We were fairly certain that listeners would pay for more in-depth and detail-oriented content based on what we know about their interests, but we couldn't know for sure until we did the work and actually made it available for sale.

Consider the nature of your podcast and then determine if more in-depth coverage of that same topic would sell well to your audience. Typically, the more the information allows them to improve some aspect of their personal or business lives, make more money or save them time, the better suited the information is for a pay-per-download model. Also, the more difficult it is to find that same information elsewhere, the greater the value to the listener and the more you can charge.

Subscription models

Subscription models are also something to consider, although it is more of a commitment on your part to produce ongoing premium content. Pay-per-download is typically the better choice, especially if it is of an "evergreen" nature where the information isn't particularly time sensitive and doesn't become stale because it can be sold for years without additional work on your part.

However, if your podcast deals with topics that are time sensitive and are usually of greater value at the time they are recorded, you may want to consider offering a monthly subscription to more detailed shows. I say monthly instead of annually because a monthly subscription allows you more freedom to stop offering the premium content should you so desire.

Offer your podcast for free initially to build your audience numbers. Then when you have earned their trust, you are better able to offer special shows on a subscription or pay-per-download basis because they will be familiar with the quality of your content. TIM'S TIP

There are not many examples of podcasters offering monthly subscriptions with consistent success at this point. My experience has been that listeners are more likely at this point to pay one time rather than on a monthly basis. However, David Lawrence (http://www.OnlineTonight.com), a podcaster who has been involved in radio and traditional media for many years, charges a monthly fee of $7.00 for listeners who want commercial-free versions of shows he broadcasts on XM Satellite radio.

David has also recently launched ShowTaxi.com (Figure 15.7), a service that allows podcasters to sell subscriptions to their content easily via PayPal. ShowTaxi.com collects the subscription fees and then pays the podcaster on a monthly basis.

I would also suggest using other ways to get distribution for your premium content with more traditional methods like selling downloads via iTunes (in addition to your own Web site) and CDs and DVDs on Amazon.com.

Sell via a Third-Party Aggregator

Most podcasters know they can submit their free podcasts to the iTunes directory. However, many don't know that you can sell your premium podcasts through major distribution channels like Amazon.com.

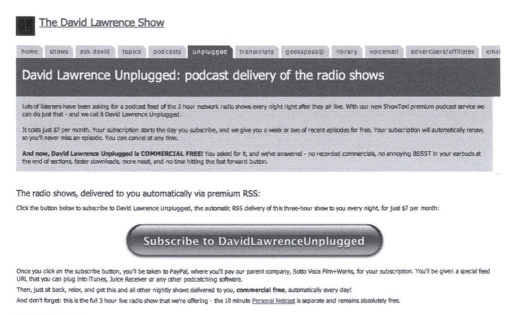

FIGURE 15.7
David Lawrence's paid podcast subscription page.

CustomFlix.com, an Amazon-owned company, offers an easy way to sell your premium content on Amazon.com and also via Amazon.com's new UnBox service for digital downloads. Sign up for the Customflix.com "Unbox Download to Own/Download to Rent" feature, send them a master DVD and collect a 50/50 split on revenue. Then, wait 5 business days to get into the system and another 30 to be available in Amazon's UnBox catalog for digital download.

These types of services allow you to gain wider distribution than your own Web site and email list—an important step if you want to bring in "real" revenues on your premium content.

Each of these methods allows you to gain wider distribution than your own Web site and email lists—an important step if you want to bring in "real" revenues on your premium content.

"Best of" CD/DVD/Download Sales

Re-purposing content that you have already made public and packaging it as a "best of" series is an excellent way to sell your work without doing a great deal of extra work in the process. "Best of" compilations of your most interesting shows can be sold even when all of the shows in the group are available for free on your Web site. I highly recommend that you give your listeners a choice when purchasing—download or CD in the mail. The CD in the mail choice seems old fashioned but keep in mind that there are still a lot of commuters out there (especially here in Southern California where I live) that don't have MP3 player integration in their car stereo and would welcome the opportunity to conveniently purchase a CD they can play in their cars.

Although you can have success re-packaging existing shows without any new content included, you can give a nice boost to your sales by including some things that are not available on your regular site. A new podcast, for example, that is not available in your RSS feed or on your Web site and available only in your "Best of" compilation will entice listeners who might not buy otherwise to make the purchase. (By the way, this is also a great tool to use to build your email newsletter list. Occasionally include a podcast that only goes out to your email newsletter subscribers to encourage listeners to sign up).

Record a podcast with someone who is well known and important in your industry and hold that podcast for a year-end "best of" compilation that you can sell. This is a perfect opportunity to "dip your toe" into selling premium content to your audience. People love top ten lists, "most memorable moments" shows and "Best of" television and radio programs. Your podcast can take advantage of the same thing and generate some nice income for your company.

Special Episodes

Occasionally, you should produce and release a "special episode" that is full of practical "how to" information that your listeners can use immediately in their own personal or business lives. It's an excellent way to build interest in your podcast early on and will hopefully be different enough to be worthy of putting out a press release to build buzz several weeks before it is released.

Releasing special episodes is an excellent way to also increase the number of RSS subscribers you have. For those listeners who are new to RSS and are simply visiting your Web site to hear the content, you can also mention that these special episodes are occasionally available only to RSS subscribers and will not be posted on the Web site or sent in the email newsletter. Your goal should be to ideally get every person who visits your podcast Web site to either subscribe to the email newsletter *and* the RSS feed, ensuring you have several lines of communication with them.

This builds a deeper relationship with your listeners and ultimately a loyal group of people who will help you spread the word about the great content you are producing.

Paid Syndication on Other Web sites

With RSS being relatively open, anyone can take your RSS feed and incorporate it on their own Web site to automatically get updated content. The first thing to keep in mind is the copyright you associate with your show. Many podcasters just associate the most liberal Creative Commons (www.CreativeCommons.org) license with their content, thinking that this way anyone can easily repurpose their content in order to get wider distribution.

However, I recommend using a standard copyright on your show, even if you are using the podcast to gain more exposure for your company products and services and don't mind if others take your feed and display your podcast on their own Web site. Using a regular copyright simply allows you to keep greater control of your content and where it is displayed. Consider the damage to your brand if an adult Web site decided to show your podcast on their site—which would be totally legal with a license that is too liberal. That's a "worst case" scenario, of course, but with a regular copyright you can approve all those who request to syndicate your content and decline those your company deems inappropriate. Obviously, if you are simply looking for as many listeners as possible because your podcast is a marketing tool for a product or service, then a copyright will simply protect your content from landing somewhere you don't want.

With a standard copyright, you can also reserve the right to charge other Web sites to display your content (or play your podcasts) on their own Web sites. This represents another opportunity to generate revenue. Your company may be spending a significant amount of money and personnel resources to produce top-flight content and they deserve to be compensated when others use that content to drive traffic to their own Web sites.

Syndicating your content to other Web sites can generate several thousand dollars each month for your company. For whatever reason, too many content creators greatly underestimate the value of their media. Even though your content may be inexpensive to produce compared to traditional media, it does not mean it worth less. If Web sites ask to carry your content on their sites, the choice of whether or not to charge them is yours of course.

However, don't discount the value of your content to draw traffic to others—traffic business people are willing to pay for.

Selling Your Podcast

The final "direct revenue" method of generating profits from your content is the sale of the podcast itself. From the very first episode you publish, you are building value in something that can be monetized for years, if not indefinitely.

EndurancePlanet.com was a podcast I started in January 2005. For more than 2 years, we posted three episodes per week with triathletes, marathon runners, and adventure racers. Although the site was started as a hobby, we began to treat it more as a regular media property of the business and sporadically sold sponsorships of the episodes. However, it was the "odd duck" of our portfolio and eventually got pushed to the back-burner more and more often when our business and finance-related media properties needed attention.

We decided it was time to sell and took an offer from a triathlete who partnered with USA Triathlon, the governing body of the sport to carry on the torch. It was the first sale of a podcast (that I'm aware of) and the amount, although not enough to retire to a private island, was respectable and fair.

One interesting point: We thought the value was in the listener base itself that included the RSS subscribers, email newsletter subscribers, and general Web site traffic. While that was important to the buyer, what they really saw value in was the 2 years of archives we had built with hundreds of shows and athletes. The lesson was that different people see different values in content so don't underestimate the value of what you will be building.

TIM'S TIP

The value of the content you have built may lie in different areas for the buyer. Don't assume that they see value in the same thing you do. They may see value in the archives, while you see the value in the RSS subscription numbers.

As mentioned earlier in this chapter, your podcast is an asset that you very well might leverage one final time by selling it to a company that can take it to the next level and perhaps leverage it against existing content they are already producing.

Determining the sales price and the actual value of the content to a company is more art than science. As with most things, the value is simply what someone is willing to pay for it. However, you will most likely be able to get a higher price by selling it to a company that is already producing similar content to a similar audience. This also saves you from having to endure a long transition period where you need to train the new owner on producing the content. Sell the podcast to someone who is already "in the business" of producing audio or video content for the Web and the transfer to the new owner will be a much smoother process.

Indirect Revenue Streams from Your Podcast

Now that we've covered the "hard dollar" options you have in the business, it's time to talk a bit about the "softer" side of podcasting—making money in indirect ways by increasing your influence and popularity in the industry you cover.

The Value of Recognition as an Expert

After publishing just a few episodes a funny thing will begin to happen. You'll begin to get phone calls from listeners and people referred to you by listeners as an expert on the topic you are covering. Becoming recognized as an expert is beneficial in several ways, including the benefit of indirect revenue.

Lead generation

The more you are considered an expert in the field, the more people will call you for information. You and your company will benefit from the contacts and relationships you'll make from the doors that begin to open. Podcasting is probably the best long-term lead generation tool you can start today. Your listeners will begin to understand your level of knowledge and passion for the subject so that by the time they call for a consultation or with a question, they feel like they already know you. Each and every listener is a potential new customer that you are slowly gaining the trust of before you ever make a sales call to one of them.

If your business involves cold-calling to generate new business, you'll find that you have to do less and less as new prospects begin to call you. The stock brokerage that produces a podcast on the "stock of the day" or the tax advisor firm that produces a "deduction of the week" podcast will find that a podcast can quickly generate interest in their company's products and services.

Every business, no matter the industry, can benefit from creating content that is interesting and educational to their target market, for example, the plumbing company that does a home improvement podcast, the day care center that does a parenting podcast—the examples are endless.

You are, in a very real sense, conducting your own PR campaign to promote yourself and your company in a positive light that will pay dividends for years to come.

Branding and exposure

Your growing reputation of expertise will also help you get mentioned more often in the press. Normally, reporters are not likely to call your company because they assume you'll simply want to pitch your products and services. However as the host of your company podcast, you become more of a resource than a company representative.

You can increase the speed at which you become well known as the "go to" person by doing press releases around special episodes and leaving interesting comments on blog posts with your podcast URL under your name.

There's also one important thing many podcasters forget to do at the beginning and end of each episode—ask your listeners to "tell a friend" to help you spread the word about your show.

Each of these things will indirectly lead people to your company and the products and services you are ultimately looking to sell with your content.

Speaking gigs

Your company probably already participates in tradeshows and conferences to gain exposure. Your newfound "celebrity" status as the show host will no doubt lead to speaking invitations at conferences around the country.

You may need to reach out yourself initially, but once you speak at a few conferences and knock their socks off (and you'll need to take your speaking gigs seriously and prepare), you'll find that you are invited to speak elsewhere as well, leading to more listeners, which will lead to more business for your company and more listeners for your podcast.

As a tradeshow organizer myself, I have a few tips for you when you are submitting a speaker proposal:

1. Do not have your PR firm submit the proposal for you. Speakers we choose for our conferences usually submit themselves as a speaker because it shows the speaker is serious about wanting to participate in the conference.

2. When submitting your topic title and description of the session you intend to teach, be as detailed as possible. Conference organizers can smell a sales pitch a mile away so never submit a session that mentions your company product or service. Instead, think from the attendee point of view and make your title and description sound like it is information they cannot afford to be without. If your presentation offers valuable information the audience can use immediately in their own personal or professional lives, you'll get more inquiries for your products and services than you ever will with even a subtle sales pitch.

Encouraging the Community of Listeners: Future Business

As Greg mentioned in a previous chapter, as your listener numbers grow, you'll find that the community you are building wants to interact with each other as well as you. Foster this in every way you can, because it can lead to a loyal following and new business! Here are some ways:

1. Create a message board forum so that listeners can comment on every episode of your show, ask questions of the community, and talk about current events in the industry. If your company already has a user support forum up and running, ask the administrator to create a section of the board just for your podcast and listeners.

2. Ask for email feedback from your listeners and read at least two or three of those emails "on the air" each show. The more emails you read, the more you'll get; you want to encourage that two-way communication with your listeners because they'll feel more connected with you, your show, and your company.

3. Host regional "listener appreciation events" around the country where you can interact face-to-face with your audience. This is also a great opportunity for your CEO or other executive to say a few words and thank the audience for coming (and I do mean "few"—don't let it turn into a blatant commercial).

If your audience is likely to be gathering already at a large industry trade-show, this is a great opportunity to piggy-back on that and have your reception at the same time so that the audience can make the most of your time.

A table or display at the back of the room where people can ask questions about your products and services is completely appropriate and I encourage you to do so.

If you have partners in the business, you might consider covering the costs of such events by selling them table displays or small sponsorships of the event. Remember, the audience of listeners that you are bringing together is very valuable to others, and charging for the privilege of reaching them at events you produce is an excellent way to make the events pay for themselves.

Writing White Papers

Another way to capitalize on your "expert" status is to research, write, and sell white papers on topics relevant to your industry. Certainly you can offer them for free to promote your company, but if the information is solid and you've invested time and resources to compile the information, why not offer it for sale as one of the "direct revenue" items you mention in your podcast?

White papers are an excellent way to promote your company and your podcast while providing needed information to your industry. They don't need to be long—a 5-page white paper that is to the point and contains information that is not available (or at least time consuming to find) else-where can be sold for several hundred dollars.

eBooks or other electronic documents are simple to sell and require little work beyond the initial production. With your built-in audience, you have an immediate channel through which to sell your text content.

Producing Podcasts for Others

Finally, let's discuss producing white-label podcasts for other companies. The fact that you are reading this book shows that you are taking the time to gain the knowledge you need to produce a great podcast. Other companies will want to do their own shows, but don't have the time or resources and are willing to pay someone who does have the knowledge for their time. Podcast consultants are doing very well these days, pro-ducing content for other companies who don't want to take on the task themselves.

After your partners and associates in the industry hear your podcast and see the success you begin to have with lead generation and marketing, they'll definitely want to start their own as well. You've worked hard to learn how it all works and that information is valuable—don't undervalue it! You can charge anywhere from $500 to $5000 per episode you help record, edit, and publish.

If you feel this gets too far away from your core business, that's fine. But also remember that every company is now a media company regardless of whether or not they create audio or video as part of their core business.

Advertising in Other Podcasts

Another indirect way of generating revenue for your company is to advertise in someone else's podcast. The same services that are outlined in the sponsorship section of the chapter can be used to not only get sponsors for your own show but to find podcasts to advertise in as well.

Most podcasters do not have formal advertising policies in place so you'll probably have to reach out to each podcast individually that attracts the target audience you want to reach.

You should be asking for all of the same exposure you would be giving to a sponsor, including audio mentions, banners/links in the RSS feed, on their Web site, and in any email newsletters they publish.

Remember: A Podcast is an Asset, Not an Expense

If there is one theme from this chapter I would like you to take away, it's that your podcast is an asset—not an expense. Yes, there will be expenses when you start including the purchase of recording equipment and time spent learning how to post your shows, but consider those as investments.

The content you are producing can earn revenue for you in both direct and indirect ways because the shows themselves, as along with the audience you build, are very valuable. Learn how to capitalize on that work, and you'll have a way to generate leads for your sales team year-round.

Finally, the value of showcasing your company in a positive light and earning the trust, respect, and loyalty of customers who "tune in" each week will be immeasurable.

Now go forth and monetize!

Lessons Learned

- Your content has value from the very first episode.

- Podcasting can result in savings when the middleman between you and your audience is eliminated.

- Successful content meets all of the five "E's": entertains, engages, educates, easy to consume, and encourages action.

- You can choose to do direct sales of sponsorships for your podcast or use one of the third-party services now available.

- There are many other ways to monetize a podcast besides advertising, including direct sales of products, affiliate programs, pay-per-download of special episodes, and premium subscription memberships.

- Mentions in the audio of your show should be just a small part of the exposure your advertiser receives.

- It's your job to help the advertiser or sponsor see the ROI.

- Encouraging your listeners to communicate with you can lead to additional sponsorship and a fast-growing audience.

16

Putting It All Together

Greg Cangialosi

We have now covered nearly everything you need to know in order to research, produce, promote, and measure your organization's own podcast initiative. As you have seen, podcasting is not necessarily a complex communications medium to deploy, but there are certain steps that must be executed correctly in order to reach your audience and maximize your return on investment (ROI). As you embark on your own podcasting ventures, hopefully you will not only find them to be beneficial for your organization, but also fun and interesting to put together.

A podcast initiative will ultimately, if not immediately, be a valuable asset for your organization. Even if your podcast isn't necessarily a sales machine, the benefits of incorporating this medium into the fold of your marketing and communications efforts are too strong to ignore, especially when compared to the relatively low costs of production. Podcasting is a new and powerful medium, and the uses are just now being explored and refined. Now that we've explored the ins and outs of podcast production and promotion, it might be helpful to review the many different ways that you can use podcasting for your organization.

What Podcasting Is Capable of Today

As outlined throughout the book, podcasting appeals to niche markets and is still very much in its early stages of development. The medium embodies and in many ways defines the changing media landscape from the captive audience to the on-demand culture.

As podcasting content continues to increase in popularity with independent content producers and other media outlets, businesses and other organizations are also finding ways to utilize this medium for communications, advertising, and marketing. As a marketing tool, organizations have been finding podcasting useful for branding and increasing product awareness. Podcasting is particularly attractive as a marketing tool because of the high likelihood that the content and information being published will be shared with an interested audience.

Marketing

Marketing professionals know that it is important not to reach just any audience with their message, but rather an audience that is interested in the information or product that is being promoted. In many cases, podcasting eliminates a substantial amount of guesswork for marketers, since the message is not being published to a general audience, of which maybe 1 percent is interested. Rather, the audience self-selects the information they desire, thereby narrowing them into a market that is more likely to engage with the message being conveyed rather than tune it out. The ability to target a specific market that is interested in your product, service, or industry is a huge asset and a rare commodity when considering traditional means of communication and marketing.

Public Relations

Podcasts have not only made an impression as a marketing and branding tool, but also as a means of launching public relations campaigns that bypass traditional forms of media entirely. The ability of podcasts to reach consumers directly means that your public relations message does not run the risk of being lost or misinterpreted by traditional media like newspapers or television. Of course, you still want your news to be picked up by the media, but having your message—your media—directly available for all to consume allows for clear and unfiltered communication. The information is put directly into the hands of the consumers, who can then engage with the content at their leisure. Such direct organization–consumer interaction builds a stronger relationship between the two parties and allows for you to maintain complete control over your public relations message.

Advertising

Because of its niche market reach, advertisers are looking at podcasting as an additional venue for reaching new audiences and consumers. Similar to its appeal for marketing, podcasting is attractive to advertisers since it offers them a chance to tap new markets that are focused and unique. Advertisers have the opportunity, for instance, to run a magazine ad for a set dollar amount and reach a set number of readers, bearing in mind that only a percentage will have an interest in the ad. Conversely, advertisers can spend significantly less on a 10-second ad run on a podcast or a series of podcasts that reaches a smaller but focused audience, but the chances of the audience having some interest in the ad is likely to be much higher. Clearly, there will be a better ROI for the advertiser using the later approach since the audience is already interested and engaged in the content, rather than spending dollars and hoping to reach the target.

Training

The target audience is key when determining how you will use your podcast. For example, many organizations are finding that podcasts are an excellent training tool. When used for internal communications, podcasts offer your employees or members the opportunity to listen to the information at their leisure, and can convey more emotion or generate more enthusiasm than simply the written word. Additionally, the portability of podcasts makes them incredibly useful for education and training, since they can be listened to repeatedly whenever the listener desires. This makes podcasting an ideal medium for teaching languages or new selling techniques.

Overall, your podcast is designed to share information and communicate directly with your audience. Whether your intention is to sell, promote, inform, or educate, the core of the podcast is your content—information or stories that appeal to the market you are striving to reach. The uses that we have described are not the final word in how you can use your podcast. Those who are already involved in the podcasting industry are continually finding new uses for podcasts and exploring ways to increase the effectiveness of current uses and beyond.

What is it that makes podcasting so important to your organization? After all, traditional methods of promoting your organization or selling products have obviously worked in the past—otherwise your organization would not be where it is today. So if these methods have worked before, won't they continue to work in the future? Why consider a podcasting initiative at all?

The Changing Social Media Landscape

Podcasting should be a crucial element of your organization's strategy largely due to major shifts in social media and the way in which the public consumes information and entertainment. Social media, as you know, is embodied by the emergence of Web 2.0 and the tools that correspond with this new era, including blogs, social networks, wikis, and podcasting.

These tools have changed the way in which consumers interact with each other and organizations as a whole. Social media has put the power of content generation into the hands of individuals instead of organizations, so that now the public can produce and publish their own content instead of only consuming what is being produced for them by organizations. The shift in power for content generation has created a situation in which the consumer can now dictate what type of information or entertainment they desire. By taking on content generation, the public is changing the way in which organizations interact with their key audience.

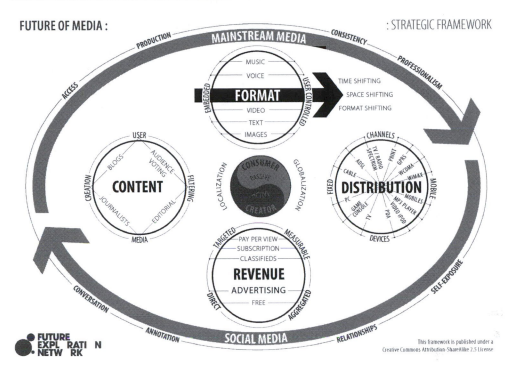

FIGURE 16.1

The symbiosis of social media and mainstream media. *Source*: Future Exploration Network (www.futureexploration.net) via Ross Dawson's Trends in the Living Networks Blog www.rossdawsonblog.com (March 2, 2007).

Social media tools empower audiences beyond the creation of their own content and enable them to get the content they want on demand. On-demand culture is a new phenomenon that has taken hold of mainstream culture (Figure 16.1). This phenomenon became well known with the onset of TiVo and other DVR devices that freed television viewers from the constraints of watching TV programs as they were broadcast. These technologies allow people to record and enjoy programs at their leisure, often skipping over advertisements and other filler in TV programs.

Social media has brought this same on-demand experience to the Web, particularly through podcasting. Overall, social media caters to the desires of an audience, and the nature of the tools and technologies around social media allows organizations to respond quickly to inquiries, comments, and opinions from that audience. In the case of podcasting, really simple syndication (RSS) feeds and popular aggregators like iTunes enable users to receive notifications when new content is available, and in most cases download the new file directly to the user's computer or digital media device. Once the file is downloaded, the audience now has control over when and how they consume the content. Gone are the days of the purely captive audience—on-demand culture is changing the way media is consumed and, thus, the way media is produced. Podcasting is a natural fit for on-demand culture.

Other forms of social media such as blogs can be very time sensitive and require that a participant engage almost immediately if their contributions are to be pertinent. Though podcast content can be time sensitive in nature, it is meant to be enjoyed when the listener so chooses. This structure fits well into the changing media landscape, where the audience has more choice and control over the content they are interested in consuming.

Now that consumers have been given the opportunity to focus on the content that really captures their attention, it is hard to imagine that they would ever want to give that up.

This is one reason that podcasting is here to stay. Audiences have become fed up with traditional models of entertainment and communication, not to mention the inundation of irrelevant advertisements that go along with them. When you figure that for most hour-long primetime television shows, only 40–45 minutes is dedicated to the actual program—and that time is continually interrupted—or that most radio programs dedicate between 12 and 16 minutes of air per hour to advertisers, you can see why on-demand communication has an increased appeal to consumers.

Podcasting will not be a lasting force as a communications and marketing tool simply because audiences have become more focused on getting what they want when they want it. Podcasting will remain an important tool because of its ability to reach niche markets that traditional means have been incapable of effectively targeting. The power and ability to reach niche markets is perhaps one of the most attractive aspects of podcasting. Because of the vast amount of content available for consumers today, they are now self-selecting the material they desire, which not only makes them harder to reach with a general message.

Organizations can use podcasting to capitalize on these targeted markets. Podcasting allows organizations and advertisers alike to maximize their budgets by focusing on an audience that has, by their own admission, an interest in the content. This translates into greater ROI, particularly because podcasts are relatively inexpensive to produce, especially when compared to traditional marketing and advertising tools. The affordability of podcast production puts the power to reach markets within reach for small businesses and organizations just as it does for larger ones. One need not have massive amounts of capital and revenue to implement an effective and successful podcasting initiative.

It is true that the audience reached with a podcast is significantly smaller than one that would be reached through a more general message; after all, podcasting is not meant to replace your entire communications strategy. But the quality of the audience that you can reach through podcasting is higher, in that a larger percentage of that audience will be interested in what your organization has to share than if you launch a message to the general public. Broad messages to the public have their place, but ultimately you are only reaching a small percentage of the audience, even though you're paying to cast a very wide net. Podcasting can act as a powerful means for deepening your organization's reach into your market.

The way in which consumers seek out their information has changed, and podcasting offers organizations a means of reaching consumers in a way that is agreeable to them. In the world of Web 2.0, the targeted message will rule. Narrower interests and the means to indulge in these interests and *only* these interests dictate a changing game in which wide-sweeping communication and advertising efforts will not be as effective as targeted efforts. As the audience changes, so must the tactics to reach them. We have seen this adoption within all online advertising mediums, from geo-targeting to behavioral targeting and beyond. Podcasting fits right into this mix.

Now Is the Time

Overall, taking on a podcasting initiative does not have any significant drawbacks. The costs for entry are low, the manpower required is minimal, and promotional efforts are either free or very low in cost. The potential for that podcasting initiative to bring growth to your organization, however, is great. When you examine the case for podcasting, you should be looking at the low production costs and relatively effortless maintenance, and weigh these factors against the possible end results. Even if your podcast does not promise to be a profit center for your organization, there are benefits that extend from launching a podcasting initiative.

Naturally, not every podcast is going to be a raging success, and occasionally cutting the initiative may be the better option than continuing forward. This is true for any medium—blogs, television, print, and Internet advertising—and for any purpose, be it communications, sales, or public relations. That being said, a failed podcast will not be nearly as costly as an ineffective advertising campaign. The barriers to entry are so low, what do you have to lose?

Even if your podcast doesn't accomplish exactly what it was designed to—increase sales, for instance—it will likely serve you in other ways. Adding a podcast to your online communications mix also offers you the ability to get more content out into the search engines and can therefore improve your rankings if optimized correctly. Also, depending on how you promote your podcast, you can also increase overall traffic to your Web site or increase awareness around your organization. Obviously, the preferred outcome would be for your podcast to both meet its objective *and* bring along additional benefits, but the fact is that either outcome is positive.

Now, more than ever, is the time to launch a podcasting initiative, while it is still an emerging medium. Podcasting, being as unique and new as it is, lacks many restrictions and boundaries that older and more established mediums have. This translates into more freedom to explore and experiment with its uses and means of production. As any medium increases in popularity it becomes more exposed to possible restrictions and regulations that may tie its hands regarding its efficacy. Being one of the infants in the world of social media, podcasting is currently free of such debates and regulations.

As I have stressed throughout the book, podcasting is more than just a passing fad, and soon more organizations will enter the market to take advantage of the power of getting their message out via audio and video. Launching your own initiative now gives you the edge in establishing an audience and fostering loyalty *now*. Remember that most podcasts do not become overnight successes; rather, it can take a minimum of 6 months to a year to build a sizeable audience. As you are well aware by now, building your audience is not a small undertaking if you are starting from scratch. There is research that should take place, an ongoing integrated approach to marketing your podcast, and then the task of building community around your efforts. Starting now allows you to reap the benefits ahead of your competitors since you have a head start on building a loyal audience. Starting now also allows you to participate in a medium that is still new and exciting and can set you apart from the rest of the pack. Podcasting is far from being seen as a "standard" for communications. Again, let's look at blogs. Once a new and unique tool, blogs can now be found for nearly every major television network, news source, business, non-profit, or other organization.

The percentage of people who know about and listen to podcasts is still small when compared to overall Internet usage, but it is growing and will grow fast. By 2010, the audience for podcasting is projected to be over 50 million strong, up from an audience of 10 million in 2006 (Figure 16.2). With such a substantial growth, it makes sense to begin exploring podcasting now so as to work out what works for you and what does not, as well as start fostering a relationship with your audience and begin community building efforts. By starting now you get that competitive edge knowing what works and what doesn't for your audience.

Once podcasting becomes more established, you will not have the same luxury of time to try different formats and approaches until you get it right. Instead, as more organizations become aware of the value of podcasting, the competition for an audience will become fiercer. Experimenting and adapting now will position you for greater success in the future when knowledge and experience will be the commodities that separate your podcast from others. As any successful professional knows,

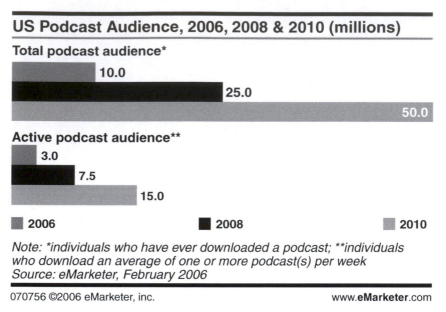

FIGURE 16.2

Podcasting audience growth as projected by eMarketer. *Source*: eMarketer, February 2006—US Podcast Audience 2006, 2008, 2010.

experience can be one of the biggest assets when conducting any sort of business or interaction. The same rule applies to podcasting, and now is the time to build that experience, when you still have some leeway in what you can try simply because it is an immature medium.

Podcasting offers you the ability to start engaging your market in direct dialog and establish a relationship that will carry your organization forward as Web 2.0 continues to expand and take hold in mainstream culture. The new wave of social media is not about corporations and networks dictating what the public can consume. Rather, it is about individuals publishing the content they desire, and seeking the company and conversation of others in their pursuit of this content. Organizations have the chance to participate in this medium by aiding their market and audience in producing and consuming content that is not only relevant but also engaging.

This concept of dialog between consumers and organizations is a common thread that runs throughout all the sweeping changes of social media. Web 2.0 has empowered individuals to not only gain more knowledge and form better-informed opinions, but also to vocalize them on a global scale. While some organizations fear this onset of strength and power on the part of the consumer, others see it as an opportunity to learn more about their market. One of the most basic human urges is the need to communicate and be heard. With these tools, consumers are able to tell the world what they think and what they want. Knowing the mindset of your audience is an absolute gift when you are looking to convey some message or information.

Podcasting opens the door to learning more about markets and audiences. As we discussed in the section on metrics, the data that can be ascertained from podcasts will range from basic demographic data, like gender and geographic location, to more elaborate and complex psychographic data. Putting this tool to use within your organization will give your organization further insight that will allow you to refine your message, or modify your service in a way that will better meet the desires and needs of your audience. The more you are able to cater to exactly what they need, the more engaged your audience would become with your production.

Producing a podcast that appeals to your market not only gives your audience what they want, but it also creates the space for you to maximize your exposure to your market. Additionally, it creates the space for dialog and collaborative content creation. The insights such collaboration can offer into your market cannot be obtained in a focus group or survey. The sort of information you can gain about your market is the kind you would get if you personally knew your audience.

The impact of social media on the consumer–organization relationship is only going to increase as time goes on. When you consider the benefits of starting now and the low barriers to entry, it is clear that the time to begin podcasting is sooner rather than later, so that your organization can capture a sizeable piece of a growing audience.

The Next Step

The very fact you have picked up this book shows that you are aware of the changes in social media and are willing to explore the benefits that podcasting can bring to your organization. Hopefully what you have learned throughout this book is that adding podcasting to your outreach efforts can offer you more than just another means of communication. Rather, podcasting offers you the opportunity to evolve as an organization into the world of social media, ready to engage in dialog, and share information through collective efforts.

By now, you have learned that podcasting is part of a change in social media that will only grow stronger as Web 2.0 technologies become more and more mainstream. Podcasting brings a great deal to your organization by way of niche marketing, dialoguing, and obtaining demographic and psychographic data that will boost your organization's understanding of your market's demands and needs. This, in turn, gives you the ability to refine your message and optimize your other communication efforts—all in addition to the chance to be a pioneer in a burgeoning industry.

I invite you to now take what you have absorbed in this book and apply it to your business or organization. I am confident you will find that your efforts will result in many successes and a rich, rewarding understanding of your market. The impacts of social media have been widespread, and still we are working to understand the true power and potential of these mediums. As we continue forward, with both individuals and organizations adapting these technologies for a variety of purposes, we realize that the journey is just beginning, but the end results will be astonishing.

Below are some additional podcasting resources to utilize:

Our main site: http://www.podcastacademy.com
Our Active Podcasting Forums: http://podcastacademy.com/forum/
Podcast Academy Channel on Gigavox Media: http://pa.gigavox.com/
Great Podcasting Resources:
http://www.podcastfreeamerica.com
http://www.podcastingtricks.com
http://www.podcast411.com
http://en.wikipedia.org/wiki/Podcast

Index

Made in the USA
Columbia, SC
17 December 2021

51912675R00243